Sharif Maghraby

THE 7 GATES OF PHI
(Progressive Human Integration)

*Knowledge, inspiration, and key applications
for the journey of self-development*

authorHOUSE®

AuthorHouse™
1663 Liberty Drive
Bloomington, IN 47403
www.authorhouse.com
Phone: 1-800-839-8640

Published by AuthorHouse 1/8/2013

ISBN: 978-1-4772-6880-3 (sc)
ISBN: 978-1-4772-6878-0 (hc)
ISBN: 978-1-4772-6879-7 (e)

Library of Congress Control Number: 2012916967

"Read in the name of thy Lord and Cherisher, Who created -
Created man, out of a clot of congealed blood:
Read and thy Lord is Most Bountiful,
He Who taught (the use of) the pen,
Taught man that which he knew not."

The Holy Qur'an (96:1–5)
(Yusuf Ali English Translation)

PREFACE

The 7 Gates of Phi is a journey of self-discovery and progressive transformation. Anyone with the conviction and desire to change can apply the principles in this book to help them bring out their best potential.

Each gate represents an important milestone in the reader's journey.

Starting with basic self-awareness concepts and moving through each gate until the final module prepares the reader to enter the phase of 'Change'—where they face the challenge of self-mastery.

The gates are further divided into sub-modules that represent the key skills required to 'open' that specific gate. You don't have to read the book in order—but I highly recommend that you do.

I am still on my journey, still have many questions, and still seek many new experiences. This book is a synthesis of information that has helped me on my journey—a set of skills that continues to assist me to realize my true potential.

I have made many mistakes—some out of ignorance and others out of simply being human. However, as I have come to know the value of these skills—such as how to actively listen, how to project confidence, and how to recognize the subtle cues of social intelligence—I have begun to see the world differently. Simultaneously, the world has begun to react in a much more interesting and dynamic way.

I believe that certain prerequisites had to be met before I could compile this knowledge.

The first of these was an internal driving force that kept pushing me beyond my mediocre artistic creations and my grandiose concepts. It was a knife that slashed away at the narcissist who sat proudly in the back of my mind. My internal self-critic was insatiable and in constant need of evolution and progress.

Another crucial factor in the journey of my self-development has been the need to be humble and assume ignorance. To choose to learn from everyone and everything—no matter who or what they are.

It is only natural that the importance of spirituality be touched upon, because it is the pillar of my balance. It is my conviction and faith in the oneness of my Creator, Allah, that has granted me gratitude and given me my own sense of morality. It yields my values, my strength at times of turmoil, and my patience. There are so many paths to travel to find our spiritual homes, and we will all open different doors. My faith allows me to be confident, assertive, and accept others with respect and an open mind.

Integrity, respect, and dedication—those values have never let me down, and letting go of them is a sure way to nourish my nightmares.

I don't take life too seriously. I love to play with reality, and I live to laugh. I always keep a part of my mind open like that of a child. I am receptive to opportunity; I keep active and always value the scarcity of time.

I will not say that I am anywhere near the point where I have skillfully and successfully applied the principles in this book—but I will say that I will always continue to try.

The first gate awaits you.

SELF

KNOWING YOURSELF: YOUR VOCATION AND PURPOSE

Everyone has his own specific vocation or mission in life; everyone must carry out a concrete assignment that demands fulfillment. Therein he cannot be replaced, nor can his life be repeated, thus, everyone's task is unique as his specific opportunity to implement it.

—Viktor E. Frankl

Personal Portraits

A few months before my sixteenth birthday, I found myself thrust into the world of college. I really had no clue what to do with my life or what to study. In the first year alone, I changed my area of specialization from engineering to computer science to economics.

Sitting wide-eyed and awed in my calculus class, trying to make sense of difficult concepts like integration and differentiation, I felt that I might have made the wrong choice. Perhaps I would find my calling in the liberal arts, I thought. I dabbled in the fields of philosophy, sociology, and psychology. I have to admit that I discovered many interesting concepts in the field of psychology. I decided to enroll in various psychology courses to learn more. I still feel very passionate about the study of the human mind. However, as a college student, I had yet to find something that really inspired and motivated me.

I recall returning home one day to find my older brother and his friend camped out at the dining room table. They were trying to come up with ideas for a marketing campaign for a new product. As I stood in the corner of the room and listened to the flurry of ideas about television commercials, radio jingles, brand strategies, storyboards, and communication design, I had a eureka moment.

I remember asking my brother if he and his friend were discussing some side project that they were working on. He explained that it was an assignment for a mass communication course. It was at that moment that I realized I had found my true calling.

The next morning, I marched into the mass communication department and changed my major for the last time.

The Man in the Tree
Driving down the wrong road and knowing it,
The fork years behind, how many have thought,
To pull up on the shoulder and leave the car,
Empty, strike out across the fields; and how many
Are still amazed among dock and thistle,
Seeking the road they should have taken?

(Damon Knight, 1984)

The Background

Really knowing yourself is the mother of all knowledge.

Consider the following questions: What drives you? What are you passionate about? Why are you here? Where are you going with your life? Are you contributing to your personal growth? Are you contributing to other people's happiness? What is it that drives you to work? Is it money, fame, power, or purpose?

If you don't regularly ask yourself those questions, you can never realize your true potential. However, the only thing worse than not knowing yourself is believing that you know it all—as the old saying goes, "Jack of all trades, master of none."

In his book *Good to Great: Why Some Companies Make the Leap ... And Others Don't,*[1] management guru James C. Collins uses a simple parable to explain what he calls the "hedgehog concept." It is fairly simple, but it contains powerful truths that can be used to discover just who you are and what your purpose may be.

> Every outward journey begins with a
> journey within. (Anonymous)

Here is the story:

One day, a hedgehog and a fox meet in the forest. The fox is a cunning, shrewd, and intelligent creature who believes in his ability to do anything he puts his mind to—anything at all. The hedgehog, by contrast, is a

---

1   Collins, James C. (2001). *Good to Great: Why Some Companies Make the Leap ... And Others Don't.* New York: HarperCollins.

humble creature who is not very good at many things, except for one—rolling into a ball to protect himself.

Suddenly, from a nearby thicket comes a ferocious beast, hungry and intent on finding dinner. The fox reacts by panicking and running through his considerable list of tricks to escape the beast, going from one to the other. However, in his panic and haste he cannot manage to get away from the beast and, unfortunately, is eaten.

The beast does not want to have anything to do with the hedgehog, though, who curls himself into a ball for protection at the first sign of danger, his sharp spines poking outwards. The beast soon leaves, and the hedgehog is left alone—alive.

What is the moral of this story? That it is better to do one thing extremely well than to be mediocre at many things and not do them nearly as well.

Remember the hedgehog as we go through this discussion.

> A hero is an ordinary individual who finds the strength to persevere and endure in spite of overwhelming obstacles. (Christopher Reeve)

Definitions

Purpose: a reason, motivation, or underlying cause of an action; a sense of who one is and his/her ambitions, desires, and skills.

Vocation: a regular occupation, especially one for which a person is particularly suited or qualified.

The Process

> When a man does not know what harbor he is making for, no wind is the right wind. (Seneca)

When you think about yourself, what comes to mind? What purpose do you think you have?

If you say, "Well, I'm not sure I have one," you will be relieved to know that everyone has a purpose. You just have not found yours yet, and that's okay.

That comes with personal development and the growth process. Every person has a purpose, some reason why he is here. We will talk more about purpose and why it matters later. But first, we will talk about something that can be just as important: your vocation.

You Are What You Do

Your work or your job is your self-portrait. You must paint it with excellence. If you are not happy in your job, ask yourself why you are still in it.

Quite simply, you are what you do.

Vocation is not necessarily just a job, by the way; it is what you dedicate your life to doing, which is similar to a purpose. For many self-aware people, their vocation happens to be their job. However, some work at a particular place of employment for money but view themselves, for example, as artists even though they do not make a living from their artwork.

Either way, you are what you do. We define ourselves by the effort and labor we put forth, so our vocation tends to determine how we feel about ourselves.

> A warrior ... feeds his body well; he trains it; works on
> it. Where he lacks knowledge, he studies. But above
> all he must believe. He must believe in his strength of
> will, of purpose, of heart and soul. (David Gemmel)

Your Vocation and Your Happiness

Our sense of happiness is a complex concept that depends on a variety of factors. As mentioned above, most people derive their happiness about or discontent with life largely from their jobs. In fact, a recent survey conducted in the United States found that the majority of workers—55 percent—were dissatisfied with their jobs, and this dissatisfaction was causing significant unhappiness in their lives.

Here is why this is so important.

You spend so much time at your job or vocation that it has a significant impact on your self-esteem and self-image.

If you want to be happy, you have to find a way to be happy with what you do. That is why vocation matters.

> You will recognize your own path when you come
> upon it, because you will suddenly have all the energy
> and imagination you will ever need. (Jerry Gillies)

Why Purpose Matters

"Okay," you say, "vocation matters. But what about purpose?"

Purpose matters as well—in fact, having a strong sense of purpose in your life may be the one key factor that determines whether or not you are truly happy.

You can be successful in life without a clear purpose, but does this mean you will be happy, or even content? No. There are plenty of successful individuals in the world who are not content with life because they have not yet found their true purpose—their calling—in life.

Let's face it: not doing what you are supposed to do—not fulfilling your purpose in life—and not being who you are supposed to be is no way to live. It feels empty and will never give you a sense of satisfaction or happiness.

> I think the purpose of life is to be useful, to be responsible,
> to be honorable, to be compassionate. It is, after all, to
> matter: to count, to stand for something, to have made
> some difference that you lived at all. (Leo C. Rosten)

So what does a purpose—a calling in life—look like? And how does it benefit you?

Motivation

A purpose, first and foremost, is powerfully motivating. When you know your purpose, your calling, you are driven to succeed and pursue it—whatever it may be. This will impact other areas of your life as well.

Passion

A purpose gives you passion about a particular topic or subject. You become so captivated with what you are doing that life is filled with exuberance and joy. What you do in pursuit of your purpose may be dreary and disappointing at times, but the passion is always there.

Direction

Having a purpose gives you a strong sense of direction. In this day and age, direction is always a good thing. As humans, we are forward-looking creatures. We want to know what's coming up ahead. Having a clear direction allows you to accomplish truly great things—once you know your purpose.

> When you see what you're here for, the world begins
> to mirror your purpose in a magical way. It's almost as
> if you suddenly find yourself on a stage in a play that
> was written expressly for you. (Betty Sue Flowers)

Finding Your True Purpose

Ask yourself these three simple questions:

1. What is it that you are truly passionate about? What energizes you and gets you excited as you start each day?

2. What are your primary strengths, skills, and talents? What do you excel at? (This could pertain to a hobby that you've never really considered pursuing as a career. It could also be related to a skill you have mastered.)

3. What would drive your economic engine? What can you do to make a living from this hobby?

Now, review these answers and look for the common thread that flows through them. The area where your answers overlap is your "hedgehog" (remember the story at the beginning of this module?). That is where you shine—what you do best. It is something you do extremely well that stirs your passion and can support you financially.

Mind you, this small exercise may not give you all the answers, but it can definitely help you to start thinking and move you toward finding your true purpose and calling in life.

> True happiness is not attained through self-gratification,
> but through fidelity to a worthy purpose. (Helen Keller)

Exercises

Now that you have determined your purpose and figured out what you'd really like to be doing with your life, here is an action plan for implementing the necessary changes to make it happen.

1. Evaluate Your Life's Roadmap

   On a piece of paper, make an outline of where you would like to go with your life. Brainstorm about your life's purpose. Start with your hedgehog. Be creative and don't limit your thoughts. Think of the impossible. Believe it and you can achieve it.

2. Ask Yourself More Questions

   ✓ What are you naturally interested in?

   ✓ What activities motivate and energize you?

   ✓ What do you want to accomplish in your life?

   ✓ What would you do if you knew that failure was not an option?

   ✓ What would you do if money was not a limitation?

   ✓ Do you believe that people have power and influence over the results they get in their lives?

3. Evaluate Your Job

   ✓ Identify and acknowledge the problems with your current job.

✓ Next begin to visualize your dream job; one that would make you truly happy and make the best use of your skills and personal resources.

✓ Ask yourself what you like about your job now. What would you need to do to leapfrog from your current job profile to your dream profile?

4. Track Your Progress

✓ Keep a record or journal of your discovery of your purpose. Review your journal periodically.

People who consider themselves victims of their circumstances will always remain victims unless they develop a greater vision for their lives. (Stedman Graham)

You Can Do It!

Hopefully you now see how extremely important vocation and purpose are to your life. Remember: always try to examine yourself objectively and evaluate your life.

Who are you? What do you want to do? Who do you want to be?

Step away every now and then and look at where you are going. We are all unique, and we all have a unique purpose and calling. Find yours. The rest will begin to happen on its own.

I've come to believe that each of us has a personal calling that's as unique as a fingerprint—and that the best way to succeed is to discover what you love and then find a way to offer it to others in the form of service, working hard, and also allowing the energy of the universe to lead you. (Oprah Winfrey)

Further Reading

Collins, James C. (2001). *Good to Great: Why Some Companies Make the Leap ... And Others Don't.* New York: HarperCollins.

Leider, Richard. (1997). *The Power of Purpose: Creating Meaning in Your Life and Work.* San Francisco: Berrett-Koehler Publishers.

Self-Motivation

A journey of a thousand miles begins with a single step.

—Chinese proverb

Personal Portraits

Apparently, I'm an excellent guitarist, songwriter, and live performer. This is not my inflated opinion of myself, but something I have been told many times by many different people. I have never studied music formally and actually hated music classes in school. So how can this be?

Well, I found my path to music later in life. There was a point in time before Jimi Hendrix, Pink Floyd, and jazz when I was lost in the mundane madness of the charts. It was meaningless to me. However, I recall a turning point in my life when I was fifteen and first heard a live album by Dire Straits called *Alchemy*. That was my first "real" exposure to progressive rock music.

So my mother bought me a classical guitar as a graduation present. I hadn't a clue as to what to do. I bought books, spoke to guitarists, watched films, and basically locked myself up for six months. My friends actually remember that time in my life where I disappeared to form a bond with my new guitar. And when I emerged, I was playing music.

I removed the strings and stuck colored dots on certain notes on the guitar fret board so that I could learn the scales in my mind. I practiced ten hours a day until my fingers bled and calluses grew on my fingertips. I learned about chords, harmony, scales, modes, and the art of song writing. I still recall the feeling when I actually managed to play for about twenty seconds without the strings buzzing, without being out of time, and without messing up the chord shapes. It was a moment of simultaneous realization and joy—"Oh my God! I'm making music!" I was also surrounded by guitarists, drummers, poets, and artists at the time who inspired me and taught me.

Eighteen years later—I still play my guitar every day.

What could you accomplish in your life if you were self-motivated? Who would you be?

If you are like most people, with the right amount of self-motivation you would do, achieve, and be everything you've ever wanted. Nothing could hold you back. Nothing could stop you from being fulfilled, accomplished, and successful.

If only you had that elusive and powerful personal force known as self-motivation.

The Latin root of the word *motivation* means "to move"—to take action. In order to achieve anything in life, you must first act. Action is fueled by self-motivation. It takes a lot of work to become a fulfilled individual; self-motivation is a significant part of the process.

In this module, you'll find powerful insights about self-motivation that will help you fully realize your talents and strengths.

The Background

Let me relate a story to you of a young man who wanted nothing more than to be a great warrior. The problem was that he was born with only one arm and was constantly told by everyone that he could never be a great warrior.

He didn't listen. He set out every day from a young age to work at his dream—exercising, practicing, and learning the arts and crafts of his trade. With years of hard training, he built his mind and body, bit by bit, into a finely honed instrument. But, because he had only one arm, all the other warriors in his village mocked him for his foolish efforts.

One fateful day, the village was attacked and every man in the settlement drew up arms and ran into battle. The tide of the battle was turning against the villagers, who were desperately looking for any chance at victory. The invaders outnumbered them, and soon the survivors were facing destruction.

The one-armed young man seized the opportunity. He drew his weapon and charged into battle. The years of hard, relentless practice had turned him into a truly powerful and disciplined warrior. With his leadership and skill, the village turned the tables and defeated the invaders.

This young man realized his dream—not because someone told him he was worthy or gave him constant support. He had the one powerful attribute that carried him through the years of hard effort to the ultimate payoff.

> But with a purpose, everything in life seems to fall into place. To be on purpose means you're doing what you love to do, doing what you're good at and accomplishing what's important to you. When you are on purpose the people, resources, and opportunities you need naturally gravitate to you. (Jack Canfield, *The Success Principles*)

Self-Motivation

Self-motivation plays an incredibly important role in becoming the person you want to be. You see, at the end of the day *you* are the only one who can really motivate you to do anything at all. At some point, your external support will fail. When that day comes, if you lack self-motivation, what will happen?

Definitions

Self-motivation: the ability to motivate, inspire, and drive yourself without any outside help.

Initiative: an introductory act or step; one's personal, responsible decision to take action.

Empowerment: a feeling of self-reliance, self-motivation, and/or initiative that enables you to take action.

The Process

Beginning any journey in life requires three things:

- a plan or direction,
- a purpose,
- and a first step.

You probably won't succeed if you skip any of those three things. If you have a purpose and a first step but no plan, how will you know where you are going? If you have a plan and a first step, but no purpose, how will you know why you are going in that direction? And if you have a plan and a purpose but no first step, when will you ever begin? You must have all three if you ever want to accomplish anything. *But* there is something else you need, one other quality that unites all three.

It is the power and drive of self-motivation - the quality that sets you up for success when you begin to achieve the goals you have established for yourself in your life.

How Self-Motivation Works

Self-motivation is one of those concepts that sound so simple and obvious. You just have to convince yourself to do something, right? Well, while it may sound simple, a lot of people have problems properly motivating themselves. I've met countless people who have all the talent and skills to succeed but somehow can't get themselves to actually take action.

This is where initiative and empowerment come in to play. Self-motivation allows you to empower yourself and seize the initiative to do whatever you want to do. There are three components of self-motivation: positive thinking, a forward-looking perspective, and goal setting. Let's look at these more closely.

Positive Thinking

There's a moving story about two shoe salesmen who went to an isolated village in the middle of nowhere to research the potential of the shoe market there. They reported back to their boss with an update the next day -

The first salesman seemed distressed and said, "Boss, that village has no potential—nobody wears shoes."

The second salesman was much more excited and reported, "Boss, that village has great potential—nobody wears shoes!"

As you can see, the second salesman was thinking in a much more positive way and he chose to have an optimistic view of the situation. I don't think anyone who can really motivate themselves if they perceive the situation in a negative manner.

> Whether you think you can, or you think
> you can't—you're right. (Henry Ford)

Forward-Looking Perspective

Here is a quick lesson on what separates winners from losers. Winners see potential for victory; they motivate themselves by looking forward to the finish line. Losers, on the other hand, see potential for defeat and they look at every possible reason for why they will *not* succeed and both perspectives end up becoming self-fulfilling prophecies.

Self-motivation requires a forward-looking perspective. Your brain is wired to spur itself into action based on how you look at the future. If you can look forward and see a positive future, you can begin to generate the force of self-motivation.

Goal Setting

We will talk about goal setting in more detail later on in the journey of personal development, but it needs a mention here because it is so important to self-motivation.

When you are motivating yourself, you are really taking action towards achieving a goal that you have set. These goals—the places you want to go and things you want to achieve—represent the finish line you should always keep your eyes on.

Put all three together—positive thinking, a forward-looking perspective, and goal setting—and you have self-motivation. When you are in a village where no one wears shoes, do the smart thing and open up a shoe store.

> The only limit to our realization of tomorrow will
> be our doubts of today. (Franklin D. Roosevelt)

Common Obstacles to Motivation

Fear

Kurt Lewin, a German psychologist, made a startling discovery about the achievement of goals. He found that the closer a person gets to accomplishing something - the more likely they will encounter the potentially negative consequences of reaching that goal. As a result, the person begins to avoid reaching the goal.

Do you know why? It's fear.

Lewin found that, most of the time, the fear of the consequences was worse than the consequences themselves. He called this the "approach-avoidance" theory. It shows how fear—fear of failure, fear of embarrassment, or fear of something unknown—is one of the main obstacles to motivation.

Recognizing that the fear is often far worse than the consequence itself is the key to staying self-motivated.

Rewards and Punishment

When you were a child, chances are you were disciplined based on a system of rewards and punishment. If you were good, you were rewarded. If you were bad, you were punished. This conditioning often continues into our adult lives, creating serious problems when it comes to motivating ourselves. As humans, we're not very good at rewarding or punishing ourselves. In fact, experts like Edward Deci have found that people are more successful at motivating themselves when they seek to do a task based on the task itself, not because of reward or punishment.

Think about that for a moment. That suggests that a big part of self-motivation comes from focusing on the task itself, as well as how it benefits you and makes you feel, rather than worrying about rewards or punishment.

Taller Than the Tallest Problems

In considering the life and achievements of Rousseau, sociologists have often raised a provocative question: how did it come about that a man born poor, who lost his mother at birth and was deserted by his father, who was afflicted with a painful and humiliating disease, who was repudiated by society and civilization, who was driven from place to place as a dangerous rebel, who was suspected of crime and insanity, ... how did it come about that this man, after his death, triumphed over Voltaire, transformed education, elevated the morals of France, inspired the Romantic movement and the French revolution, and influenced the philosophy of Kant?

Whether or not we wholly agree with their evaluation of Rousseau, his accomplishments seem truly remarkable when viewed against the stressful conditions of his early life. Although he suffered from serious emotional difficulties, he reached an unusually high level of achievement.

If he could do it, surely you and I can attempt the same.

Exercises

To help you better understand self-motivation, here are a few exercises.

1. The Power of Positive Thinking

   The simple goal of this exercise is to help you get started with thinking positively. Take a piece of paper and write down five positive attributes you have. These should be things about yourself that you value. Review this list regularly.

2. The Three-Goal List

   Take another piece of paper and write down three goals you have: one short-term goal (1–2 weeks), one mid-term goal (1–2 months), and one long-term goal (6–12 months).

3. What Motivates Me?

   Take some time to consider what motivates you. What gets you really excited about a task?

Action Plan

Okay, this is where the real work begins. This is how you can actualize the potential you were born with and motivate yourself to realize all your dreams and goals.

If you follow this action plan closely, you will soon realize the power of self-motivation.

1. Establish a Goal

   ✓ Every time you come across something you want to achieve, establish a goal. Be specific about what you want to accomplish. Write it down, and remember what you want to happen.

2. Establish "First Steps"

   ✓ Getting started with any task is often the most difficult part. With regard to your chosen goal, what are the first tangible steps you can take to get started?

3. Daily Tasks

   ✓ Find inspiration wherever you can, such as in quotes, music, or literature; whatever motivates you, read it, watch it, or listen to it daily.

   ✓ Affirm yourself. Consider your positive traits and abilities (e.g., "I'm thoughtful and compassionate"); remind yourself of them often.

4. Track Your Progress

   ✓ Keep a record or journal of your journey. Write down the things you are doing to develop self-motivation. Review your journal regularly.

You Can Do It!

Anyone can develop self-motivation—no matter who they are or what their circumstances are. You have the incredible power within you to motivate yourself, reach your goals, and become the person you long to be. Stay positive, look to the future, and set goals. Always look for ways to affirm yourself and find inspiration in the world around you. You'll quickly discover that you can motivate yourself—and that is a very powerful thing.

> Destiny is not a matter of chance, it is a matter
> of choice. It is not a thing to be waited for, it is
> a thing to be achieved. (Jeremy Kitson)

Further Reading

Deci, Edward. (1995). *Why We Do What We Do: Understanding Self-Motivation.* New York: Penguin Books.

Covey, Stephen. (1989). *The Seven Habits of Highly Effective People.* New York: Free Press.

COURAGE AND CONFIDENCE

Courage is resistance to fear, mastery of fear—not absence of fear.

—Mark Twain

Personal Portraits

One of the strangest things that I have learned about myself is that my internal state and self-talk affects my reality in such a profound way that sometimes I feel that the results I get in life are totally related to the inner workings of my mind. In other words, if I believe I am powerful and confident and strong—and really have conviction—everything in my environment reacts accordingly. And if I feel weak or insecure or passive, I get negative results. To some of us this is common sense, but for others who don't know how to quiet the random thoughts that our subconscious minds conjure up, it can be a difficult struggle.

I remember my first job after graduating from college when I was nineteen. I was inventing toys to help sell hamburgers to children. That's true. My official title was "Kid's Marketing Coordinator." It was definitely a fun job for a fresh graduate. Three months into the role, I was sent to Hong Kong and then asked to make a presentation to the board of directors. I felt extremely anxious and afraid. I thought about everything that could go wrong. I imagined scenarios in which I would just freeze in front of the management or I would forget my lines or I would trip or faint or something else terrible. But the strange thing is, I never imagined my success. I didn't see myself being bold, walking straight and proudly, and delivering the presentation with authority and confidence. That was the moment when I realized that sometimes I have to be conscious of these thoughts and try to control them.

When I began to imagine and believe that I had the resources, strength, and confidence to excel at my task, I began to act that way. And the more I focused on my preferred results, the more my behavior became congruent with my positive vision.

I gave an outstanding presentation to a board of twelve senior executives—and I was just a nineteen-year-old kid, fresh out of college. This was all because I chose to focus on the desired outcome and to harness the strength and courage to be confident in my delivery, even though deep down inside, I was still extremely scared.

Are you a courageous person?

When you think of courage, what comes to mind? If you're like a lot of people, you may envision powerful warriors striding into battle, brave explorers and adventurers, risk-takers, or death-defying daredevils. What many people do not realize is that anyone can be courageous—and being courageous may not be quite what you think.

In this module, you'll discover what it really means to be courageous and confident. What you learn may surprise you, but it will also definitely enlighten you and provide you with ways to gain more courage and confidence in your own life.

Background

What is courage, and why is it important? Why do you need confidence? Is there a difference between confidence and arrogance?

We will discuss why confidence is such an important trait—and how, sometimes, being confident means having courage. We will also explore what courage really means as opposed to what people often think it means.

Most successful people have both confidence and courage—an unshakeable belief in their own abilities. Even when they lack confidence, they know that if they act as *if* they are confident, they'll succeed.

If you have issues with confidence or courage, don't worry. Everyone does at some point. Remember the Cowardly Lion in the *Wizard of Oz*? Or Sinbad during his seven voyages? Both faced trials and tribulations, and both had to muster up enough courage to overcome them.

You can, too. With a bit of courage and confidence, you can make it through anything.

Find yourself, for courage and confidence are
as easy as breathing to the person who really
knows who he is. (Vernon Howard)

Definitions

Courage: acting in the presence—not absence—of fear.

Confidence: assurance; freedom from doubt; belief in yourself and your
abilities.

Perseverance: steady persistence in a course of action; continuing a purpose
despite difficulties.

The Process

It is not the critic who counts; nor the man who
points out how the strong man stumbled, or where
the doer of deeds could have done better.

The credit belongs to the man who is actually in
the arena; whose face is marred by dust and sweat
and blood; who strives valiantly. If he fails, at least
he fails while daring greatly; so that his place shall
never be with those cold and timid souls who know
neither victory nor defeat. (Theodore Roosevelt)

In pre-Islamic times around the year 525, a poet and warrior by the name
of Antarah Ibn Shaddad was born in Najd (northern Saudi Arabia). He was
placed into servitude at an early age but did not remain a slave for long. He
quickly made a name for himself as a brave and courageous warrior who
helped his master's tribe defend itself from a rival in battle. As a result, he
was granted his freedom and went on to become a great poet who often
wrote about courage and heroism in battle. Antarah's works have become
noted for representing courage and chivalry—and serve as a good example
for us of what courage means.

And, verily, I remember the advice of my uncle, in the
battle, when the two lips quiver from off the white teeth
of the mouth, In the thick of the battle, of which the

warriors do not complain of the rigors, except with an unintelligible noise. When my people defended themselves with me against the spears of the enemy, I did not refrain from them through cowardice, but the place of my advance had become too straight. (Antarah Ibn Shaddad)

Being Courageous

Courage is the ability to act in the presence of fear. Some people may think that being courageous means having no fear, but there is nothing wrong with being afraid. There is something wrong, however, with not being able to act when you're afraid. You don't want fear to paralyze you so that you take no action at all.

Courage, then, is making the decision to act even if something worries you, concerns you, or frightens you. Dealing with fear, obstacles, and problems takes more courage than dealing with positive, stress-free situations.

If you lack courage and confidence, the goal is to overcome your fear of fear.

A Winner's Prayer

Let me win. But if I cannot win, at least let me
be brave in the attempt. (Anonymous)

Actions As Well As Thoughts

Being courageous isn't just about how you act—it's also a mindset. Think about how you handle adversity. Did you know that how you see a situation determines how you act in that situation? It's true. To be courageous, you must adopt the mindset of a courageous person—that you will carry on and persevere, *no matter what*. This brings us to prerequisites.

Prerequisites

Courage requires two prerequisites—determination and motivation. After all, sometimes getting past fear just means turning a blind eye to what scares you and pressing on.

Being courageous means you have something motivating you to act—some purpose that is worth the difficulty. Remember our discussion about self-motivation? That is absolutely crucial to developing courage in yourself.

Now let's look at how courage and confidence go hand in hand.

Keys to Confidence

How would you describe a confident person? Someone who looks confident? Speaks confidently? Confidence is, simply put, a belief that you can accomplish whatever you set your mind to. When you are confident, you are optimistic, relaxed, calm, upbeat and positive. When you lack confidence, you are pessimistic, stressed, worried, frantic and negative.

Fortunately, confidence comes through three simple routes: positive thinking, strong beliefs, and perspective.

Positive Thinking

We have already discussed how positive thinking can help with self-esteem. It also plays a big role in confidence. If you think positively, it's easy to feel confident. This is because a positive mindset allows you to see the possibilities in anything. Remember this: confidence, like so much else, is a self-fulfilling prophecy. If you think you have confidence, you will be confident. If you don't think you are confident, you won't be. You are what you think; you become what you think about.

> Life shrinks or expands in proportion
> to one's courage. (Anais Nin)

Strong Beliefs

Confident people have strong values, beliefs, and standards. They rest on them as a house rests on a foundation. To be confident means to have strong beliefs about not only yourself, but also what you do and your purpose in life.

Perspective

It always helps to remember to pay attention to perspective. One trick to gaining confidence is to look at it from another person's perspective. Is what you are facing really as bad as your mind makes it out to be?

When you keep things in perspective you'll find it easier to be confident.

Acting in the Presence of Fear

Of course, both courage and confidence involve acting in the presence of fear. Remember: everyone feels fear at one point or another. It's not about feeling afraid; it's about what you do when fear arises.

Here are three ways to act even when fear is present.

Visualization

Picture the problem in your mind. Try to "see" the situation and your fear. Imagine the fear. Visualizing fear or doubt allows you to understand it, and understanding it is the best way to make it insignificant.

Affirmation

Tell yourself constantly that you are confident, courageous, and capable of handling whatever lies before you. Keep in mind that what you tell yourself is what you believe, and what you believe will become a self-fulfilling prophecy.

Strength and Weaknesses

Know yourself—your strengths as well as your weaknesses. When you have an accurate opinion of yourself, you know your limits and what you can and cannot handle. That will make you more confident and assured in any situation.

An Example of Courage and Confidence—Nelson Mandela

In 1962, a man by the name of Nelson Mandela was arrested in South Africa for opposing the South African government, which favored a policy of racial segregation and oppression known as apartheid. Mandela stayed in prison for twenty-seven years—twenty-seven long, dreary years, doing hard labor in a depressing and miserable place. During this time, he was allowed only one visitor and one letter every six months. It was a terrifying existence.

But one day—on February 11, 1990 to be exact—Nelson Mandela walked out of prison a free man. He eventually became the president of South Africa and has become a symbol for courage and strength in the midst of terrible adversity.

Exercises

Below are three exercises that can help you cultivate courage and confidence in yourself.

1. Facing Your Fears

   Write down three to five of your biggest fears. Be specific. What makes you afraid of them?

2. Positive Thinking

   Reflect on one positive trait you've identified. Does this make you feel confident?

3. Courage and Confidence around You

   Take a look at your family, friends, and co-workers. Are any of them confident and courageous? What makes them that way? What can you learn from them?

Action Plan

Being confident and courageous is all about thinking and acting confidently and courageously. Here is an action plan that can help you develop those strengths and use them down the road to change your life for the better.

1. Facing Your Fears Again

   ✓ Identify actions you can take to counter or get over the fears you listed previously—and then make a commitment to do them.

2. SWOT Analysis

   ✓ SWOT stands for "Strengths, Weaknesses, Opportunities, Threats." Whenever you encounter a situation that causes fear, concern, or doubt, do a "SWOT analysis" for the situation. Think of your strengths and weaknesses that apply to the situation. Then, look at whether you feel threatened by the situation. Also, consider what opportunities you will gain by dealing with the situation.

3. Goal Accomplishment

   ✓ Identify three short-term goals that you can achieve fairly quickly and easily.

   ✓ Accomplish them. When you set reachable goals for yourself and fulfill them, you build a track record of success—which in turn gives you confidence.

4. Track Progress

   ✓ Keep a record or journal of your journey and what you are doing to develop courage and confidence. Review your journal periodically.

You Can Do It!

A "fearless" warrior has not learned to live without fear; he has instead learned to fight even though he is afraid. A person who rushes into a burning building to save someone is not acting without fear; he is choosing to act even though he is scared. He acts because he has an overriding reason for doing so.

You can be like these people every day of your life. Make a commitment to living with fear instead of without it, because living without fear is impossible. Remember: you become what you think about.

Stay positive and determined. As American president Franklin D. Roosevelt famously said, "We have nothing to fear but fear itself."

> I learned that courage was not the absence of fear, but
> the triumph over it. The brave man is not he who does not
> feel afraid, but he who conquers that fear. (Nelson Mandela)

Further Reading

Anderson, Walter. (1998). *The Confidence Course: Seven Steps to Self-Fulfillment*. New York: HarperCollins.

Warrell, Margie. (2008). *Find Your Courage: 12 Acts for Becoming Fearless at Work and in Life*. London: McGraw-Hill.

SELF-ESTEEM

A person's worth in this world is estimated according to the value they put on themselves.

—Jean De La Bruyere

Personal Portraits

I really believe that everyone is capable of greatness. We are blessed with time, reason, love, and creativity. Why not create art, write books, build cities, make music, invent gadgets, and achieve self-actualization?

I wrote *Paper Forest* when I was a teenager. It was a frenzy of poems, ideas, prose, and raw unabridged emotion. For ten years, it lay in the dusty bottom of some creased box—waiting. Then came the time to complete it. So I typed it all, which took me about three months of on and off work. Next, I self-published it and made sure there was a copy sent to the US Library of Congress. Why? Because I value the creative talent that God has given me, and I felt that I deserved to publish my own poetry book. And when I did, it felt incredible. The first time I held it in my trembling hands and flipped through the pages, glimpsing sentences and phrases that I had written ten years earlier printed and bound in this little book ... I felt extremely proud of myself.

I could now the accolade of "author" and "poet" to my list of achievements.

There once was a small child who dreamed of becoming a great professor. He wanted to travel the world, speak several languages, read piles of books, deliver lectures to the masses, and bring knowledge and culture to the world.

As he grew older, he began to see that perhaps these great ambitions of his were a little too far-fetched. After all, although he thought he was smart, he didn't believe he was that smart, and he definitely didn't see himself as wise. He revised his dream and decided instead to become a pretty good professor at a great university that was closer to home.

As the boy approached adulthood, he began to see himself differently. Failures and difficulties had tempered his outlook on life. He revised his dream yet again. Surely someone as flawed as him couldn't even be a pretty good professor. Instead, he would merely teach secondary school or, perhaps, just tutor students.

The boy eventually became an adult. As he passed through the years, he continued to doubt and degrade himself. Then, one day he woke up and realized that he was now an old man who had been working as a janitor at a local school for many years.

At the beginning, the child said, "I can do great things because I am great!" Now, the old man said, "I did not do anything great, because I was never great."

Who do you think is correct?

> You yourself, as much as anybody in the entire
> universe, deserve your love and affection. (Buddha)

Background

One of my favorite photos is that of a kitten looking in a mirror, and the reflection it sees is a lion. The caption says, "What matters most is how you see yourself."

Those are powerful words because a major part of who you are is how you see yourself and how you feel about yourself. Your feelings and perceptions about yourself make up your self-esteem. Self-esteem plays a huge role in everything you do. Like the boy in the story above, people who have high self-esteem can envision great things in their future. They will strive to accomplish them. However, people who have low self-esteem will see negativity wherever they look. They'll talk themselves out of every dream they have.

What does it mean to have self-esteem? Just how important is it? And how do people increase their self-esteem and feel better about themselves? This module will provide answers to those questions.

> Nothing splendid has ever been achieved except by
> those who dared believe that something inside of
> them was superior to circumstance. (Bruce Barton)

Definitions

Self-esteem: psychologist Nathaniel Branden, a renowned expert on self-esteem, defines it as "the experience of being competent to cope with the basic challenges of life and being worthy of happiness."

Self-image: how you see yourself and how you perceive others' views of you.

> No one can make you feel inferior without
> your permission. (Eleanor Roosevelt)

The Process

Your self-esteem—i.e., how you see yourself—is incredibly important. After all, if you don't see value in yourself, no one else will. And even if someone does, you won't believe them.

Self-esteem is more than thinking you are good or bad at a task, role, or occupation. It is more than how you rate your skills and inabilities. Self-esteem is how you value yourself—how worthy you think you are of having love, happiness, and satisfaction in life.

Here's another way to look at it: think of self-esteem as fuel for your car. If your car runs out of fuel, you won't be able to drive it anywhere—you'll be stranded. Without self-esteem, you'll be "stranded" or stuck in life—never really going anywhere.

While most people seem to know what self-esteem is, they don't fully understand it. Let's look at a few more aspects of self-esteem that you may not know.

Self-Esteem Can Be Changed

Self-esteem isn't something that is set in stone—it can be changed. If you suffer from low self-esteem, it can be improved significantly. You can develop a much better view of yourself—and that is where true change starts to take place.

Self-esteem Is Directly Related to Happiness

Self-esteem is directly related to happiness and satisfaction. People who have low self-esteem, yet consider themselves happy and fulfilled, are extremely rare.

Self-esteem also impacts how you relate to other people. I once knew a person who had very low self-esteem, had very few friends, and treated others poorly because he didn't think anyone could actually like him.

> People are like stained-glass windows. They sparkle
> and shine when the sun is out, but when the darkness
> sets in their true beauty is revealed only if there
> is light from within. (Elisabeth Kübler-Ross)

Sources of Self-Esteem

As you can see, self-esteem is vital to anyone who desires to live life fully. Let's look at the three primary sources of self-esteem:

1. Accomplishments

   Many people feel good about themselves because of the things they've accomplished. The sense that you can accomplish things is called self-efficacy. Increasing one's self-efficacy by reaching goals (even very small ones) and successfully completing tasks is a tried and true way to help build self-esteem.

   Of course, what happens when you fail at a task, or your accomplishment isn't quite as great as you had hoped? Well, if you rely solely on self-efficacy as a source of self-esteem, you'll almost definitely end up disappointed.

2. Validation from Others

   Another common source of self-esteem is validation from other people, such as family, friends, and co-workers. People feel good about themselves when they receive compliments, praise, affirmations, or rewards from others.

Unfortunately, other people can also do a lot of damage to your self-esteem—e.g., when they criticize you, judge you, put you down, or treat you with disrespect. And you can't control other people's actions.

As you can see, neither of the first two sources of self-esteem is reliable. That leaves us with …

3. Validation from Within

Ideally, your self-esteem should come from within you. You should base it on how you see yourself, not how others see you. In order to do this, you must recognize your strengths and all the wonderful qualities you possess.

Self-esteem also involves positive thinking and self-acceptance.

The Importance of Accepting Yourself

It took me a long time not to judge myself
through someone else's eyes. (Sally Field)

What does it mean to truly accept yourself?

You are a unique individual. Out of over seven billion people on this planet, there is *no* one else exactly like you. For all your flaws, you are you, and that is who you will always be. Accepting yourself means acknowledging that you are not perfect—*no one is*—but you *are* a unique individual with many great qualities.

It's impossible to have strong, positive, loving self-esteem if you do not accept yourself. Hard as it may seem, look at yourself for who you really are. Accept your imperfections and spectacular traits—everything that makes you *uniquely* you.

As Eleanor Roosevelt once said, "Somehow we learn who we really are and then live with that decision."

Did You Know?

Self-esteem, self-efficacy, and self-concept are all related concepts in psychology.

Self-concept is a collection of beliefs about yourself that is arranged in hierarchical order and directly influences your behavior.

Self-esteem promotes an overall feeling of worth and value for oneself.

Self-efficacy involves a judgment of one's specific capabilities to do a task in comparison to others. Self-efficacy is therefore a more focused concept limited to domain-specific tasks.

A Role Model of Healthy Self-Esteem

One of the best role models of healthy self-esteem is the legendary boxer Muhammad Ali. He is famous for his unwavering belief in himself and frequent proclamation, "I'm the greatest!" He truly believes in himself and sees the value and worth he possesses. Granted, at times he has come across as a bit arrogant. However, everyone has been able to see the pride, self-acceptance, and amazing self-confidence he possesses.

Take a look around you. If you know people who are self-assured, confident, happy, and satisfied with life, they most likely have a positive view of themselves.

> It's lack of faith that makes people afraid of meeting challenges, and I believed in myself. (Muhammad Ali)

Exercises

These exercises will help you see yourself in a different, more positive way. They will also help boost your self-acceptance.

1. Identify Three Positive Characteristics

    Write down three positive characteristics or traits that you possess. Don't write down accomplishments; look at your attributes and qualities and explore the traits you possess that you feel good about.

2. Accept Yourself

    Write down five self-affirmations. These are statements that say something positive and uplifting about you. For example, you could say, "I am a kind person who cares about other people."

3. Rosenberg's Self Esteem Scale

   Psychologist Morris Rosenberg developed a scale to evaluate self-esteem. Find the "Rosenburg Scale" on the net and take the short test to see where you rank.

   If you really put a small value upon yourself, rest assured that the world will not raise your price. (Anonymous)

Action Plan

As you have come to realize by now, every module comes with a good action plan to jumpstart the change in your life. Here are some tangible steps you can take to improve your self-esteem:

1. Give Yourself Active Self-Feedback

   ✓ Give yourself accurate, honest, and objective feedback on a routine basis. Tell yourself how you feel about something you say, think, or do—and be honest. Don't be harsh, and don't be afraid to give yourself a compliment.

2. Reward Yourself

   ✓ Be nice to yourself once in a while. Know that you are worthy of rewards—regardless of what you may have been told in the past. So reward yourself often.

3. Reverse Your Thoughts

   ✓ Whenever you hear or recall a negative comment about yourself, reverse it. Turn it into something positive. Embrace your positive qualities and don't put too much stock into your negative traits.

4. Track Your Progress

✓ Keep a record or journal of your journey and what you are doing to develop your self-esteem. Review your journal periodically.

A successful person is one who can lay a
firm foundation with the bricks that others
throw at him or her. (David Brinkley)

You Can Do It!

You really can improve your self-esteem and change how you see yourself. People with self-esteem are able to accept criticism and learn from past mistakes. They are self-confident without being conceited, and they are open with others and self-assured. They don't worry about looking foolish. They are accepting of themselves and others, and they are able to laugh at themselves.

Remember: who you are is just as much a function of who you think you are as it is anything else. Be positive. See yourself in a positive light.

By being yourself, you put something wonderful in
the world that was not there before. (Edwin Elliot)

Further Reading

Branden, Nathaniel. (1995). *Six Pillars of Self-Esteem*. New York: Bantam.

Burns, David D. (1999). *Feeling Good: The New Mood Therapy (Revised and Updated)*. New York: HarperCollins.

OVERCOMING YOUR FEARS

If we let things terrify us, life will not be worth living.

—Seneca

Personal Portraits

I used to be really afraid of approaching strangers on the bus or in the grocery store. I used to have many assumptions about such a situation. How will people judge me? What if they don't like me? What if I sound stupid? My mind used to construct these and hundreds of other scenarios based on absolutely no evidence. I don't have that fear anymore, because I have learned to approach and interact with everyone in all situations. I play with children, start intellectual conversations with taxi drivers, and flirt with cute waitresses. The reason for this is that, inevitably, we are a social species, and isolating ourselves is not a healthy option. We were created to interact with and learn from each other, and grow together as a community.

When I realized that the fear I used to create in my mind was purely self-imposed and that it was false, I was freed from my own negative self-talk. I am not afraid to talk to strangers anymore. I have met business partners, potential employers, lifelong friends, and beautiful women in the most unlikely places and under the strangest circumstances. In certain situations, I tell myself that our paths have crossed for a reason, and I make the decision to forget my fear and turn it into courage—I choose to interact. The positive outcomes of such moments of courage have given me incredible fulfillment and satisfaction, opened up doors for me, expanded my business and social network, and created a positive feedback loop that continues to reinforce my behavior. A friend asked me what I say to strangers when I approach them, and I replied, "Just relax, smile, make eye contact, and then introduce yourself—what's the worst that could happen?"

"The first time I won Boston, I didn't think I even belonged in the race," said wheelchair athlete Jean Driscoll. Winner of seven consecutive Boston Marathons (1990–96), Driscoll's success has helped change public perception of athletes with disabilities. It has also opened doors for more female athletes with disabilities to overcome their fears and follow their dreams.

Fear is a universal human emotion. Everyone experiences it.

Spiders, flying and public speaking are some of the things that are terrifying people everyday and the common factor in each fear is that each one evokes powerful mental, physical, and even spiritual reactions.

> Confront your fears, list them, get to know
> them, and only then will you be able to put
> them aside and move ahead. (Jerry Gillies)

Fear is everywhere—and no one is immune to it.

Background

What exactly is fear?

We all know what it is like to fear something - everyone experiences fear. Part of learning how to deal with life and how to be successful in your personal journey is learning how to meet fear head on—and overcome it.

Everyone has fear—there are no exceptions. Even the biggest, loudest, alpha-type men have fears. While fear is inevitable—at some point you will be afraid of something—it can be overcome.

Let me repeat that: *it can be overcome.*

Definitions

Fear: a distressing emotion aroused by impending danger, evil, pain, etc., regardless of whether the threat is real or imagined. Fear is almost always related to the future and comes from the expectation of some form of possible harm.

Phobia: a persistent, irrational fear of a specific object, activity, or situation that leads to a compelling desire to avoid it. Not all fears are phobias, because not all fears are irrational.

Fear conditioning: the process by which we are made to fear something. Most fears are learned by repeated interactions with others and the environment around us.

The Process

> When a resolute young fellow steps up to the great
> bully, the world, and takes him boldly by the beard,
> he is often surprised to find it comes off in his
> hand, and that it was only tied on to scare away the
> timid adventurers. (Ralph Waldo Emerson)

Think about a time when you were really scared. Do you remember how you reacted? Do you remember how you felt? Do you remember what you thought? Those reactions, feelings, and thoughts are a basic part of human nature. Unfortunately, they can be truly terrifying. One way to combat these fears is to understand fear itself. The more you understand something, the less power it has over you and the less it will terrify you.

How Fear Develops

Most fear arises as a result of past conditioning. We learn how to fear something because we dwell on the bad consequences we experienced in the past. For example, if you burned yourself badly with hot coffee in the past, you may now fear a steaming cup of coffee. We teach ourselves to expect negative events in the future based on past negative experiences. That expectation creates fear and worry about the future. You learn to be afraid of something through fear conditioning. This means that you can

- identify a possible event or consequence that is negative,

- imagine yourself experiencing that negative consequence,

- and associate your body's reactions with that event and consequence.

That's how fears develop.

Take public speaking, for instance.

Imagine a manager who is preparing for an important presentation that will be beneficial for his career. His boss mocks him in front of the board and he feels degraded by the experience. As a consequence, he develops an irrational fear of public speaking and pictures himself being mocked again—and embarrassed and humiliated as a result. Over time, he becomes conditioned and associates public speaking with those painful reactions.

Any fears you have likely developed in the same way, especially if the fear involves you having to perform in any way.

Tips to Control Fear

- Consider your foundation,

- fuel yourself with positive resources,

- and learn to control worry.

How Fear Interferes with Life

Fear is one of the most disruptive and paralyzing emotions we can experience. Do you remember times you've been afraid? You no doubt experienced a variety of physical reactions, such as sweaty palms and a racing heart. These physical reactions are caused by the fight-or-flight response - a built-in safety mechanism designed to protect you when you perceive any kind of threat. The fight-or-flight response is actually a burst of adrenalin that helps you survive when we encounter real danger in your life. It is an ancient biological response that was crucial to the survival of our species when faced with man-eating tigers and fierce warriors.

Unfortunately, that adrenalin still kicks in today, despite the fact that the vast majority of things that scare us aren't real threats (such as public speaking or fear of the dark). Far too often, it—and the fear that accompanies it—keeps us from moving forward in life. You become afraid to take action and, instead, avoid the object or situation as much as possible.

Fear interferes with your life by creating a vicious cycle that can keep you stuck.

Franklin D. Roosevelt said that the only thing we have to fear is fear itself. Here is the second part to that quote: "Fear—nameless, unreasoning, unjustified terror which paralyzes needed efforts to convert retreat into advance."

That is what we're up against—and that is what we need to overcome.

Traits Necessary to Fight Fear

When it comes to overcoming fear, several traits are required. Being aware of these required traits is the first step to learning how to overcome your fears:

- Determination and resolve

    - You must be determined and dedicated to overcoming fear.

- Ability to set goals

    - Setting a goal gives you a light at the end of what can be a very dark tunnel.

- Self-worth/self-esteem

    - Fear tends to dissolve quickly in the presence of high self-esteem.

- Realism and perspective

    - Realize that most fears are exaggerated and far worse than the actual situation itself.

- Perseverance

    - Keep moving forward, as some fears may take years to overcome.

- Confidence

    - This is the cornerstone. If you are confident, fear will have no power over you.

    Fear is never a reason for quitting; it is only an excuse. (Norman Vincent Peale)

Two Types of Fear

To overcome fear, it's helpful to understand the two types of fear: incapacitating fear and motivational fear.

Incapacitating Fear

This is a very common—and destructive—type of fear. It can significantly interfere with your life because it causes worry, panic, and paralysis. It prevents you from taking constructive action. In most instances, the fear of fear is worse than the fear itself. The trick, then, is to turn incapacitating fear into …

Motivational Fear

Motivational fear is actually a good type of fear. It's constructive and beneficial, because it motivates us to take action and move forward. An example of motivational fear is the student who studies harder because he's afraid of failing, or the person who practices a speech over and over because they are afraid of messing it up. Allow your fear to motivate you and drive you toward improving yourself.

> Fear is only as deep as the mind allows. (Japanese proverb)

Exercises

These exercises can help you overcome your fears by making them familiar to you. The more familiar they are, the less power they will have over you.

1. Honesty Exercise

   Identify a fear you have. Be honest with yourself as you document in detail how that fear makes you feel and how it limits you.

2. Prioritization

   List your fears, and rank them based on how strong they are. Which one scares you the most? That's the one you should address first.

Action Plan

You can also use previous action plans to help you with overcoming your fears. Remember: everything flows together and it's all one process.

1. Recognize the Problem

   ✓ When faced with a fear, be honest with yourself. Identify what scares you. Recognize that fearing fear causes more anxiety than the fear of the situation itself.

2. Motivate Yourself

   ✓ Identify the benefits you would receive if you overcame the fear. Give yourself something to shoot for; it will help keep you going.

   ✓ Affirm yourself daily that you can and will beat the fear.

3. Systematically Desensitize Yourself

   ✓ Systematic desensitization involves acknowledging and confronting your fear while using relaxation techniques to lower the intensity of the fear. After you encounter your fear over and over again, you will become desensitized to it—and it will disappear.

   ✓ Find ways to encounter your fear. When you do, use relaxation techniques (e.g., prayer, meditation, music, self-affirmation, or whatever calms and relaxes you) to soothe your anxiety. Continued practice will help you overcome the fear.

4. Analyze the Two Types of Fear

   ✓ Take your list of fears and determine which category (incapacitating or motivational) each fear fits into.

   ✓ Think of ways you can turn each incapacitating fear into a motivational fear.

   ✓ Analyze just how much of a threat each situation poses. Be objective.

    ✓ Think of ways you can use your motivational fears to better yourself.

5. Track Progress

    ✓ Keep a record or journal of your journey and what you are doing to combat your fears. Review your journal periodically.

You Can Do It!

Fear can be overcome. People all over the world overcome fear every day—people just like you. It can be done. Remember: fear is worse than the consequence itself, because the consequence may never happen. Fear will always happen—*if* you allow it. Overcome your fears, and become a better, stronger person throughout your journey.

> Inaction breeds doubt and fear. Action breeds confidence and courage. If you want to conquer fear, do not sit at home and think about it. Go out and get busy. (Dale Carnegie)

Further Reading

"All About Fear." *Psychology Today*. http://www.psychologytoday.com/basics/fear

Pillay, Srinivasan S. (1999). *Life Unlocked: 7 Revolutionary Lessons to Overcome Fear*. New York: Rodal Books.

EMOTIONAL MANAGEMENT

*The sign of intelligent people is their ability to
control emotions by the application of reason.*

—Marya Mannes

Personal Portraits

The traffic in Cairo is a nightmare, and everyone knows this. It is normal to waste four hours every day commuting, stuck in traffic and daydreaming until you arrive at your destination. One of my good friends has a very short temper and is incapable of controlling his emotions. I recall one time we were stuck in traffic, and he was swearing at the other drivers, shouting at me, and beating his fists on the dashboard—wasting his energy completely.

I felt really bad for him and asked him a question that was related to a concept I had read about in psychology.

"Do you have any influence over the flow of traffic?" I asked.

"No."

"Then why are you wasting your energy being concerned about it?"

I went on to explain to him the difference between the "circle of influence" and "circle of concern."

I really find no reason to become anxious or agitated about matters that are outside my own circle of influence. Watching the news makes me feel sad about the state of the world, but this is out of empathy and not out of anger. I really could not care less about how long it takes me to get out of a traffic gridlock, because there is absolutely nothing I can do about it. And when I see the crowded public bus filled to the rim with hundreds of people, squeezed together like sardines in a can and staring down at me, I feel grateful that I am sitting in my cool air-conditioned car, listening to inspiring music and enjoying a casual phone conversation.

Robert Pirsig's book, *Zen and the Art of Motorcycle Maintenance*, has a powerful story about the South Indian monkey trap which was developed by villagers to catch the ever-present small monkeys in that part of the world. The trap is a hollowed-out coconut chained to a pole. The coconut contains rice, which is visible through a small hole. The hole is just big enough for the monkey to put its hand in but too small for its fist to come out once it grabs the rice. Tempted by the rice, the monkey reaches in and is suddenly trapped. It doesn't realize that its desire for the rice is what traps it. It wants the rice too much to let it go, even though doing so would free it from the trap. So the villagers capture him.

Just as the monkey's greed trapped it, your emotions can blind you and "trap" you by interfering with your ability to make rational choices.

Do your emotions control you—or do you control them?

Emotions are one of the most dynamic forces in our lives. They can be uplifting, inspiring, and motivational—or depressing, deflating, and unwanted. They can make you smile and laugh, or frown and cry. We experience emotions on a daily basis. Managing your emotions is vital to developing yourself and taking control of your life.

This module will help you recognize your emotions and learn how to control them. You'll be able to see just how emotions can work for you instead of against you.

Background

What is an emotion? Emotions are basically feelings—how we respond to what happens to us. Psychologists define emotions as having three distinct parts:

- Physiological changes

  - What happens to your body when you experience an emotion; e.g., elevated blood pressure, heart rate, facial expressions, etc.

- Behavioral expression

  - What you tend to do in reaction to an emotion; e.g., frown, yell, cry, panic, etc.

- Subjective experience

  – What you feel when you experience an emotion.

When we say "emotion," most of the time we are referring to the third part—subjective experience.

Imagine you are faced with an overload of projects at work. They all have deadlines that are rapidly approaching, and you don't think you'll have enough time to complete them. Think of the physical response your body will have. Think about how you will react. Think about how you will feel. That is what it means to experience an emotion. Emotions can be positive or negative; they can help you or hurt you. Either way, when they are out of control, the consequences are almost always negative. That's why controlling your emotions is so important and vital.

> Take control of your consistent emotions and
> begin to consciously and deliberately reshape your
> daily experience of life. (Anthony Robbins)

Definitions

Emotion: a mental state that arises spontaneously rather than through conscious effort. A primary emotion is what you feel first in response to an event or an action. A secondary emotion is what you feel in response to the primary emotion (e.g., hurt is the primary emotion, followed by anger in response to the hurt).

Emotional intelligence: the ability, capacity, or skill to identify, assess, and control your emotions, as well as to have empathy for others' emotions.

> You cannot always control circumstances, but you can
> control your thoughts and emotions. (Charles Popplestown)

The Process

Have you ever experienced such powerful emotions that they completely overpowered you? Do you wish you had a better understanding as to why you felt that way and how you could have regained control? We all have felt this way at one point or another. For thousands of years, people have tried to control their emotions in various ways. Yoga, for example, was created to harness the spirit while achieving a sense of calm and balance. Meditation has been used to enhance focus and bring about inner peace.

You can manage and control your emotions so they don't interfere with your life and cause distress. You may not be able to prevent emotions from happening—they happen pretty much without our consent. But you can at least deal with them effectively when they occur.

Cognitive-Motivational-Relational Theory

One of the most important discoveries in emotional management was made by a renowned psychologist named Dr. Richard Lazarus. He was one of the first to assert that emotions were connected to thought and not merely uncontrollable responses to external events. This was the premise of Lazarus' cognitive-motivational-relational theory. In a nutshell, this theory states that how we feel about an event—our subjective experience—is determined by how we interpret it. To put it another way, you can control your emotions by using your brain.

Think about something that triggers your emotions. By changing how you interpret the event—e.g., by choosing to see the positive aspects of the event rather than the negative ones—you can influence your emotional reaction. That is wonderful news, because it shows that being able to control your emotions is possible. You are in the driver's seat when it comes to how you feel.

Relationship Between Stress and Emotions

One of the main factors that comes into play when we talk about emotional management is stress. We're all familiar with stress, and most of the time, we hate it. Sure, stress can be good—it can motivate you to achievement and accomplishment. But, most of the time, it seems that being stressed out is a purely negative thing.

Many experts agree that there is a direct link between stress levels and emotions. Specifically, the more stressed out we feel at any given time, the more likely we are to experience negative emotions—and be unable to control them. Reducing stress, then, is a vital part of emotional management. You can reduce stress by finding ways to relax. There are many different ways to relax, such as exercising, listening to music, or reading a good book. Finding what helps you to relax—what calms you down—is essential to reducing stress.

> A leader's intelligence has to have a strong emotional component. He has to have high levels of self-awareness, maturity and self-control. She must be able to withstand the heat, handle setbacks and when those lucky moments arise, enjoy success with equal parts of joy and humility. No doubt emotional intelligence is rarer than book smarts, but my experience says it is actually more important in the making of a leader. You just can't ignore it. (Jack Welch)

Why Emotional Management Is Important

If you don't learn to manage your emotions, there will be negative consequences. These may include the following:

- erosion of self-confidence,

- de-motivation,

- decreased work ethic and productivity,

- strained interpersonal relationships,

- and unhealthy situations.

Unaddressed emotions also tend to spiral out of control quickly. It's common to ignore unpleasant emotions, but that can lead to the negative consequences listed above—and more. Therefore, it is crucial that you learn how to control them.

Managing Emotions

Here are ways you can manage your emotions and keep them under control, so that you decide what you feel and when you feel it. You will find that when your emotions are under control, you can achieve more and be happier as a result.

Keeping Cool

One key to emotional management is keeping cool which basically means staying emotionally detached and objective whenever a conflict arises. In other words, stay calm, patient, and relaxed instead of reacting. Remember: you are in control. As long as you keep perspective, you can manage your emotions from a position of strength, not weakness.

Covey and Responsibility

Personal development expert Dr. Steven R. Covey has made a career out of helping people develop healthy habits for living. One of the habits he promotes is proactivity. Covey believes that people who are successful are proactive—they focus their efforts on things they can control and do something about. Proactive individuals take responsibility for their own lives and do not allow their feelings to control their actions.

Responsibility is the name of the game. According to Covey, managing your emotions means taking responsibility for what you feel and learning from your mistakes. It also means managing your personal "emotional bank account"—which he says is similar to a bank account. You can make deposits or withdrawals from each of your relationships. Covey tells us to make a conscious effort to make meaningful deposits in our relationships and when we make a withdrawal—apologise and correct the mistake.

Much of the emotional stress we experience comes from our relationships with other people—something we will focus on later in our journey together. What Covey says also applies to you. When you are self-aware, you can control what does and does not affect you—therefore, you can control your emotions.

Anger is a brief madness. (Horace)

Fear and Courage

We have talked quite a bit about fear and courage. This is because fear and courage are at the center of many actions and decisions you make in life. Emotional management is no different. Remember: fear interferes with your life. When you are afraid to face your emotions, you are magnifying the negativity and increasing the bad consequences. Facing your emotions takes courage—and courage is merely acting in the presence of fear. When you are courageous, you can control your emotions. That is the key to emotional management.

> The first duty of man is to conquer fear; he must get
> rid of it, he cannot act till then. (Thomas Carlyle)

Exercise

For this module, try this exercise:

1. Emotion List

   List the emotions that you experience throughout an average day. Identify how often you experience each emotion. Which emotions occur most frequently? This gives you an idea of balance—and lets you see what needs to be fixed or controlled.

You might also try this on-line exercise:

2. Dealing With Our Emotions Worksheet (Dr. Don Gilbert)[2]

   > When sadness comes, just sit by the side and look at it and say, "I am the watcher, I am not sadness," and see the difference. Immediately you have cut the very root of sadness. It is no more nourished. It will die of starvation. We feed these emotions by being identified with them. (Bhagwan Shree Rajneesh)

Action Plan

The action plan below will help you build on the things we covered previously, and it will enable you to develop a plan to manage your emotions and develop your emotional intelligence.

1. Face Your Emotions

   Whenever you experience an emotion, be honest with yourself. Identify what causes it. Try to interrupt the

---

2   Gilbert, Don. "Dealing with Our Emotions Worksheet." *ebookbrowse.* http://ebookbrowse.com/dealing-with-emotions-worksheet-pdf-d26583949

response between the event and your reaction. Move from what is "natural" to what is controlled. The more you can take time to think before you react, the more you will be able to control what you think and feel.

2. Brainstorm about Emotional Management

   ✓ Look at your emotion list. Think of a counter to each negative emotion.

   ✓ For example, you can say something like, "When stressed, I can calm down by …"

   ✓ Or, "When I am angry, I can reach peace by …"

   ✓ Develop positive plans for each negative emotion you experience.

3. Track Progress

   ✓ Keep a record or journal of your journey and what you are doing to control your emotions. Review your journal periodically.

Control your emotion or it will control you. (Anonymous)

You Can Do It!

Emotions can be wonderful things. Laughing at a hilarious joke with friends; enjoying a romantic sunset; feeling pride when you accomplish something great—all of these are feelings that make life worth living. However, emotions can also interfere with your happiness and success and take control.

Emotional management is one of the best ways to keep your emotions in check so that you are in control of what you think and feel. With all of the skills you have read about in this first gate (Self) you are well on your way to fulfilling your journey of personal development.

Realize that now, in this moment of time, you are creating. You are creating your next moment based on what you are feeling and thinking. That is what's real. (Doc Childre)

Further Reading

Schinnerer, John L. (2006). *Guide to Self: The Beginner's Guide to Managing Emotion and Thought.* Bloomington: AuthorHouse.

Witz, Paul, and John Witz. (1999). *One Powerful Mind: The Complete Approach to Emotional Management at Home and at Work.* Upper Saddle River, New Jersey: Prentiss Hall.

MIND

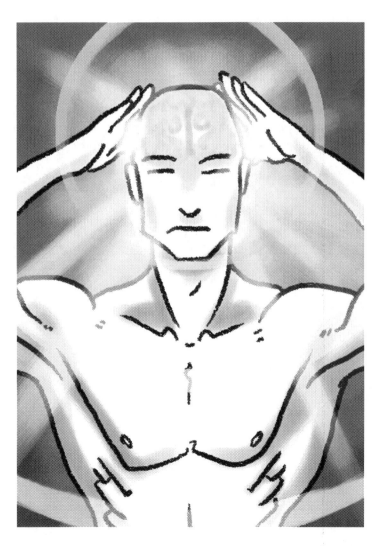

Vision

Personal Portraits

"I will compile, summarize, and disseminate knowledge and draw upon my own life experiences to aid people to reach their greatest potential." That was the vision statement I wrote that started me on the path to create the *7 Gates of Phi*. I believe that this type of knowledge is not something that we are taught at school or university—unless of course we actively seek it out or study psychology. Also, many people who find themselves attending some random training course on leadership or emotional intelligence either fail to retain and apply that knowledge in their own lives, or they don't see the full picture of how all the pieces of the jigsaw fit together.

I am very passionate about the content of this book because I believe that everyone can find some value within these pages. I have designed the content in such a way that I can also deliver it as audio modules via mobile or other digital platforms—because there are many people out there who are illiterate. I have also studied to become a trainer/facilitator so that I can conduct workshops and seminars around this content. I will aim to translate the content into Arabic, Indian, Chinese, and other languages. Why am I doing all of this? Because I have a vision, and when this vision comes true (*In Sha Allah*—God willing), I will be recognized for my positive contribution to society, I will probably make lots of money doing something that I love to do, and I will have helped someone somewhere become a happier person—and that sure beats selling hamburgers to children.

Do you have a vision? You should—because it's hard to go through life without a vision to guide you.

A professor teaching a course on business once asked a classroom full of students to spend half an hour coming up with as many ideas as they could to make ten dollars. The students broke up into groups and went to work, brainstorming for ideas—any ideas at all—to make just ten dollars. At the end of the thirty minutes, they reported back to their professor.

The professor asked the students, one by one, to share their ideas. Some ideas were great, and some were terrible. Some were serious, and some were humorous. At the end, the professor asked, "No matter how good or bad the idea, don't you agree that by the end of the day, you could probably take any of these ideas and make ten dollars?"

The class agreed.

The professor then asked, "Now, can any of these ideas make a million dollars?"

The class thought about it for a second or two and agreed none of the ideas were good enough to make a million dollars. The professor nodded and gave his class a very astute piece of wisdom: "You can't get million-dollar ideas from a ten-dollar vision."

That is what we will discuss in this module.

Background

> We create happiness by providing the finest in entertainment for people of all ages, everywhere. (Disney)

What do we mean when we say "vision"? What is a vision, and why do we need one? Part of developing your mind is creating a path to the future, to your goals. Without a path to follow, you will most certainly get lost. A vision is a broad perspective on the future. You use it for inspiration, not just as a description of what you want in life.

A vision points the way for your journey of personal development. Developing your vision requires creativity and imagination, combined with your goals and aspirations. Together, these will give you a powerful roadmap for your life.

Definitions

Vision: where you see yourself going and how you see the world.

Strategy: a broad, overarching plan to achieve an objective.

Mission: a specific purpose, designed to achieve a goal or objective.

A vision is where you want to go, a strategy is how you will get there, and a mission makes it happen.

The Process

> Vision without action is a daydream. Action without vision is a nightmare. (Japanese proverb)

There is a reason why we are addressing vision this early in the process. This gate is all about developing the mind and vision plays a big part in that. More importantly, a vision will guide you and remind you of your purpose—why you are doing what you are doing, day in and day out.

How Vision and Goals Are Related

You have probably already figured out that vision sounds an awful lot like having a goal. And, you're absolutely right—a vision is a path to your goals. It's based on what you want for yourself—where you want to go, what you want to achieve, and who you want to be.

Do you create the vision first, or set your goals first? Well, since a vision points you to your destination, you need to have a destination in the first place. Figure out what you want in life—be mindful of your goals—and then craft a vision to get you there.

How Vision and Motivation Are Related

In addition to goals, vision is also related very closely to motivation.

Imagine that you are driving a car to a destination, say, a vacation spot. It is night and pitch dark outside. The headlights that pierce the darkness and illuminate the road in front of you so you can drive safely and see where you are going represent your vision. The destination is a nice, luxurious beach resort and that represents your goal. The fuel in your car's gas tank that propels your car forward and allows you to drive represents your motivation.

You have to have motivation in order to fulfill your goals and your vision. In the previous gate, we discussed the importance of self-motivation and how it must be present in order for you to succeed. The same is true for your vision.

> Cherish your visions and your dreams, as they
> are the children of your soul, the blueprints of
> your ultimate achievements. (Napoleon Hill)

Importance of Vision throughout History

If you search through the pages of history—from the earliest days of human civilization to now—you will see many, many instances of how vision has played an important role. Every famous person, every notorious character, every noble warrior and wise sultan and genius inventor, no matter who they were or what they did, had a vision to guide them.

In the seventh century, a man named Musa bin Nusair was approached by a nobleman from the Iberian Peninsula (present-day Portugal and Spain). The nobleman told Musa tales of oppression, injustice, and cruelty inflicted by their king, Roderick. Musa was so moved by the stories, he decided to take action. Over the course of eight years, Musa Bin Nusair and his generals invaded the Iberian Peninsula. They conquered the land, ruling it for eight hundred years. It was Musa's vision that made this great feat possible. He created goals, developed a strategy, and achieved his goals because of the powerful vision that guided him.

Of course, you do not have to be a famous general to have vision. Vision is useful for anyone, no matter who he may be.

> A vision is not just a picture of what could be;
> it is an appeal to our better selves, a call to
> become something more. (Rosabeth Moss)

Vision and Creativity

Vision is also tied to creativity. As humans, we are all highly creative beings—even if we don't think we are. We love art, music, writing, dreaming, and imagining amazing things. We create and design and envision. We use creativity in every aspect of our lives on a daily basis.

The playwright George Bernard Shaw said it best: "Imagination is the beginning of creation. You imagine what you desire; you will what you imagine—and at last you create what you will."

You must tap into your creativity in order to create your vision—to imagine what you want to be. Just as a musician envisions what melody he will use for a song and what lyrics will accompany it, you use creativity to envision what you will do and where you will go in life.

Creating a Vision

To create a vision - you can start by answering these questions:

- What are your five most important values?

- What are the ten things you most enjoy doing?

- Where would you like to see yourself in five years? Ten years?

- If your life ended tomorrow, what would you most regret not doing, seeing, or achieving?

- What are your strengths and weaknesses?

Consider your answers to these questions, and then think back to what we discussed in the first gate. After you've done that, simply write down where you see yourself going—where you would like to go, what you would like to accomplish, and who you would like to be.

John F. Kennedy's Vision and Mission Statement

In 1960, John F. Kennedy crafted the following mission statement: "We will put a man on the moon by the end of the decade." This was his very public mission statement for the USA's space program. There was a clear objective and a specific time frame to achieve the goal. And it happened— Neil Armstrong took that famous "one small step for man, one giant step for mankind" in 1969.

Even though his mission statement may sound simplistic now, it had a strong impact on the entire world back then. Your mission statement should have a significant impact on your career and the choices you make in life as well.

The soul never thinks without a mental picture. (Aristotle)

Exercises

Following are three exercises that not only help you create your vision but also improve your creativity:

1. Visualization

    Picture a goal in your mind. Imagine yourself accomplishing that goal. Capture the feelings and emotions that you have.

2. Night and Day

    Take five minutes and make a list of fifteen to twenty common words, such as night, apple, sun, heavy, etc. Then, take ten to fifteen minutes and list as many opposite words as you can for each word you listed. For example, for *night* you can list *day*, *awake*, *light*, and so on.

3. Brick storming

    Think of a legacy brick—a brick inscribed with a person's name and achievements—to be placed in a wall or along a brick path as a commemoration of that person's life. A brick is not very large, so there is limited room for writing. With this in mind, write down what you would want inscribed on your legacy brick.

Action Plan

When carrying out this action plan, remember the previous lessons you've learned and keep in mind your motivations, goals, and aspirations.

1. Create a Vision Statement

✓ Take a piece of paper and write out your vision statement. Write it as if you are telling it to yourself. Be confident and assertive—this is who you will be.

2. List Personal Goals

✓ Beneath your vision statement, list your personal goals. Be as specific as possible.

3. Desired Trait List

✓ Beneath your personal goals, create a list of traits you want to develop. Rank them in order to priority. Then, list three ways to improve the trait at the top of your list.

4. Track Progress

✓ Keep a record or journal of your journey and what you are doing to control your emotions. Review your journal periodically.

You Can Do It!

Now you know what a vision is, why it is important, and how you can create one of your own. Congratulations! A vision is a remarkable achievement. Without a vision, you will not really accomplish anything meaningful, because the vision is what gives your life meaning and purpose. Keep the quote below in mind—and keep moving forward.

> Vision without action is a dream. Action without vision is simply passing the time. Action with vision is making a positive difference. (Joel Barker)

Further Reading

Burgess, Tobin. (2006). *The Personal Vision Workbook*. Florence, Kentucky: Delmar Cengage Learning.

Krippner, Stanley (2007). *The Mythic Path: Discovering the Guiding Stories of Your Past—Creating a Vision for Your Future*. Fulton, California: Elite Books.

Discipline

It is better to conquer yourself than to win a thousand battles. Then the victory is yours.

—Buddha

Personal Portraits

I've always struggled with my weight, and there have been points in my life when I have been extremely fit and also extremely fat. I need more discipline in that area of my life. However, I do remember six months before my wedding when I realized that I really needed to get into shape, because I was 20 kg overweight. So, as usual, I researched and studied the different ways that I could achieve the best results in a healthy and sustainable way. I took control of every aspect of my life, from scheduled fitness sessions to fancy shopping lists. I always maintained a constant awareness of my goal—to lose 20 kg in six months.

The actual diet was difficult because of the preparation and time required to cook large volumes of healthy food. I even found a catering company that sent me a personal chef to cook meals that I would freeze for the whole week. It sometimes felt like airplane food—so dull and redundant. I soon realized that I had to cook myself.

Thanks to my parents, I am a creative cook, and I did manage to create five amazing recipes for my meals. I allocated four hours every Saturday to preparing my nutrition plan for the whole week. The roasted oregano chicken with sweet potato was a personal favorite. I also discovered the perfect recipe for my famous tuna salad. The point is that I learned to enjoy the process. I also followed a very strict fitness plan that was built around twelve weeks of progressive growth and strength building.

I laid down some strict rules, too—no coke, no sugar, no white bread, eat small meals, eat more often, and sleep light.

On the day of my wedding, I weighed in at 94 kg, which fell short of my goal. But that didn't matter, because I felt incredible—healthy, fit, and confident. My tuxedo fitted perfectly, and I felt more alive than I had ever felt in my life.

Inevitably, I regained more than 15 kg, but I had proved to myself that with the right mindset, discipline, and focus, I could achieve my goals.

The journey toward self-fulfillment is typically a long and difficult one. Most people experience disappointment, distraction, and defeat along the way. Staying on the path can be exhausting. The temptation to quit can be fierce. Sadly, many people abandon their journeys long before they arrive at their destinations.

Genshin Fujinami is a forty-four-year-old Buddhist priest who completed an astounding seven-year spiritual journey in 2003 that had him running—literally—up and down mountains, in the heat of summer and cold of winter, while praying and meditating daily. By the time his journey ended, Genshin had covered 24,800 miles throughout Japan, wearing nothing but a white robe and a flimsy pair of straw sandals. Only forty-six other monks—called "marathon monks"—have ever completed this ritual. Far more have failed. Any monk who begins the ritual but does not complete it must take his own life. Genshin Fujinami braved countless dangers and seven years of exhaustion, fatigue, and physical and mental agony to complete his ritual and finally arrive at his destination. What could possibly have kept him going for seven years in some of the worst conditions possible, along a path filled with danger and defeat?

Discipline.

Background

> Discipline is the bridge between goals and
> accomplishments. (Jim Rohn)

The story of Genshin Fujinami is remarkable—but you do not have to be a marathon monk to have discipline. Discipline is one of the most important qualities you can possess, but it is also one of the hardest to develop and keep. Remember the car analogy from the previous module? If you are driving in a car and your vision is your headlights, your fuel is your motivation, and your goal is your destination, then discipline is the car itself—the frame and everything that holds it together. Discipline is what keeps you going where you should go. Think of it as a train on train tracks. As long as those tracks are there, the train will go exactly where it should.

In this module, we will discuss how we can keep the train on the train tracks.

Definitions

Discipline: control gained by enforcing obedience or order.

Locus of control: your perception of the underlying main causes of events in your life.

- Internal locus of control: you believe you primarily are in control of what happens to you.

- External locus of control: you believe that others are in control of what happens to you.

Gratification: satisfaction or pleasure in response to the fulfillment of a desire or goal.

- Instant gratification: seeking satisfaction now rather than later.

- Delayed gratification: seeking satisfaction later rather than now.

The Process

Discipline can be a tough subject to figure out—but, in the end, it is well worth the effort. In this module, I will explain discipline so you can understand exactly what it is. I will also show you how to develop discipline in your life to help you with your journey.

Discipline, the Environment, and You

Finding Your Locus of Control

Recall those definitions we talked about earlier. Discipline is basically self-control—control over what you think, feel, and do.

People generally have two different views of discipline and what—or who—is in control of their lives. These views are referred to as loci of control. You can either have an internal locus of control or an external locus of control. Do you believe that you are primarily responsible for what happens in your life? If so, you have an internal locus of control. You have an external locus of control if you typically feel helpless when it comes to controlling your life because other people or forces control it.

The most successful people have an internal locus of control. This means they take responsibility for what happens to them. This is what you should have—you should believe that you are in charge of the results that you get in your life.

Motivation

Motivation plays an incredibly important role in discipline. The more motivated you are, the more likely you are to discipline yourself. However, the relationship goes both ways. Once you get into the habit of disciplining yourself, you can keep going even if you don't always feel particularly motivated. That will happen at times.

Discipline and Self-Esteem

Discipline is also closely related to self-esteem. Individuals who have a strong, healthy self-esteem find it easier to discipline them selves. Those with low self-esteem, however, tend to be less disciplined.

It all comes down to how you see yourself. If you see yourself as having worth and value, and believe that you deserve good things, you'll discipline yourself so you can achieve them. However, if you don't see yourself as worthy or deserving, then you won't see the point of disciplining yourself and staying on track.

> Half of life is luck; the other half is discipline—and
> that's the important half, for without discipline you
> wouldn't know what to do with luck. (Carl Zuckmeyer)

Steps to Discipline Yourself

Fortunately, while actually disciplining yourself can sometimes be tough, the general concept of how this happens is pretty straightforward. There are three general steps that are involved—commitment, process, and feedback.

Commitment

Discipline starts with a commitment. Genshin Fujinami made a commitment to himself that he would finish the perilous seven-year journey. And, he did.

Process

Process involves the steps you will take to carry out your commitment. Studies have proven that people are far more likely to achieve a goal and carry out a commitment when they develop a concrete process, complete with specific steps and timelines.

Feedback

If you do not take the time to evaluate how you are doing, you can easily derail yourself and slip right off the tracks. Feedback helps you stay on track by giving you a way to measure how you are doing. Journaling, keeping records, and self-evaluating all help you discipline yourself because you can quickly see your progress and learn from any mistakes you've made or setbacks you've had along the way.

Building Good Habits

> We are what we repeatedly do. Excellence then
> is not an act, but a habit. (Aristotle)

In the end, discipline is all about building good habits. Scientists have found that, in general, it takes forty days of consistent effort to create a habit—regardless of whether the habit is a good or a bad one. If you can create a routine for a specific activity—for example, going out and exercising daily—and keep it up for forty days, you can create a habit. Once you do, you'll feel like something is missing when you don't carry out the activity. This is a great way to build discipline and keep yourself going.

Your Vision and Goals

In addition to habits, discipline has to involve your goals. You see, you must have something to shoot for—some destination in mind—or you won't have the motivation, guidance, or discipline to continue.

Tie in everything you do to a greater purpose. Find a reason for everything. When things get tough or you start having thoughts of giving up, remind yourself of these reasons. When you do this, you can control your sense of gratification.

Many times we fail because we want instant gratification—and we will sacrifice our goals in order to get pleasure or satisfaction when we want it. With discipline, you don't need immediate gratification to keep going. You can delay gratification. Delayed gratification allows you to feel genuine satisfaction when you achieve your goals instead of sacrificing them for cheap and fleeting pleasure.

> It's easier to go down a hill than up it but the view
> is much better at the top. (Henry Ward Beecher)

Exercises

Want to develop more discipline in your life? Here are two exercises to help you get started.

1. Create a Goal Tree

    Start with a broad personal development goal you have. Then, write smaller and more specific goals that relate to that first goal. Continue until you can identify specific tasks that will be required to reach your goal.

    For example, if you want to be more productive, you can put that at the top and below it write goals like "Earn more money," "Write a book," etc. Then, underneath those goals, you can write more specific goals until you reach the actual tasks you'll need to do them. If you're writing a book, one specific task could be "Write an outline" or "Chapter structure."

2. Keep Your Vision in Mind

Refer to the vision statement you made earlier. Identify three ways your goals relate to your vision.

Action Plan

This action plan is very important for instilling discipline, so make sure you follow it as closely as possible.

1. Create a Schedule for a Task

    ✓ Identify a task you want to accomplish. Be specific.

    ✓ Create milestones to track your progress, and set up a schedule. Be reasonable with your deadlines; don't give yourself too much time or too little.

    ✓ Writing down a schedule helps you stay on track and stay committed.

2. Reward Yourself

    ✓ When you accomplish something, reward yourself with your favorite activity, food, etc. Give yourself a treat because you have earned it.

3. Build a Habit Plan

    ✓ Identify a good habit you would like to begin. Then, set up a forty-day calendar that you can use to make sure you do your habit every single day.

    ✓ Remember: it takes just forty days of continuous effort to create a habit.

4. Track Progress

    ✓ Keep a record or journal of your journey and how you are developing discipline. Review your journal periodically.

You Can Do It!

Discipline can be tough—but without it, you will not be successful. You do not have to be a superhero or an incredibly gifted and talented person to achieve great things in life. Genshin Fujinami is a normal person, but he achieved something remarkable because he disciplined himself. You can do the same. Never lose sight of what you want, and tell yourself that you will never give up. You can do it—you can stay on track and reach your goals.

The first and best victory is to conquer self. (Plato)

Further Reading

Bryant, Theodore. (1999). *Self-Discipline in 10 Days: How to Go From Thinking to Doing.* Seattle: HUB Publishing.

Tracy, Brian (2010). *No Excuses! The Power of Self-Discipline.* New York: Vanguard Press.

KNOWLEDGE

Ignorance is the death of the living.

—Arabic proverb

Personal Portraits

I have more than three hundred books that cover subjects so unrelated that I sometimes wonder why I ever got interested in such diverse subject matter. I've actually decided to give away half of them for free, because that goes in line with my vision and purpose of knowledge transfer. Besides, there are many titles that have been gathering dust on my bookshelf for years, and I still haven't read them or don't refer to them anymore.

I think my love for knowledge stemmed from my early memories of my father keeping us at the lunch table for hours after we had completed our meal to tell us fantastic stories about astronomy, history, science, and religion. I remember the feeling of curiosity and excitement as I opened the heavy, red leather-bound volumes of the *Encyclopedia Britannica* and read some random entry about the world. I used to read the dictionary as well, and l loved watching documentaries and factual programs. I do not know if this passion for knowledge is genetic or due to my exposure to learning at an early age. I do know that I will always continue to invest in my mind and absorb knowledge and wisdom.

With all the science and technology we have today, we still do not know the potential of our own limitless brainpower.

In 476 AD, the last emperor of the Roman Empire was removed. This event marked the fall of the Roman Empire and the beginning of the European Dark Ages. Following the fall, Europe's pursuit of knowledge and wisdom fell into a decline for the next eight hundred years. However, this pursuit continued to flourish in Eastern centers of learning, such as Damascus, Baghdad, and Cairo. Great strides were made in art, literature, architecture, astronomy, chemistry, and mathematics in this part of the world, and new discoveries were made—discoveries that changed the world for years to come. We owe much of what we know and have today to the advances we made in those eventful years.

It's been said that knowledge is power—not just for the world at large, but for each and every person.

Background

What do we mean when we refer to knowledge? Is it just trivia, facts, dates—random knowledge that we read in books and see on television? Or is it something more? The simple answer is that knowledge is everything you know and everything you've learned. It is the fuel for success and growth, because you can only build from something you know about and are familiar with. Knowledge is like having a flashlight to guide you when you're trying to find something in the dark. Just like that light, knowledge enables you to see what you couldn't see before.

That being said, knowledge is only as valuable as what you do with it. You see, it's one thing to know something; it's another to make something useful out of what you know. For example, I used to read constantly when I was a kid. I would read anything I could get my hands on—books, encyclopedias, magazines, newspapers—everything and anything that came my way. I devoured the written word and feasted on it as if I were starving. Did that make me a smart kid? Absolutely—I could recite facts and figures off the top of my head. But did all that information make me wise? Did that knowledge ultimately mean anything?

No—and that is what we will talk about in this module: why learning is so valuable, and how to turn the knowledge you gain into something incredible.

Definitions

Knowledge: familiarity, awareness, or understanding of a concept.

Wisdom: a deep knowledge of a concept, such as life, coupled with sound judgment pertaining to action.

> I am learning all the time. The tombstone
> will be my diploma. (Eartha Kitt)

The Process

Why is knowledge important? Why is it important to learn—and use your knowledge wisely?

Here's a little story to help answer those questions. Once there was a dog that loved to eat eggs. It would break into chicken coops and eat eggs constantly—and relished each and every one of them. One day, while the dog was out exploring, it came upon a beach by the ocean and noticed an oyster concealed in the sand. Thinking it was an egg, the dog eagerly gulped it down. The unfortunate dog soon developed a terrible stomach ache that made it very ill. Barking in pain, the dog thought to itself, *Oh, I deserve all of this pain for assuming that everything that's round must be an egg.*

The above fable may be amusing, but it also illustrates an important lesson: Knowledge is the key to avoiding mistakes and failures in life. After all, you don't want to eat an oyster because you thought it was an egg.

> Not to know is bad; not to wish to know
> is worse. (African proverb)

Knowledge: The Foundation for Growth

One way to better understand the importance of knowledge is to think of a tree. A tree needs certain things to grow—air, water, and nutrients from the soil. Take away any of these, and the tree will quickly wither and die.

Just like a tree, we need certain elements in order to grow and become successful in life. Knowledge is one of those vital elements. Take a moment to consider everything we have covered so far in this journey. Everything you've learned thus far is knowledge—and all of it can be put to good use to help you develop physically, mentally, and spiritually.

Let's take a closer look at knowledge.

Three Types of Knowledge

There are three different types of knowledge—knowing yourself, knowing others, and knowing the world.

Knowing Yourself

Knowing yourself is one of the most important forms of knowledge you can possibly have. After all, if you don't really know and understand yourself, how will you be able to improve yourself? How will you be able to use your strengths and work on your weaknesses?

We'll spend a bit more time on knowing yourself later.

Knowing Others

Knowing others means understanding how to work with people and effectively communicate with them. It also means understanding people close to you—their likes, dislikes, needs, wants, and desires.

Knowing the World

Knowing the world means being aware of the world around you, of the environment in which you live and what lies beyond. One of the hallmarks of a successful person is the desire to learn as much as possible about the world around them—to be genuinely curious about life and everything in it.

Why Knowing Yourself Is So Important

Knowing yourself is extremely important because, as I said above, without self-knowledge you'll never be successful or accomplish anything truly worthwhile—at least not without a lot of luck.

Part of knowing yourself is being aware of your strengths and weaknesses. When you know what those are, you can use your strengths to your advantage while improving your areas of weakness. When you know your strengths, for example, you can choose a career that utilizes them—one that is well suited to your talents and skills. When you're aware of your weaknesses, you can take steps to improve them. For example, if you're not good at math, you can get a tutor or find a lesson to help you understand a particular concept.

> If I could know me, I could know the
> universe. (Shirley MacLaine)

Having a Thirst for Knowledge

A thirst for knowledge is a trademark of successful people. People who achieve success personally and professionally want to know as much as they can about what they do and—more importantly—who they are.

The legendary physicist Albert Einstein developed a thirst for knowledge at an early age. As a child, Einstein was always building models and mechanical devices. He was also reading advanced books on mathematics and physics— devouring anything he could find like a sponge soaking up water. Years later, he won the Nobel Prize and revolutionized science as we knew it. Imagine if he had never developed that thirst for knowledge. The world would be drastically different—and progress would have suffered considerably.

Applying Knowledge

Of course, having knowledge is not the same as using it well. That is where wisdom comes in. Some wisdom comes only with experience and time. Some wisdom, however, comes from good habits.

Three good habits that will help you develop wisdom are the following:

1. Patience—to avoid being reckless and making snap decisions.

2. Practice—to consistently apply what you've learned.

3. Prudence—to evaluate all your options in order to make the best decisions.

A Lifelong Endeavor

Learning is a lifelong endeavor—even for the most successful people on the planet. Warren Buffet would tell you that the most successful people know that the most important investment they'll ever make is the investment they make in themselves.

Any knowledge that increases your self-esteem and broadens your horizons is priceless. Winners constantly seek out opportunities to enhance their knowledge. If there is one thing that separates winners from everyone else, it is their voracious appetite for more knowledge. Successful people learn from their past experiences and observations of what's going on around them. In the words of Steve Jobs, the founder of Apple, "They stay a little hungry; a little foolish" all the time. They are constantly looking for newer and better ways of doing things. No matter how much they may have learned or how much they may have accomplished, they realize they'll never know it all.

The failure to invest in yourself is the biggest mistake you could make in life. Regardless of your age or your previous education or training, there is always room to learn and grow, to discover new things.

Never stop learning.

> Anyone who stops learning is old, whether
> at twenty or eighty. (Henry Ford)

Exercises

The exercises below will help you with the three types of knowledge.

1. Knowing Yourself

   Write twenty-five one-line descriptions of yourself. For example, "I am a man. I am a teacher. I am a husband." Identify traits about yourself—not accomplishments.

2. Knowing Others

   List three acquaintances you do not know very well. Find out more about each of them by asking them questions about their likes, dislikes, hobbies, interests, accomplishments, etc.

3. Knowing the World

   List four topics related to personal development and your interests—topics you would like to know more about. This will enhance your curiosity.

Action Plan

Knowledge without action is just useless information. Here is a plan to help you put your knowledge to good use and make a difference.

1. Create a Reading List

    ✓ Become an avid reader. Reading broadens your horizons and gives you powerful knowledge to make the best choices in your life.

2. Three-Step Action Plan

    ✓ Identify a goal that you want to achieve.

    ✓ List key things you will need to learn in order to accomplish your goal.

    ✓ List ways you can then implement this knowledge. Make sure these actions are practical and concrete.

3. Track Your Progress

    ✓ Keep a record or journal of your journey and what you are learning. Review your journal periodically.

You Can Do It!

Knowledge is power—and power can be used to achieve great things in your life and to enhance the lives of others. However, the key is what you do with your knowledge is the key. Developing wisdom to use your knowledge in the best possible way is the gateway to a lifetime of success. Never stop learning. The world is filled with wonders yet to be explored so get out there and explore.

> Knowing is not enough; we must apply. Willing is not enough; we must do. (Johann Wolfgang von Goethe)

Further Reading

Allen, Roberta. (2003). *The Playful Way to Knowing Yourself: A Creative Workbook to Inspire Self-Discovery.* New York: Mariner Books.

Benjamin, Harry (1989). *Basic Self-Knowledge.* Newburyport, Massachusetts: Red Wheel.

CONTROLLING YOUR THOUGHTS

A pessimist sees the difficulty in every opportunity; an optimist sees the opportunity in every difficulty.

—Winston Churchill

Personal Portraits

Regardless of our varied backgrounds, we probably all share common emotional wounds that can manifest as negative emotional energy in our lives.

I have learned to deal with much of my childhood trauma through various techniques related to NLP (neuro-linguistic programming) and meditation, and also by taking a very lighthearted approach to life. Regardless of the details, it is a constant effort and struggle for me to be consciously aware of my own thoughts. I have learned to apply some of the principles of NLP, such as reframing, sub-modalities, and positive visualizations, to assist me in times of trouble.

One of the interesting techniques relies on detaching myself from a specific experience and, instead of reliving it inside my memory, choosing to observe it instead. For example, instead of recalling the experience in full vivid color, I turn it into an old black-and-white movie. And instead of the scary monster screaming at me, I turn him into a cartoon character with a funny voice. And instead of the painful memory filling up my entire head, I make it smaller and move it to a tiny corner in my mind.

After I practiced these techniques, I realized that I could actually control my thoughts and, in turn, control my involvement and my emotional reaction to them. This was very liberating and empowering because it made me feel that I was not a slave to the random messages generated by my subconscious. By consciously managing my thoughts and focusing on positive experiences, I have trained my mind to be my friend, not my foe.

Here's a little experiment for you to do: for the next sixty seconds, don't think about a blue elephant.

How did you do? Were you successful? Was the first thing to pop into your mind a blue elephant?

More than likely, you thought about a blue elephant and then tried desperately to think of something else. You may have succeeded initially, but no matter how hard you tried, your mind stubbornly kept going back to that lovely blue elephant.

You see - your mind works in a particular way to process the information that it receives from the world around you. How we deliver information and how we think about and interpret that information plays a significant role in how we act upon that information. This is why controlling your thoughts is as much a part of developing yourself as controlling your behavior—because, as you will discover in this module, the two are one and the same.

Background

Have you ever had an unwanted thought?

Have you ever had a song stuck in your head that just would not go away?

Have you ever found yourself regretting that you had a thought and then you acted on it—for example, thinking about that rich creamy chocolate bar in the kitchen cupboard and eating the whole thing, only to really wish you had more control over yourself?

All of us have experienced the things above at one time or another. That's because, as human beings, we have active, powerful brains that can seem too difficult—if not impossible—to control at times. But is that really true?

You can learn to control your thoughts through mental discipline. Remember the discussion we had about discipline? The same lessons and principles apply here; however, this time they apply not just to your actions, but to your thoughts as well—the thoughts behind the actions.

So what does this mean, exactly? And why is it so important that we learn to control our thoughts? After all, until we act on it, isn't a thought just a thought? Yes, but what you will come to realize in this module is that *your thoughts drive your actions.* As a result, controlling what you think goes a long way toward helping you control what you do—and, ultimately, the person you become.

> If you don't control your mind, someone
> else will. (John Allston)

Definitions

Focus: a central point, as of attraction.

NLP: neuro-linguistic programming. The connection between how you think, how you speak, and how you behave. NLP focuses on changing your behavior by changing your thoughts.

Self-talk: the ongoing internal dialogue we have with ourselves, which influences how we feel and behave.

Downward spiral: an emotional state in which a person becomes more and more depressed.

The Process

How do you discipline what is arguably the most powerful thing you possess—your mind? The process is actually not as difficult as you might think. As with anything else involved with discipline, it just takes practice. (For some it may take a *lot* of practice—but the benefits are well worth the effort.)

However, let me first fully explain mental discipline to give you a solid understanding of the concept before jumping into how to put it into action.

The Importance of Mental Discipline

In the world of modern archery, the Koreans are clearly head and shoulders above the rest. Korean archers have long dominated the sport. They routinely win world championships and Olympic gold medals in every event. Do you know why they are able to do this? It's because they train hard. They practice for hours and hours every day. They have extremely high standards and practice constantly to uphold them. They also have incredible mental discipline—in fact, they are perhaps the most disciplined athletes you'll find anywhere in the world.

One technique used by Korean archers (as well as other archers and athletes in general) is known as "mental rehearsal." This essentially involves picturing a technique or skill in your mind—seeing yourself go through all the steps and motions—and repeating it over and over and over again, until it becomes something they do automatically. Studies have proven that mental rehearsal can measurably improve an athlete's performance. It can do the same for you.

That is why mental discipline is so important. It boosts your performance and helps you achieve anything you desire—and it keeps you focused and on track.

> Self-discipline begins with the mastery of your thoughts.
> If you don't control what you think, you can't control
> what you do. Simply, self-discipline enables you to
> think first and act afterward. (Napoleon Hill)

Practical Applications of Focus

When you learn to focus, you'll reap the following benefits:

- You'll feel less stressed during a task,

- you'll be more efficient and timely,

- you'll be more successful in completing a series of tasks,

- and you'll be capable of more complex and difficult tasks.

Focusing on something—placing all your attention on one thing—is one of the ways you can control your thoughts and develop mental discipline. Korean archers focus on the target and their technique. They focus on every little detail—from how they are standing and holding the bow, to the rate of their breathing and where their eyes are centered.

When you focus, you are essentially doing the same thing as a Korean archer—placing your "arrow" right on target every time you snap the string.

> Most people have no idea of the giant capacity we can
> immediately command when we focus all of our resources
> on mastering a single area of our lives. (Anthony Robbins)

Controlling Negative Thoughts

One of the most practical benefits of controlling your thoughts is the
ability to manage negative thoughts and behaviors.

Perhaps you've heard the term "downward spiral." This occurs when you
have a negative thought or emotion that begins to spiral out of control—
eventually dominating all your thoughts. A downward spiral can be very
destructive. For example, when you're under a lot of pressure, negative
thoughts can literally knock you off your feet if you don't know how to
control them. Self-doubt can start creeping in as a result of stress. You may
start questioning your ability to complete the task at hand or reach your
goal. If those thoughts continue, you're destined to fail.

Learning how to stop negative thoughts can help prevent downward spirals
from occurring—whether you're thinking about yourself or someone
else.

> Keep your mind on the things you want and off the
> things you don't want. (Hannah Whitall Smith)

Self-Esteem

Self-esteem is one of the main tools you have in your toolbox to combat
negative thoughts and prevent downward spirals. The more positive your
self-perception, the more capable you are of combating any negative
thoughts that creep in and filling your mind with positive thoughts
instead.

Changing Your Perspective

It also helps to change your perspective whenever you encounter a negative
thought. Don't try to ignore the thought—you'll only end up thinking
about it more, just as you thought about the blue elephant a while ago.
Instead, confront the thought and change your perspective. You can
change your perspective by looking for the positive—the opposite of what
your mind is trying to make you believe. This involves positive self-talk,

a wonderful tool to use to change your perspective and challenge those intrusive negative thoughts.

> The difference between a stumbling block and a stepping stone is whether you are cursing your bruised knee or admiring the view. (Silent Owl)

NLP

Another fascinating component of controlling your thoughts is a relatively new concept known as NLP, which stands for neuro-linguistic programming. As defined above, it explains how your behavior is influenced by how you think and how you communicate with yourself.

The human brain is programmed a certain way. We are hardwired in a particular direction, and reprogramming the brain can help defend against negativity and out of control thoughts. For example, if you don't want someone to become angry, rather than telling him, "Don't get mad," say something like, "Relax."

Similarly, you can create ideas in your head called "anchor thoughts." Anchor thoughts are ones that you associate with certain events or situations. They can be related to a sense (sight, touch, smell, sound, etc.), a thought, or a memory. Let's say you want to create an anchor thought for relaxation to help you in stressful situations. So the next time you are relaxed, try this: visualize your relaxed state—where you are, what you feel, etc.—and focus on it intently. As you're focusing, place your hand over your heart and keep it there. Associate the two—the feelings you experience while your hand is over your heart—and link them in your mind. Whenever you are stressed, place your hand over your heart. I bet you'll feel relaxed. That's just one example of how you can reprogram your mind.

> If you focus on results, you will never change. If you focus on change, you will get results. (Jack Dixon)

Exercises

For this module, try these two exercises:

1. Rate Your Focus Ability

On a piece of paper, rate your ability to focus in different areas of your life (e.g., work, school, family, etc.) on a scale of one to ten. This will give you an idea of what areas need work.

2. Distraction List

List ten things that distract you on a regular basis. What are some practical ways you can avoid these distractions?

Action Plan

Building on what we discussed in the discipline module, here is an action plan you can use on a regular basis to develop mental discipline and control your thoughts.

1. Create Anchor Thoughts

   ✓ Create anchors as described above for situations that require focus, calm, and other positive emotions. Use them to combat unwanted thoughts and negative emotions.

2. Task Management

   ✓ Whenever possible, break tasks up into smaller, more manageable tasks. Also, try to focus on one thing at a time instead of multitasking (which actually decreases your productivity).

3. Develop Relaxation Techniques

   ✓ Make use of breathing patterns, meditation, or any other activity you find to be soothing and peaceful whenever you need to help control your thinking.

4. Track Progress

   ✓ Keep a record or journal of your journey and what you are doing to control your thoughts. Review your journal periodically.

You Can Do It!

Controlling your thoughts is definitely possible. It's also necessary if you want to become a person who is in complete control of your life. Build mental and physical anchors. Work on changing perspectives. Turn the negative into positive, and face your thoughts head on. Talk to yourself. Think out loud.

Act like you are in control of your thoughts, and you will be in control of your thoughts.

> Rule your mind or it will rule you. (Horace)

Further Reading

Leaf, Caroline. (2008). *Who Switched Off My Brain? Controlling Toxic Thoughts and Emotions. Nashville, Tennessee, Thomas Nelson International.*

McKay, Matthew. (2007). *Thoughts and Feelings: Taking Control of Your Moods and Your Life.* Oakland, California: New Harbinger Publications.

BODY

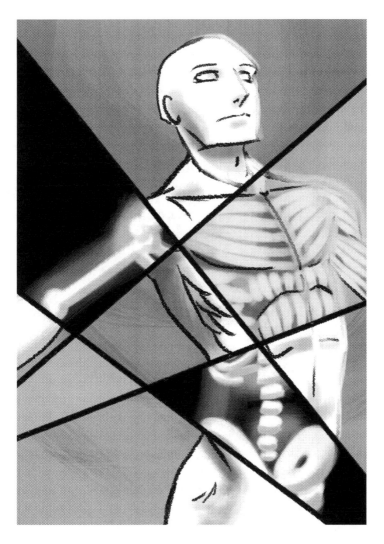

Basic Physiology

When you consider yourself valuable, you will take
care of yourself in all ways that are necessary.

—M. Scott Peck

Personal Portraits

I hate smoking and see no reason why any smart and sensible human being would smoke.

I've been a smoker for 20 years now.

I am totally aware of the damage that cigarettes cause my body, and I'm also ashamed that I have not yet found the strength to quit smoking. The first time I decided to quit was about ten years ago, after the holy month of Ramadan. It was easy, because during Ramadan I hadn't smoked throughout the whole day, and even after sunset I would smoke only about five or six cigarettes, so I realized that I could do without them. Unfortunately, it took less than two months for me to get back to my old habit.

The second time, I decided to try a new acupuncture method and actually invested time and money to get outside help. That lasted four months, and I still remember how great it felt to be free of nicotine. Unfortunately, I found my way back to my old habit again.

The third time, I decided to gradually cut down my daily intake. I reached a point where I was down to three cigarettes a day—but I was still smoking. I stopped buying the "cancer sticks" and used to take them off my friends and strangers at the bus stop. That was not good at all, so I found my way back to my old habit again.

I am aware of the power that cigarettes have over me, and one would think that the very nature of this book would give me the strength to quit—but so far, I have been unable to. I sometimes wish I could wake up one morning and find no cigarettes being sold anywhere because of a nationwide health awareness campaign. If you think about it, cigarettes are the only products you can buy in a supermarket that have absolutely no health benefit (as food does, for example) or household function. They are just poison, and nicotine is one of the most addictive substances known to humankind.

That, however, is a victim mentality and is not going to get me very far. So I will continue to work on this aspect of my journey. My body deserves to be treated better than that, and there is absolutely nothing to gain from the habit of smoking.

So far during this journey of personal development, we have spent most of our time discussing the inner workings of the mind and spirit. While both are incredibly important to who you are as a person, there is another equally important part we haven't talked about yet.

Your body.

Your body is more than just a bunch of skin, bones, and muscle; it is the vehicle you inhabit and operate throughout your lifetime. It's hard to get through life without a strong, healthy body, especially since your body has a direct relationship with your mind. That's why taking good care of your body and keeping it in the best possible condition is a must.

If your body is a vehicle, then you want to make sure your engine is running well, your tank has plenty of fuel, your chassis is strong, and everything else is working just as it should. Besides, when your body is functioning as it should, you'll be lot less likely to get into a wreck.

The Chariot Analogy

In Hindu mythology, our body is analogous to a chariot. The rider is the spirit. The horses represent the sense organs. The reins represent the mind. The charioteer is the intellect. If the intellect does not hold the reins tight, it won't be long before the horses go astray.

Background

What does it mean to be healthy? And why is your health so important? After all, aren't people less healthy now than they were decades or even centuries ago? People eat more poorly, stress their bodies with long work days, and participate in generally unhealthy lifestyles compared to our ancestors.

Being healthy is incredibly important, Every bit of work you put into your mind and spirit—increasing your self-esteem, building your confidence, changing your perspective, instilling discipline in yourself, etc.—is all for nothing if you don't take care of your body.

Let me share a story with you. There once was a young man whose goal was to be the wisest man in the world. He locked himself in a library and read constantly—for hours and hours each day—devouring as many books as he could. He studied tirelessly, until he mastered subject after subject. He spent decades in his place of solitude, until at last he'd acquired all the knowledge in the world. Ready to share his vast knowledge with the world, he went to the door, flung it open, and ran outside—only to die of a heart attack.

For all of those decades he'd locked himself away to study, he never exercised at all. He was far too busy learning to be bothered with something as trivial and nonsensical as fitness. He also failed to watch what he ate. In fact, he barely had time to wolf down basic sustenance before returning to his studies. Despite all his great knowledge, he had neglected his body. In the end, he sacrificed his health to develop his mind. In the end, his body was unable to take care of him.

Remember this poignant story as we talk about staying healthy throughout this gate.

Definitions

Physiology: the study of the function of a living organism.

Health: a state of complete physical, mental, and social well-being—not merely the absence of disease or illness.

Metabolism: the physical processes occurring within a person that are necessary for the maintenance of life.

The Process

Ask yourself this question: how much do you really know about your body?

Do you know how it works? Do you know what it needs—and doesn't need? The more you understand your body and know how it functions, the more equipped you will be to take care of it properly. The body is a wonderfully complex organism; in order to keep it running well, you must do your homework and know what's required to maintain it.

Taking care of your body is really just like maintaining a car. Some mechanical problems must be fixed by a trained mechanic (or, in your case, a doctor or other medical professional). But isn't it better to know how your car works anyway, so you can keep your car running well and so that repairs are minimal and infrequent?

Knowing your body and how it works is the first step toward becoming physically fit.

> Take care of your body. It's the only place
> you have to live. (Jim Rohn)

Your Body, Your Self-Esteem, and You

First, we'll talk about the importance of your body and how it ties into how you see yourself. As we've talked about previously, your self-image and self-esteem are created through a variety of factors. Your body plays a role in both your self-image and your confidence.

When I refer to how you see yourself, I'm not just talking about how your body looks. In fact, your physical appearance is far less important than how your body feels when we're talking about self-esteem. People who are healthy and energetic tend to have strong self-esteem, even if they perceive themselves as unattractive. People who are considered attractive but don't feel strong physically tend to have lower self-esteem.

This is why taking care of your body can also help improve your self-esteem.

The Relationship Between the Mind and Body

Your mind and your body are connected—and not just because they share territory.

How your mind functions—clarity, sharpness, fluidity of thought—depends directly on how you are feeling. Your brain is an organ, after all, and it requires fuel and energy just like anything else. If you are not taking care of your body, your mind will suffer, and you will not be able to think or behave appropriately.

A healthy mind complements a healthy body, and vice versa. Did you know that hospital patients who are positive and optimistic—two signs of a healthy mind—heal faster and more thoroughly than patients who are negative and pessimistic? Along those same lines, people who suffer from depression and become healthy and fit generally cope much better than depressed individuals who do not.

Your mind influences your body—and your body influences your mind.

> To keep the body in good health is a duty ...
> otherwise we shall not be able to keep our
> mind strong and clear. (Buddha)

Your Body: Systems Within a System

Now let's discuss the inner workings of one of the greatest systems on earth: the human body. Your body is a complex system that contains several subsystems. These subsystems all work together to keep your body running smoothly. Let's look at each system and what it does.

Digestive System

The digestive system—consisting of your esophagus, stomach, large and small intestine, and rectum—breaks down food into the nutrients that your body needs in order to run. Your body then uses these nutrients for energy, growth, and healing.

Respiratory System

The respiratory system is comprised of your airway (trachea) and your lungs. When you breathe in, you are feeding your body with oxygen. The oxygen is transported through the body via the blood stream. Oxygen is critical when it comes to the healthy functioning of the millions of cells in your body. Your body then expels the waste—via carbon dioxide—from your body.

Circulatory System

The circulatory system uses the heart and an extensive network of arteries, veins, and capillaries to send blood to and from different parts of your body. Without blood, your body cannot receive oxygen and other nutrients.

Nervous System

The nervous system effectively controls your body. This amazing system includes the brain, spinal cord, and an extremely large network of tiny nerves that transmit electronic signals back and forth throughout your body. The nervous system not only controls and regulates your body but also tells you when you are hot, cold, in pain, feeling pleasure, etc.

Immune System

The immune system is your body's defense system. It's designed to fight off invaders in the form of foreign substances (such as bacteria and germs) that make you sick. A healthy immune system is vital to a healthy body.

Muscular System

The muscular system, along with the skeletal system, helps support the entire body and all the subsystems within it. Do you enjoy exercise? If so, you can appreciate your muscular system—it's this system that enables you to be active.

> If you have health, you probably will be happy, and if you have health and happiness, you have all the wealth you need, even if it is not all you want. (Elbert Hubbard)

What Being Healthy Means

Now that we've reviewed the body's systems, let's talk about what it really means to be healthy. When we speak of health, we're not just talking about the absence of illness or injury. After all, you can be free of illness, disease, and injury and still not be healthy. Being truly healthy means that your body is operating just as it should—at or near its optimal level of performance. In practical terms, this means you

- feel great more often than not,

- have plenty of energy,

- feel fully alive,

- can focus, concentrate, and think clearly,

- do not have any serious disease or illness,

- and can use your body to the fullest extent possible.

A healthy body is absolutely crucial to a healthy mind and spirit. The three work together in tandem, enabling you to accomplish your goals and have a life filled with success.

> If the mind, that rules the body, ever so far forgets itself
> as to trample on its slave, the slave is never generous
> enough to forgive the injury, but will rise and smite
> the oppressor. (Henry Wadsworth Longfellow)

Exercises

The exercises below will help you get started on keeping your body healthy and running strong.

1. Identify Body Goals

   List your top five goals for your body. What would you like to do in order to be healthy? Be as specific as you need to be—e.g., do you want bigger muscles, do you want to lose a number of pounds, or do you just want to have more energy? Write it down.

2. Rate Your Energy Level

   Rate your energy level on a daily basis from one to ten. See how it changes over time, and see what factors cause it to go up or down. (Hint: pay attention to your sleep; you should get at least seven to seven and a half hours of sleep per night for a healthy lifestyle.)

3. Take a Body Survey

   It is a very good idea to take a health assessment to identify how healthy you are. You should schedule a visit with your doctor for a complete evaluation, but here is a link to an informal assessment you can use to get a general idea of your health: http://www.fittogethernc.org/hra.aspx

Action Plan

To get you started on the right track, here is an action plan you can use to begin the process of building a healthier, stronger body.

1. Commit to Working on One Specific Body Goal

   ✓ Make a written commitment to one of your body goals. Think about a plan you might use to put it into action later with what you will learn.

2. Write a Mission Statement

   ✓ Create a mission statement about physical health. What do you want to do to improve your body? Record your desire and commitment to becoming healthier, and write a mission statement for each goal.

3. Track Progress

   ✓ Keep a record or journal of your journey and what you are doing to ensure your general health. Review your journal periodically.

You Can Do It!

The body is your vehicle for life. Without it, you can be stranded on the side of life's highway as life passes you by. You deserve to live a full and vibrant life. In order to do this, you have to be healthy. That is why this gate is so important—so you can learn how to maintain and care for your body and keep it running strong.

> He who has health has hope; and he who has
> hope, has everything. (Arabian proverb)

Further Reading

Cash, Thomas F. (2008). *The Body Image Workbook: An Eight-Step Program for Learning to Like Your Looks.* Oakland, California: New Harbinger Publications.

Gilbert, Edwige. (2008). *The Fresh Start Promise: 28 Days to Total Mind, Body, and Spirit Transformation.* Woodbury, Minnesota: Llewellyn Publications.

Eating Right and Nutrition: Part I

*Those who think they have no time for healthy eating
will sooner or later have to find time for illness.*

—Edward Stanley

Personal Portraits

When I was younger, I was completely ignorant of good nutrition or the concept of conscious, healthy living. We would stuff ourselves with melted cheese sandwiches, doughnuts, chocolate, fried chicken, brownies, potato chips, and ice cream—all on the same day. The next day we would order kilos of sushi followed by cold rice milk pudding and chunky mango juice. Then, on family Fridays, we would gorge on homemade traditional Egyptian *koshari*—which is a macaroni and brown lentil mix covered with crispy fried onions and smothered with a red hot chili sauce. We really loved to eat and all had huge, hearty appetites.

I recall an incident when I had a date with a cute girl that I really liked. As I was walking out of the house, I caught a glimpse of myself in the mirror and was struck by what I saw. I had grown really fat, and my self-esteem was suffering badly. I felt lethargic and had severe acne all over my face. I freaked out and cancelled the date. That day, I made a stand with myself. I suddenly realized that it was all a matter of habit, which I could change by becoming more aware of my food intake.

I began to do the research to understand nutrients in food and how those affect my performance. I've always been very active, which helped me get back into shape as soon as I changed my eating habits. Understanding the basics of carbohydrates and fats, how protein plays a big role in muscle development, and technical concepts, such as resting metabolic rate and after-burn, helped me start to become healthier. I told our live-in maid who cooked for us not to use butter and sugar in my food. She would make me salads and grilled chicken for lunch. I realized the perils of processed foods, preservatives, and chemicals and how those affected my body. I made a conscious effort to enjoy salads and fruit. I cut out the junk food completely and gave up on carbonated soft drinks.

Of course, I still get weak and dive into in a deep-dish pepperoni pizza at two in the morning. However, I am aware that this is not something I can enjoy every day and am trying to achieve a balance between wholesome nutritious foods and the occasional guilty pleasures.

If you're like a lot of people, you love your "junk" food. Do you have any idea what's really in the chocolate, burgers, pizza, French fries, and other highly processed foods that you eat? They have limited nutritional value, and they're loaded with fat, sodium, and other unhealthy things that can increase your risk for health issues like diabetes and heart disease.

In the previous module, we talked about being healthy—how important it is for your body to maintain its health so it can keep running as it should. In this module, we'll discuss how to become healthy and stay healthy. It all begins with eating right and having solid nutrition as a part of your lifestyle.

Always remember this: you are what you eat. So who do you want to be? You decide.

> When diet is wrong, medicine is of no use. When diet
> is correct, medicine is of no need. (Ayurvedic proverb)

Background

As we've discussed, total personal success depends on how healthy you keep your mind and your body. Keeping your body healthy means continuously supplying it with the vitamins, minerals, and other nutrients that it needs to keep it running well.

Notice I said *well*. That's a crucial distinction.

Did you know that the human body can last up to three to four weeks without food and can live for a very long time on a minimum intake of calories? There are stories of people who have been forced to live for months, even years, with the bare minimum of calories and nutrition in their diet.

They lived—but did they really live? It's doubtful. It would probably be more accurate to say that they survived. The truth is, you can function—physiologically—by eating just about anything. But to function well—i.e., to function at an optimum level—you need a healthy, balanced diet that gives you the nutrients and energy you need. That's what we're talking about in this module—ensuring that you get the nutrition you need for peak performance, not just performance that is at a bare minimum.

After all, in this journey of personal development, we don't believe in doing just the minimum in anything.

> The greatest wealth is health. (Virgil)

Definitions

Nutrition: the process by which a person takes in and uses food for healthy living and functioning.

Calorie: a unit of heat used to measure how much energy is gained by digesting food. The more calories that are in a particular food, the more energy that is stored.

Nutrient: a substance that a human needs to live and grow. Nutrients include carbohydrates, fats, proteins, minerals, vitamins, and water.

The Process

> Don't dig your grave with your own
> knife and fork. (English proverb)

Purpose of Nutrition

What is the purpose of nutrition? Why should we care so much about what we eat? There are three primary reasons why nutrition is important and why we should care about proper nutrition. Proper nutrition

- gives your body plenty of energy,

- keeps your body—the immune system, your organs, etc. —healthy,

- helps your body grow and function properly,

- helps you perform at your best—both physically and mentally,

- and helps prevent premature aging.

We all know a tree needs certain things to grow. These include sunlight for photosynthesis, water to keep it hydrated and to supply necessary minerals, and nutrients in the soil to help it grow and flourish. In many ways, both literally and figuratively, you are very much like a tree. Which tree would you rather be—a shriveled sapling or a tall, towering oak?

Nutrition is designed to help you grow, flourish, and thrive—and to continue thriving throughout your entire life.

Effects of Improper Nutrition

Improper nutrition has many physical consequences. You will feel lethargic and sluggish. You will also be more susceptible to illness and disease. You won't be healthy, and you could become either malnourished or obese from eating the wrong foods.

Improper or poor nutrition increases your risk of a variety of physical health problems, including but not limited to the following:

- high blood pressure,

- higher body fat,

- heart disease,

- gall stones,

- sleep apnea,

- and diabetes.

Did you know that improper nutrition also affects your mental health? Improper nutrition may result in the following:

- depressed mood,

- eating disorders,

- loss of motivation,

- lowered alertness,

- and difficulty focusing and concentrating.

Nutritional deficiencies may also affect your problem-solving ability and make it more difficult for you to handle stress.

Healthy Balance Is Needed

Just as with many things in life, proper nutrition involves finding a balance. Having too little of a good thing is just as bad as having too much—and that's even if you have the good things to begin with. The truth is that in this day and age, it's too easy to find unhealthy foods—and too easy to obtain too much of any foods we do find.

Nutrition, then, isn't just what you eat but also how much you eat and when you eat it. Eating an excessive amount of a healthy food can be just as bad as eating a normal-sized portion of an unhealthy food. You also need to consider when you eat. For example, most people are in the habit of eating three meals: one in the morning, one in the afternoon, and one at dinner. However, did you know that the human body is actually designed to eat more often, but in smaller portions? It's true. Our ancestors ate four to five small meals throughout the day. They did this because eating frequent small meals is better for our metabolism. Eating the bulk of your calories in the evening at dinner or before you go to bed can lead to weight gain. Your body needs the most energy (from calories) early in the day, not at the end of the day.

Unfortunately, this is where most people get it backward. As the old saying goes, "Eat breakfast like a king, lunch like a prince, and dinner like a pauper." Of course, you're going to be eating four or five meals, not three—so be sure to eat the bulk of your calories earlier in the day, not in the evening. That being said, don't eat a breakfast that is really heavy or especially high in fat, as that can also make you feel sluggish—which is not a good way to start your day.

Knowing what to eat, how much to eat, and when you should eat it is important to having proper nutrition.

If you don't take care of your body, where
are you going to live? (Anonymous)

The Importance of Good Habits

The best way to build proper nutrition is to build good habits. We mentioned in a previous gate that it takes only forty days to create a good habit. If you can get into a healthy routine for just forty days, you can change your life for the better. Once healthy eating becomes a habit, you'll find it easier to maintain a healthy lifestyle.

Just like doing anything else, eating right is about creating the right habits. Here are four good habits you can develop to make sure you're getting the proper nutrition and living a wholesome lifestyle:

- Read the nutritional content on the food you buy. If you buy packaged food, read the list of ingredients on the label. If you buy fresh food, look up the nutritional content online. Know what you are eating. A good place to find the nutritional values of most foods online is http://nutritiondata.self.com.

- Plan your meals in advance. When you prepare your meal plan ahead of time, you are more likely to eat healthily. When you wait until it's time to cook dinner, you are more likely to eat whatever is available—which will often be much less healthy than a meal planned in advance.

- Avoid processed foods. Strive to eat fresh foods whenever possible. Processed foods typically contain a lot of preservatives. The more processed a food is, the less healthy it is. Common unhealthy ingredients to avoid are high-fructose corn syrup, enriched and bleached wheat flour, artificial colors and flavors, hydrogenated oils, saturated fats, and just about anything that you don't immediately recognize or are unable to pronounce.

- Choose organic whenever possible. While organic foods aren't necessarily more nutritious than non-organic foods, they are grown and produced without dangerous chemicals (primarily pesticides and herbicides). These chemicals have been associated with an increased risk of cancer and other health issues. Certified organic foods also do not contain anything that is genetically modified (which many health experts consider dangerous). Since organic foods are typically more expensive, if budget is an issue try to at least buy organic produce that is on the "dirty dozen" list. This list is updated frequently and shows the foods that contain the highest amounts of pesticides and other chemicals. You can find the list here: http://www.ewg.org/foodnews.

I saw few die of hunger; of eating, a hundred thousand. (Benjamin Franklin)

Exercises

These two exercises will help you start two very good habits: keeping track of your food intake and keeping a record of how nutrition impacts your life.

1. Identify Contents of Three Meals

   Take a close look at three meals that you eat regularly—one in the morning, one in the afternoon, and one in the evening. Find out how many calories, fats, proteins, carbohydrates, vitamins, and minerals are in each dish. This gives you an idea of what you are eating and teaches you to pay attention to what goes into your body.

2. Write About Nutrition and Your Life

   Think of a time you felt tired, lethargic, and listless. Also think about a time in which you were sick. What was your diet like? What was going into your body? Draw connections routinely between your nutrition, your lifestyle, and how you feel.

   Your body is a temple, but only if you treat it as one. (Astrid Alauda)

Action Plan

Here are tangible steps you can take to get on the right track and create a healthier lifestyle, complete with proper nutrition.

1. Make a Commitment

    ✓ Write down a statement declaring that you believe nutrition is integral to your overall success in life. Make a commitment each day to eat healthy and pay attention to your nutrition.

2. Weekly Reading

    ✓ Make a commitment to learn as much as you can about nutrition.

    ✓ Every week, spend at least one hour researching nutritional topics. Good sources for these include newspapers, magazines, online journals, and informative websites.

3. Track Progress

    ✓ Keep a record or journal of what you eat and how it makes you feel. Review your journal periodically.

You Can Do It!

You need your body—it's your temple, your home—and it needs you to take care of it properly. A big part of taking care of your body is giving it the right type of fuel, in the right amounts, and at the right time. That is really what nutrition is all about.

You want to be at your best—and to be at your best you must eat right. Healthy eating really is that important. Remember this: eating right, like anything else, is all about habit and routine. Start creating the good habits today that will lead you to success tomorrow.

> You cannot achieve environmental security and human development without addressing the basic issues of health and nutrition. (Gro Harlem Brundtland)

Further Reading

Willet, Walter C, Dr. (2005). *Eat, Drink and Be Healthy: The Harvard Medical School Guide to Healthy Eating.* Tampa, Florida: Free Press.

Schenck, Susan. (2009). *The Live Food Factor: The Comprehensive Guide to the Ultimate Diet for Body, Mind, Spirit & Planet.* Milpitas, California: Awakenings Publications.

Eating Right and Nutrition: Part 2

To eat is a necessity, but to eat intelligently is an art.

—La Rochefoucauld

You are what you eat.

Let me say that again: *you are what you eat.*

Your body uses what you eat to grow and to renew its cells so the food you put into your body literally becomes a part of you. That is why you need to be very careful about what you eat. In this module, we'll talk about what you should look for in the foods you choose so you'll have the information you need to create a healthy, nutritious diet.

> Sugar is a type of bodily fuel, yes, but your body runs
> about as well on it as a car would. (V. L. Allineare)

Background

Nutrition can be very complicated—but it doesn't have to be. In fact, while many people think they are incapable of figuring out nutrition because there are so many facts, figures, and scientific terms thrown around, the opposite is true. Nutrition can be simple. You don't need to be a trained, licensed nutritionist with a formal education to know how to adopt a healthy, nutritious lifestyle. All you need to know are the basics, plus a few pieces of advice on how you can put your knowledge into action. Once you have that knowledge, you can forge a stronger body for yourself through proven principles that I will share with you today.

> The best and most efficient pharmacy is within
> your own system. (Robert C. Peale)

Definitions

Protein: an organic compound that is used in the body to build, maintain, and replace the tissue in the body, such as your muscles and organs. Sources of protein include beef, poultry, dairy products, eggs, fish, nuts, seeds, and beans.

Carbohydrate: the major energy source for your body. Sources of carbohydrates include whole grains, vegetables, fruits, beans, and sugars.

Lipid: lipids, otherwise known as fats, are used by the body to store energy. They also help insulate the body. Sources of lipids include fatty meats and fish, butter, and nuts.

Cholesterol: a wax-like substance used by your body to metabolize certain nutrients in your body. There are two types: "good" cholesterol—or HDL—and "bad" cholesterol—or LDL.

The Process

> Don't eat anything your great-great grandmother wouldn't
> recognize as food. There are a great many food-like items
> in the supermarket your ancestors wouldn't recognize
> as food (Go-Gurt? Breakfast-cereal bars? Non-dairy
> creamer?); stay away from these. (Michael Pollan)

How do you know where to begin when it comes to nutrition? What do you need to know—and how do you separate the necessary essentials from the extra information that you don't really need?

Let's start with basic nutrition, which consists of knowing the following:

- the basics of essential nutrients and ingredients,

- proper eating habits,

- what foods to avoid,

- and what foods to eat.

If you can learn these basics, you will be well on your way to learning more about nutrition and improving the quality of your life.

Overview of Nutrients

Your body requires certain materials for growth and energy. These are known as essential nutrients. In other words, they are not optional, and a healthy balance of them is needed.

Vitamins and Minerals

These nutrients are required for your body to carry out a variety of biological functions. Vitamins are either fat-soluble or water-soluble. Fat-soluble vitamins tend to stay in your body over a period of time, while water-soluble vitamins are easily utilized by your body and quickly eliminated.

Minerals are inorganic elements found in a variety of foods. They add strength to your bones, tissues, and organs; help your eyesight and other senses; play a vital role in digestion; and are involved in just about every biological process that occurs in your body.

Proteins

> Proteins are the machinery of living tissue that
> builds the structures and carries out the chemical
> reactions necessary for life. (Michael Behe)

As mentioned above, proteins are essential building blocks of your body. They make up your tissues, organs, and muscles. They are used not only for growth from infancy through adolescence, but your body also utilizes them regularly during adulthood to repair and replace damaged tissue.

The average person needs about forty to seventy grams of protein on a daily basis. However, that amount can vary a lot depending on body weight (e.g., a 250-pound male requires much more protein than a 100-pound female) and how you use your body. Athletes and body builders require more protein than the average person. If you exercise regularly (which you should), protein is necessary to help you build muscle and recover from fatigue.

Other things may increase your protein needs as well. For example, if you are getting over an illness, pregnant, or under a lot of stress, your body's need for protein will be higher than usual.

Many people in the world get more than enough protein on a regular basis, especially in places where high amounts of meat, fish, and poultry—which are rich in protein—are consumed.

Carbohydrates

Carbs, as they are often called, are crucial to your body because they provide you with something you always need: energy. Carbs are the primary fuel source for the body—they help keep you going. An average person needs roughly three hundred grams of carbs per day. As with protein, athletes—particularly endurance athletes, such as marathon runners—need a higher number of carbs. At least twenty-five grams of those carbs should come from fiber. Fiber is important because it helps keep your digestive system functioning properly and reduces your risk of heart disease and other serious health conditions. Foods high in fiber include whole grains, nuts and seeds, and fruits and vegetables.

You can get carbohydrates from sugars, starches, grains, vegetables, and fruits. However, not all carbohydrates are good for you. Sugars—particularly refined sugar and high fructose corn syrup—are very high in carbohydrates and can quickly raise your blood sugar levels and stress your pancreas. High sugar consumption increases the risk of obesity, heart disease, premature aging, cancer, and many other serious health conditions.

> It is more important to eat some carbohydrates at breakfast, because the brain needs fuel right away, and carbohydrate is the best source. (Dr. Andrew Weil)

Lipids

Lipids, or fats, have a bad reputation because they are often associated with being overweight and blamed for obesity—and no one wants to be overweight. Your body actually needs a moderate amount of fat in order to survive. Most problems occur when you eat the wrong kinds of fat or too much fat.

Unhealthy fats include trans fats and partially hydrogenated oils. Healthy fats, however, can be found in foods such as egg yolks; fish high in omega-3 fatty acids, such as salmon and mackerel; healthy oils, such as coconut oil and olive oil; nuts, and seeds.

Why does your body need fat? Fat is used by your body to store energy, which you need. If you have too little fat in your body, your body will suffer, which is why extremely low-fat diets are unhealthy. Most people, however, consume too much fat. Too much fat in your diet can lead to being overweight or obese, and may cause serious issues with your respiratory, circulatory, muscular, and digestive systems.

Water

Many people don't realize that water is actually a nutrient—one you need every single day. The human body can go for weeks without food, but it will survive only three days without water. Even if you drink water every day, if you don't drink enough you will feel tired and lethargic. Proper hydration keeps your body functioning at its best.

The Institute of Medicine determined that an adequate water intake for men is roughly about 3 liters per day and for women it is about 2.2 liters of water per day.

> "We made from water every living thing." (The Holy
> Qur'an (21:30) (Yusuf Ali English Translation)

Proper Eating Habits

Knowing what nutrients your body needs is useless unless you know how to establish proper eating habits.

The Correct Eating Pattern

Try to eat four to five smaller meals instead of two or three big meals throughout the day. This will improve your metabolism, give you more energy, and help keep your weight in check. Large meals tend to overload your digestive system and make you feel sluggish. They can also lead to weight gain.

Balanced Meals

You should eat healthy, balanced meals as a part of your total diet. There are many on-line tools to help ensure that you are creating healthy, balanced meals for yourself and your family.

Additional habits (that we touched upon in the previous module) include the following:

- read the nutritional content on the food you buy,

- plan your meals in advance,

- avoid processed foods,

- and choose organic whenever possible.

Foods to Avoid

Of course, there are several things you avoid eating at all costs—and others you should limit as much as possible. These include the following:

Trans Fat and Hydrogenated Oils

These fats, simply put, are very bad for you. Consuming them will increase your risk for heart disease, obesity, and other serious health conditions. Try to avoid all foods that contain them. Foods that typically contain trans fats and/or hydrogenated oils include margarine, most packaged foods (e.g., cake mixes and convenience foods), many fast foods, most commercial baked goods (cookies, pies, cakes, etc.), shortening, potato chips, and most other types of "junk food."

Foods with Artificial Preservatives

Preservatives are used to increase the shelf life of food. Unfortunately, preservatives can seriously damage your health, especially when consumed regularly over the years. While there are many different types of preservatives used in foods today, a few common ones include propyl gallate, sodium nitrate, benzoic acid (or sodium benzoate), sulphites, and monosodium glutamate (MSG). Try to stay away from all of these.

Foods High in Cholesterol

Too much cholesterol clogs your arteries and can cause heart disease, including heart attacks and stroke. Avoid foods high in LDL cholesterol, such as ice cream, butter, pork, fatty cuts of beef, hydrogenated vegetable oils, and whole-fat dairy products.

Fried Foods

Fried foods in general are unhealthy in significant amounts because they often contain trans fat as well as other unhealthy ingredients. Frying food also removes a lot of its nutritional content. Try to limit the amount of fried food you eat. A little now and then is okay, but don't make it a regular part of your diet.

High-Fructose Corn Syrup

High-fructose corn syrup—often called HFCS for short—is used in many processed foods. It is also found in most non-diet sodas. It has been associated with many health conditions, including obesity, heart disease, and type-2 diabetes.

Artificial Sweeteners

Over the past few decades, artificial sweeteners, such as aspartame, saccharin, and sucralose, have been used in many foods and beverages to replace or limit the amount of sugar (and calories) in these foods. Many studies have linked these human-made sweeteners to a variety of serious health problems. If you are looking for a healthy sugar substitute, stevia is a natural sweetener that has been used for centuries.

Dairy or Beef from Cows Treated with Antibiotics or Growth Hormones

Unfortunately, many cows in the United States are given antibiotics and growth hormones (bST or rBGH). When you eat beef or dairy products from these cows, you are also consuming those dangerous antibiotics and hormones. Choose "certified organic" dairy and beef whenever possible, as that ensures no hormones or antibiotics were given to the animals.

Foods That Turn to Fat

According to Dr. Sam Bakhtiar, a well-known expert in nutrition, fitness, and metabolism, the following twelve foods should generally be avoided because they turn to fat.[3] As you will notice, the foods on these list overlap with many listed above.

1. Ice cream.

2. Fried foods.

3. Doughnuts and pastries.

4. White sugar, candy, chocolate, and sweets.

5. Soda.

6. Fruit "drinks" and other sugar-sweetened beverages.

---

3   From http://www.fitnessgurusam.com/

7. Bacon and sausage.

8. White bread.

9. Potato chips, nachos, and corn chips.

10. Hot dogs and fast-food burgers.

11. Cookies, cakes, and pies.

12. Sugary breakfast cereals.

Foods to Eat Regularly

Foods to eat regularly include the following:

1. Vegetables, particularly leafy green vegetables, such as spinach, and fibrous vegetables, such as broccoli which is rich in vitamins and minerals.

2. Fresh fruits, especially berries which are packed with antioxidants (very healthy nutrients) as well as vitamins and fiber.

3. Whole grains, such as brown rice and oats which contain fiber and complex carbohydrates.

4. Nuts and seeds which are good sources of fiber, protein, and healthy fats.

5. Legumes, such as beans, peas, and lentils which are an excellent source of fiber and protein.

6. Lean meat, such as chicken, turkey, and lean cuts of beef (in moderation) and protein that's low in LDL cholesterol.

7. Fish and seafood which are great source of protein and omega-3 fatty acids, an essential nutrient that isn't produced by your body.

8. Healthy cooking oils such as olive oil, coconut oil, sunflower oil, canola oil (preferably organic), and peanut oil.

Other healthy foods to include regularly in your diet include cottage cheese, flax seed, sweet potatoes, and avocados. Make these foods a regular part of your diet for optimum health.

> As I see it, every day you do one of two things: build health or produce disease in yourself. (Adelle Davis)

Exercises

These two exercises will help you build on the habits you've started to develop with the last module.

1. Record Your Meals

   For one week, keep a record of everything you eat. Look at what you are eating. Count the calories and record the percentages and amounts of fats, proteins, carbs, cholesterol, vitamins, and minerals that you consume.

2. Plan a Sample Meal

   Using what you have learned, plan a nutritious meal. Include all the nutrients that your body needs. One sample meal for breakfast could include a whole-grain bagel with low-fat cream cheese, an orange, and a glass of low-fat or fat-free milk.

   Happiness lies in health. (George William Curtis)

Action Plan

Use this action plan to get started with your healthy nutritional lifestyle and build the good eating habits you'll need for your life.

1. Plan Your Meals

   ✓ Before you get ready to fix a meal, plan it. Write down the nutritional content of each food item. When you write down your meals, you are more likely to have healthy, balanced meals.

2. Consult a Physician and/or Nutritionist

   ✓ If possible, schedule a visit with your doctor and a nutritionist. Ask them for advice about your diet and how you can make your lifestyle more nutritious and healthy.

3. Weigh Yourself

   ✓ Keep track of your weight on a weekly basis. Do research on your suggested weight.

   ✓ Track Progress

   ✓ Keep a record or journal of how you are keeping up a nutritious lifestyle. Review your journal periodically.

You Can Do It!

You need to eat food in order to survive but not just any food will do. Now you have the basic tools you need to eat a healthy diet. You know what foods to include in your diet and which ones to avoid. You also know what your body needs from your food so you can successfully create and plan highly nutritious meals.

Remember: *You are what you eat.* Now, you can move towards being a healthier, more energetic, and happier person.

> Today, more than 95% of all chronic disease is caused by food choice, toxic food ingredients, nutritional deficiencies, and lack of physical exercise. (Mike Adams)

Further Reading

Bowden, Johnny. (2007). *The 150 Healthiest Foods on Earth: The Surprising, Unbiased Truth About What You Should Eat and Why*. Minneapolis: Fair Winds Press.

Phillips, Bill. (2003). *Eating for Life*. Golden, Colorado: High Point Media.

EXERCISE FOR MEN

Exercise and application produce order in our
affairs, health of body, cheerfulness of mind,
and these make us precious to our friends.

—Thomas Jefferson

Personal Portraits

At school, besides the weekly physical education class that involved gymnastics, football, basketball, and swimming, we were always running around the playground, fighting or playing marbles. I also had a BMX bike that I used ride for hours every day and then had to carry up three flights of stairs. I had a very good basis (*il hamd lil La'ah*—thanks be to God).

My cousins and I were members of a social community called "Gezira Club," where we spent our youth exercising and bonding through sport. I have found that being involved in team sports at a young age can help the development of character and social skills. Between the seven of us, we played everything from football to basketball to tennis to squash. It was an amazing upbringing that really brought out our competitive natures and our energy in a positive environment.

During the summer, we would spend three months in the northern city of Alexandria, where we would burn thousands of calories every day, swimming, running, fishing, biking, and playing football.

The first time I realized I needed to lose a lot of weight was when I was nineteen. I had never really understood anything about weightlifting or circuit training and had only been part of team sports. I hated the treadmill, and I was really bored with having to do cardio exercise inside the gym. Six months earlier, while playing squash with my cousin, I'd hurt my back and had to spend three months in physiotherapy. It was my own fault, because I hadn't warmed up before exercising. Now I had to find a sport that I enjoyed, had the benefits I was looking for, and was not too strenuous, because I was still recovering.

I remembered how much I had enjoyed diving and swimming during the summers in Alexandria. I am someone who feels very comfortable in the water and connects greatly with the ocean. So I chose swimming. It was good for my back and was also a very good way for me to begin to lose weight and build my cardiovascular strength.

I also started to get involved in weightlifting, because I saw how some of my friends had transformed their bodies. They gave me support and helped me to learn the basics. I read in *Men's Health* that as a man ages, his hormone levels start to drop. This can cause a number of issues, including loss of muscle mass, depression, loss of libido, and lack of focus. Weightlifting is the best way to maintain your muscle mass, manage energy levels and moods, and build strength. It gives me confidence, releases endorphins and testosterone into my bloodstream, and helps keep me fit and focused.

I really can't imagine life without exercise or team sports. The more energy I invest, the more energy I seem to have. I love to feel my muscles burning and the hot blood rushing through my veins after an intense weightlifting session—it's an incredible sensation.

Being physically healthy and fit requires proper nutrition and healthy eating habits. It also requires something else: exercise. Your body is like a building. You can construct a soaring tower made of flimsy materials, such as thin wood, mud, and sticks. You can also construct a soaring tower made of concrete, steel, and iron. Which one will last longer?

Exercising regularly keeps your body strong and toned and your mind sharp—and it completes the equation for a fit and healthy body.

> It is exercise alone that supports the spirits, and
> keeps the mind in vigor. (Marcus Tullius Cicero)

Background

What is physical fitness, and what does it mean for men? Men are designed and created to be strong. It's in our blood and in our spirit. A man's body should be as strong and fit as possible, enabling it to fulfill its natural purpose.

Being physically fit doesn't necessarily mean having bulging muscles like a bodybuilder. Rather, it means that every aspect of your body is as healthy as it can be—on the outside as well as the inside.

Exercise keeps your body looking, feeling, and functioning, as it should. Just as you need to routinely tune the strings on a guitar so they can make beautiful music, you need to regularly work out your body so you can keep it—and your mind and spirit—in tune.

Nutrition and exercise together are the keys to a healthy body. In this module we'll talk about how men can create good exercise habits. We'll also discuss what men need to know about physical fitness to stay on top of their game.

> Lack of activity destroys the good condition of every human being, while movement and methodical physical exercise save it and preserve it. (Plato)

Definitions

Aerobic exercise: exercise that is primarily designed to increase the body's ability to process oxygen.

Strength training: exercise designed to increase strength, build muscle tissue, and improve muscular endurance by using resistance.

Calisthenics: exercise that is designed to increase body strength, flexibility, and cardiovascular fitness.

The Process

> The higher your energy level, the more efficient your body. The more efficient your body, the better you feel and the more you will use your talent to produce outstanding results. (Anthony Robbins)

Centuries ago, some of the most feared and capable warriors in the world were known as Mamluks. These warriors helped to carve out empire after empire for centuries. They used their formidable strength to overthrow enemy after enemy, including the Crusaders, while serving under Salah ad-Din. In 1260, a Mamluk army made history by being the first force to destroy the unstoppable Mongol hordes at the Battle of Ain Jalut—a feat that changed the course of history.

Why were the Mamluks so dominant on the battlefield? What was the secret of their success? Like the legendary Spartan warriors in ancient Greece, Mamluks devoted themselves completely to the art of war. They endured strict and rigorous military training, including physical exercise, which turned their bodies into powerful instruments of war.

Mamluks are excellent examples of what happens when you dedicate the time and effort to turn your body into a machine capable of great things. That's why exercise is so very important—a strong body and strong mind can accomplish anything.

Benefits of Exercise

When you exercise on a regular basis, you receive several benefits. Some of the benefits are immediate, while others long-lasting. These benefits include the following:

- increased energy,

- mental clarity and alertness,

- lower blood pressure and a healthier heart,

- stronger muscles and bones,

- more endurance and stamina,

- weight loss/healthy weight maintenance,

- stronger respiratory system,

- better sleep,

- less stress/greater ability to handle stress,

- improved mood and outlook,

- protection from illness and injury,

- improved self-esteem and self-confidence,

- and a much more attractive appearance.

The more you exercise, the better you feel. Even when you think you're too tired to exercise, you still can gain benefits. In fact, exercise will actually make you feel more energetic. The next time you feel like you don't have enough energy to work out, take a one mile walk. You'll be surprised how that simple physical activity will boost your energy and help you to keep going.

Testosterone

Testosterone is a hormone that is very important to men. Basically, testosterone plays a major role in building protein. It influences many bodily functions, including the metabolism of lipids and carbohydrates. It also plays a significant role in terms of your sex life and your physique.

In short, testosterone is something your body really needs. However, after the age of forty, your testosterone level gradually begins to decline. The drop is generally harmless at first, but over the years it can lead to problems, including loss of muscle, impotence, significant weight gain, and bones that become increasingly brittle.

You can increase your testosterone by increasing your muscle mass, which can be accomplished with weight training. Compound weight exercises— the type that work several muscle groups all at once—will raise your testosterone levels significantly. Squats are a good example of a compound exercise. Using heavier weights—choose one you can't lift more than five times—and doing three sets per exercise will also help boost your testosterone level.

Working out isn't the only way to increase your testosterone levels. According to a *Men's Health* article by Ron Geraci in December of 2000, the following are some other ways to boost your testosterone:

- Get down to a healthy weight, but don't try to lose more than one pound a week.

- Avoid high-protein diets (aim for a protein intake of about 16 percent of your total calories).

- Eat foods high in monounsaturated fat (e.g., olive oil, sesame oil, avocado, nuts, and peanut butter), and make sure your fat intake is about 30 percent of your total diet.

- Get sufficient sleep (seven to eight hours for most men).

- Avoid overtraining.

- Don't skip meals or go for several hours without eating.

- Limit your alcohol intake.

    A man too busy to take care of his health is like a mechanic too busy to take care of his tools. (Spanish proverb)

Types of Exercise

When we refer to "exercise," we are mainly referring to two types—cardiovascular (or aerobic) exercise and strength (or resistance) training.

Cardiovascular Exercise

As you've learned, your cardiovascular (or circulatory) system transports oxygen-rich blood through your body. Cardiovascular exercise, also known as aerobic exercise, improves your body's ability to take in oxygen and utilize it effectively—resulting in a more energetic and efficient performance.

Examples of cardiovascular exercise include running, cycling, swimming, jogging, brisk walking, and many other sports and activities. Most sports, such as football and basketball, also help improve aerobic health.

Strength/Resistance Training

Resistance training is designed to build up strength in your body by working out your muscles and helping them to grow stronger. Your body grows stronger by responding to stress. When you stress your muscles beyond their capabilities, the muscle fibers tear. Your body then has to rebuild those torn muscle fibers with protein. This process of tearing and rebuilding your muscles is what makes them stronger.

The main type of resistance training is weightlifting. Lifting weight creates resistance, which stresses your muscles to the point where they are forced to adapt and grow. This process of adaptation increases both muscle mass and strength.

    A man's health can be judged by which he takes two at a time—pills or stairs. (Joan Welsh)

What Your Exercise Program Must Include

There are a few components that every exercise program must have in order to be successful. While the specifics of your program will depend on your personal goals, every program needs to include the following core elements:

- Goals

  Without goals, you won't know where you're going. A goal can be something as simple as "lose weight" or something as specific as "add two inches to my biceps." As a general rule, the more specific and clear your goals, the more likely you'll be to reach them.

- Schedule

  You should have a schedule for every goal you set. Schedule your sessions so you know in advance what you will be doing and when you will be doing it. Stick to your schedule just as you would any appointment. This will help you stick with your workout routine.

- Aerobic Conditioning

  You don't have to run a marathon in order to be healthy. However, I recommend some form of aerobic conditioning for at least thirty minutes, three times a week.

- Strength/Resistance Training

  Even if you don't want to build muscle and bulk up, some form of strength training is good for your body. You can either do weight training or bodyweight exercises. Just as the name implies, bodyweight exercises use your body's weight for resistance. Push-ups, pull-ups, and sit-ups are three types of bodyweight exercises.

Exercise Examples

To help you find the right activity for you, here are some examples of exercises for particular types of training:

- cardiovascular training: swimming, running, jogging, basketball, cycling.

- strength: weightlifting, bodyweight exercises, plyometrics.

- general fitness: yoga, calisthenics, light aerobics.

- cross training: sports, circuit training, swimming, yoga.

Proper Scheduling

When you exercise is just as important as the type of exercise you do.

If you want to incorporate running or some other form of aerobic exercise into your routine, you can do so every day if you wish (depending on the intensity). To start, however, shoot for three days a week, thirty minutes at a time. Even when you are in shape, you should dedicate at least one day a week for rest.

Strength training should be done two to four times a week (twice a week if you work out your entire body, or four times if you split your workouts into two upper-body workouts and two lower-body workouts). If you alternate upper-body and lower-body workouts, you can work out consecutive days. Just be sure that you never work out the same muscle group on consecutive days, because your muscles need at least forty-eight hours to recover and heal from the stress.

Another element of proper scheduling is creating a well-balanced routine, complete with exercises from each major type of training. Below is a sample weekly exercise routine that is well-balanced and covers all major areas:

- Monday: run for thirty minutes.

- Tuesday: lift weights for thirty minutes, targeting the upper body; walk for twenty minutes.

- Wednesday: swim for thirty minutes; lift weights for thirty minutes, targeting the lower body.

- Thursday: lift weights for thirty minutes, targeting the upper body; walk for twenty minutes.

- Friday: run for thirty minutes.

- Saturday: lift weights for thirty minutes, targeting the lower body; walk for twenty minutes.

- Sunday: rest.

You should exercise long enough and hard enough to elevate your heart rate significantly. Just thirty minutes of walking can do this. Raising your heart rate routinely builds a stronger heart and helps to keep you healthy.

> A lack of exercise robs the body of an essential ingredient. (Karen Sessions)

Diet and Muscle Building

While you may think you're building muscle while you're working out, the actual "building" takes place while you're resting. If you want to make the most of your strength-training workouts, be sure to eat the right foods.

Experts recommend eating a combination of carbohydrates and protein not long after your workout—ideally within three hours. You can create a variety of healthy shakes that are perfect following your workout. One great combination is yogurt, fruit, and protein powder. Another good combination is milk, fruit and an egg substitute.

You can also get creative and add other power-packed foods, including oatmeal, wheat germ, flax seed, sunflower seeds, peanut butter, and/or fruit juice. MensHealth.com and BodyBuilding.com are two excellent websites to find delicious, healthy, post-workout shake recipes.

It's also important that you eat two hours before your strength-training workout. Similar to your post-workout food, choose a combination of protein and carbohydrates. This will give your muscles the amino acids they need and give you energy for your workout. Keep fiber and fat to a minimum prior to your workout.

A snack before bedtime will also help your muscle building efforts. Keep it under five hundred calories, and choose nutritious foods, not junk food. Avoid protein-rich foods for your night-time snack.

Another important diet tip for building muscle is to eat healthy carbohydrates, such as whole grains. Carbohydrates should make up 30 to 50 percent of your total food intake. Avoid (or at least limit) unhealthy carbohydrates like sugar and high fructose corn syrup—they'll sabotage your efforts.

Exercises

These two exercises will help you build on the habits you've started to develop with the last module.

1. Physical Fitness Survey

    Take a physical fitness survey with a trained physician or physical trainer so she can assess your current state of physical health. You can also use online calculators to help you see where you are right now. Your body-mass index (BMI) is a common indicator of how appropriate your current weight is for your size. You can use a metric calculator to determine your BMI score here: http://www. bmi-calculator.net/metric-bmi-calculator.php.

2. Create Two Goals

    Write down at least two personal goals you have for physical fitness. These need to be specific and measurable.

    I'll tell you one thing; you don't always have to be on the go. I sit around a lot, I read a lot, and I do watch television. But I also work out for two hours every day of my life, even when I'm on the road. (Jack LaLanne)

Action Plan

Here is an action plan that, if followed correctly and to the letter, will give you an excellent tool to help you start your fitness program.

1. Exercise Schedule

    ✓ Create an exercise schedule for the upcoming weeks.

✓ Do something physical at least three times a week, for thirty minutes at a time.

✓ Start small and simple, and gradually add more exercises and more total effort over time.

2. Build Your Own Program

✓ Come up with activities you would like to do to stay healthy.

✓ Try to choose at least one aerobic activity, one strength training activity, and one cross-training/general health activity.

3. Alternatives to Traditional Exercise

✓ Always look for some way to stay active. For example, try to walk to where you need to go whenever possible. Do housework and yard work. Anything you can find to safely raise your heart rate is a good idea.

4. Track Progress

✓ Keep a record or journal of what exercise you are doing and how it goes. Review your journal periodically.

You Can Do It!

You'll experience incredible things when you start exercising regularly—the rush of blood, the flow of adrenaline, the intoxicating feel of achievement—all of which will leave you addicted to exercising and wanting more. It will also make you look and feel better than you have ever looked and felt before, guaranteed.

There is a reason that so many men exercise on a regular basis. It does something wonderful and powerful with the male spirit—and keeps your body healthy and strong, too. What are you waiting for? Start exercising today.

Everything you want is out there waiting for you to ask. Everything you want also wants you. But you have to take action to get it. (Jack Canfield)

Further Reading

Schuler, Lou. (2003). *Men's Health—The Book of Muscle: The World's Most Authoritative Guide to Building Your Body.* New York: Rodale Books.

Dos Remedios, Robert. (2009). *Cardio Strength Training: Torch Fat, Build Muscle, and Get Stronger Faster.* New York: Rodale Books.

Exercise for Women

Personal Portraits

My neighbor was amazing. She had two kids, was working, and was also an amazing cook. When she got pregnant for the third time, I noticed that her habits at the gym didn't change. I continued to see her every day until only forty-eight hours prior to her giving birth.

I use this example sometimes when women tell me that they don't have the time or the energy to go to the gym. This working mother of two was nine months pregnant and still doing squats and Pilates. When she did give birth to a beautiful baby boy, she invited us to see him. I remember she looked incredible for someone who had just had a baby, and I told her husband that he was a very lucky man. God bless them.

From a male perspective, it's really attractive—a woman who is confident and proud and always finds the time and the discipline to look and feel her best.

One noticeable global trend lately has been the increasing number of women who are becoming more active and interested in physical fitness. This is wonderful news—mainly because traditionally, women have been less likely to exercise and stay physically fit. The truth is that women need exercise just as much as men—sometimes even more.

A woman's body is capable of enduring great physical stress, but only if it is taken care of and maintained properly. Proper care means more than just eating right—it means exercising regularly as well. Additionally, women are more vulnerable to body image issues and low self-esteem than men. Fortunately, exercise can help keep a woman's body and mind strong and fit—and also make her feel terrific.

The body is like a piano, and happiness is like
music. It is needful to have the instrument
in good order. (Henry Ward Beecher)

Background

Women are very resilient creatures. They are designed from birth to be able
to handle the stresses and pressures of the world—to create life, nurture
it, raise it, and sustain it through the ups and downs, through whatever
challenges life may throw their way.

Being a physically fit woman doesn't mean you have to bulk up and look
and act like a man. It means that your body is how you want it to be—on
the inside as well as the outside. Of course, there are differences between
how men and women approach exercise. In this module, we'll discuss
exercise from a woman's point of view. We'll also explain how women can
get the most out of looking and feeling great through physical fitness.

Take care of your body, then the rest will
automatically become stronger. (Chuang Tzu)

Definitions

Aerobic exercise: exercise primarily designed to increase the body's ability
to process oxygen.

Strength training: exercise designed to increase strength, build muscle
tissue, and improve muscular endurance by using resistance.

Calisthenics: exercise designed to increase body strength, flexibility, and
cardiovascular fitness.

The Process

In ancient Greek mythology, there lived a race of warriors so feared, so
formidable, and so strong that they became—literally—the stuff from
which legends are made. These warriors, however, were not men. They
were women, and they were called Amazons.

Amazons, as the stories go, were legendary warriors who were as strong, lithe, and as cunning as men. They lived in their own secluded territory and were incredibly self-reliant. They depended on men for nothing. Many great tales were created about Amazons, and all of them extolled the admirable virtues of this fierce yet proud people.

What can women today learn from the Amazons? The primary lesson isn't that a woman should become a fierce warrior. Nor is it that a woman should train relentlessly to become a physical machine. The lesson to be learned is that, just like men, women can become strong in body and mind. They can use both their inner and outer strength to stay healthy and fit.

> Physical fitness is not only one of the most important keys to a healthy body; it is the basis of dynamic and creative intellectual activity. (John Fitzgerald Kennedy)

Benefits of Exercise

Exercise has many terrific benefits for women. Some of these benefits are immediately noticeable; others accumulate over time with sustained and consistent exercise. A woman who exercises will reap a multitude of benefits, including the following:

- gaining more energy,
- shedding unwanted pounds,
- toning and strengthening her muscles,
- increasing flexibility,
- building a strong immune system,
- becoming more physically attractive,
- keeping her bones strong,
- improving her skin's appearance,
- reducing her stress,
- lowering her blood pressure,

- improving her sleep,

- keeping her heart strong and healthy,

- improving her mood, optimism, and outlook,

- increasing her self-esteem and confidence,

- looking and feeling more attractive,

- and reducing the risk of disease and illness.

Many women work very hard, though. They don't think exercise will do them any good because they are already tired after long, hard days taking care of their family, raising children, managing the household, and working at a job outside the home as well. The truth is that exercise is wonderful, because if you're tired, it will give you the very energy that you need. In fact, if you make time for exercise, you'll find that you feel much less tired than you did when you weren't exercising at all.

To give yourself the energy you need to keep going when you're tired, try going for a brisk walk. You'll be surprised at just how much better you will feel once you elevate your heart rate for twenty to thirty minutes. It's almost like magic.

> Exercise is good for your mind, body, and soul. (Susie Michelle Cortright)

Types of Exercise

When we refer to "exercise," we are mainly referring to two types—cardiovascular (or aerobic) exercise and strength (or resistance) training.

Cardiovascular Exercise

Your cardiovascular (or circulatory) system plays an extremely important role. It transports oxygen-rich blood through your body. Cardiovascular exercise, often referred to as aerobic exercise or "cardio," improves your body's ability to take in oxygen and utilize it effectively—resulting in a more energetic and efficient performance.

Examples of cardiovascular exercise include running, cycling, swimming, jogging, brisk walking, and many other sports and activities. Many women enjoy going to the gym for aerobic classes or spinning classes—both of which are excellent cardiovascular workouts.

Strength/Resistance Training

Strength training is designed to increase the strength of your muscles by placing more stress on them than they are used to handling. This stress makes your body respond by tearing down your muscle fibers and then repairing them. This process of tearing down and rebuilding makes your muscles stronger. Most women think of weightlifting when they hear the term "resistance training." However, there are other types of resistance training methods that many women enjoy. These include using resistance bands and medicine balls, as well as doing bodyweight exercises (e.g., sit-ups or push-ups).

Many women ask this question about strength training: "Is it really for us?" They point to the rippling muscles and bulging bodies of men who do weight training as examples of what they do not want to have. This is one of the reasons many women view weightlifting as a male-only activity and feel that strength training is decidedly unfeminine. The truth, however, is this: women can benefit from strength training just like men. Lifting weights doesn't mean you have to bulk up; in fact, many women lift weights to attain a body that is beautifully toned and slim. By using lighter weights and more repetitions, women can tone their muscles and tighten up their body without having to worry about developing bulky, masculine muscles.

> If you don't do what's best for your body, you're the
> one who comes up on the short end. (Julius Erving)

What Your Exercise Program Must Include

There are a few components that every exercise program must have in order to be successful. While the specifics of your program will depend on your personal goals, every program needs to have the following core elements to some degree:

- Goals

    Without goals, you won't have any idea where you're going. A goal can be something as simple as "lose weight," or it can be as specific as "drop twenty-five pounds." As a general rule, the more specific and clear your goals, the more likely you'll be to reach them.

- Schedule

  You should have a schedule for every goal you set. Schedule your sessions so you know in advance what you will be doing and when you will be doing it. Stick to your schedule just as you would any appointment. This will help you stick with your workout routine.

- Aerobic Conditioning

  You don't have to run a marathon in order to be healthy. However, I recommend some form of aerobic conditioning for at least thirty minutes three times a week.

- Strength/Resistance Training

  Even if you don't want to build muscle and bulk up, some form of strength training is good for your body. You can do weight training, bodyweight exercises, or resistance band training (in which large, rubber band-like devices are used instead of weights).

Exercise Examples

To help you find the right activity for you, here are some examples of exercises that women tend to enjoy and benefit from:

- cardiovascular training: swimming, running, jogging, walking, cycling, spinning, aerobics.

- strength: resistance training, weightlifting, bodyweight exercises, calisthenics.

- general fitness: yoga, calisthenics, aerobics (traditional and rhythmic)

- cross training: racquet sports, swimming, volleyball.

Proper Scheduling

One big component of proper exercise is proper scheduling. The human body can endure a lot of work, but you have to gradually increase the amount of time you work out. When you're first starting out, try doing some form of aerobic exercise for thirty minutes a day, three days a week. You should always have at least one rest day per week, even when you work up to exercising four to five times a week.

Strength training should be done two to four times a week (twice a week if you work out your entire body, or four times if you split your workouts into two upper-body workouts and two lower-body workouts). If you alternate upper-body and lower-body workouts, you can work out consecutive days. Just be sure that you never work out the same muscle group on consecutive days, because your muscles need at least forty-eight hours to recover and heal from the stress.

As far as sports are concerned, women can typically engage in low-impact sports as many times a week as they want. (They're fun, too, so that is another big advantage.)

Below is a sample weekly exercise routine designed for women who want a well-balanced program:

- Monday: strength train for thirty minutes, targeting the lower body; walk for twenty minutes.

- Tuesday: run/jog for thirty minutes.

- Wednesday: strength train for thirty minutes, targeting the upper body; swim for twenty minutes.

- Thursday: strength train for thirty minutes, targeting the lower body; walk for twenty minutes.

- Friday: run/jog for thirty minutes.

- Saturday: strength train for thirty minutes, targeting the upper body; walk for twenty minutes.

- Sunday: rest.

Whenever you exercise, focus on elevating your heart rate for at least thirty consecutive minutes. This will strengthen your heart and reduce your risk of heart disease and many other common conditions.

> To feel "fit as a fiddle," you must tone
> down your middle. (Anonymous)

Eating Before and After Exercise

It's important that you eat something before and after your workout. Prior to working out, it's best to eat something light—you don't want to work out on a full stomach. A piece of fruit or some yogurt is an excellent pre-workout snack. After you work out—especially after a strength-training session, when your muscles are starting to repair themselves—you want to be sure to eat as well. Select a combination of complex carbohydrates, protein, and healthy fats. A post-workout shake made from yogurt, protein powder, and fruit is an excellent choice. You might also add a little peanut butter or flax seed.

Be creative and experiment with different combinations. You can find some delicious recipes for healthy shakes and snacks on the internet or in your local book-store.

Exercise Tips for Problem Areas

Cellulite—exercise can help reduce cellulite. Cardiovascular exercise helps improve circulation and burn fat, while strength training helps to build and tone the muscles underneath the skin. Do a combination of both to help reduce cellulite.

Belly fat—in order to reduce belly fat, you need to burn excess fat and strengthen the abdominal muscles. A few good abdominal exercises include crunches, reverse crunches, and hanging leg lifts.

Flabby butt—squats, lunges, hip extensions, running, cycling, and kickboxing are all excellent exercises to firm up a loose butt.

Sagging upper arms—to tone your triceps, do triceps kickbacks, dumbbell triceps extensions, and triceps dips (either hanging or with a bench).

Exercises

These two exercises will help you build on the habits you've started to develop with the last module.

1. Physical Fitness Survey

   Take a physical fitness survey with a trained physician or physical trainer so he can assess your current physical health. You can also use online calculators to help you evaluate your current condition. Your body-mass index (BMI) is a common indicator of how appropriate your current weight is for your size. You can use a metric calculator to determine your BMI score here: http://www.bmi-calculator.net/metric-bmi-calculator.php.

   There are many professionals who specialize in women's health and fitness. Women have different physiological needs than men, so getting a check-up with a specialist who works regularly with female health is recommended.

2. Create Two Goals

   Write down at least two personal goals you have for physical fitness. These need to be specific and measurable.

   Exercise should be fun, otherwise, you won't be consistent. (Laura Ramirez)

Action Plan

Here is an action plan that, if followed correctly and to the letter, is an excellent tool to help you start your fitness program.

1. Exercise Schedule

   ✓ Create an exercise schedule for the upcoming weeks.

   ✓ Do something physical at least three times a week, for thirty minutes at a time.

      ✓ Start small and simple, and gradually add more exercises and more total effort over time.

2. Build Your Own Program

      ✓ Come up with activities you would like to do to stay healthy.

      ✓ Try to choose at least one aerobic activity, one strength-training activity, and one cross-training/general health activity.

      ✓ Take your current schedule and find ways to fit in your exercises.

3. Alternatives to Traditional Exercise

      ✓ Always look for some way to stay active. For example, try to walk to where you need to go whenever possible. Do housework and yard work. Anything you can find to safely raise your heart rate is a good idea.

4. Track Progress

      ✓ Keep a record or journal of what exercise you are doing and how it goes. Review your journal periodically.

Our health always seems much more valuable after we lose it. (Anonymous)

You Can Do It!

Physical fitness is a must when it comes to total personal development—for women just as for men. There's a reason that so many women exercise on a regular basis. It makes them look and feel attractive and alluring—and it keeps their bodies healthy and strong, too.

If you want to feel like a capable, independent, and positive woman, exercise is one of the best ways to accomplish that. How your body looks and how it makes you feel—on the inside as well as the outside—is within your control. Take your health in your hands and make it happen—you can do it!

Living a healthy lifestyle will only deprive you of
poor health, lethargy, and fat. (Jill Johnson)

Further Reading

Linguvic, Wini. (2004). *Lean, Long & Strong: The 6-Week Strength-Training, Fat-Burning Program for Women.* New York: Rodale Books.

Northrup, Christiane, Dr. (2010). *Women's Bodies, Women's Wisdom: Creating Physical and Emotional Health and Healing.* New York: Bantam.

HEART

First—Be Happy

If the heart is empty, the rest will soon abandon you too.

—Arabian proverb

Personal Portraits

When I was seven years old, I had an eye accident that left me nearly blind in my left eye. It was actually my fault because, like any child, I was curious and experimental with my toys. I was actually very creative in my approach—I had received a toy gun with rubber sucker-cap bullets from a birthday party I had been invited to and had become really bored with the fact that the bullets just stuck to the wall. I happened to have some Styrofoam cartons lying around and decided to remove the rubber caps and sharpen the plastic bullets so that they would penetrate the Styrofoam. I fixed pictures of the enemies of my superheroes from my comic books onto the foam and started playing a game of target practice. I was having so much fun!

Anyway, one of the bullets became misplaced in the gun's barrel. As I held the gun between my knees and forced a sharp stick down the gun-hole to load it onto the spring, the bullet slipped and went straight for my eye at very close range.

I thank God every day that my eye looks perfectly normal and that I have had no need for cosmetic or reconstructive surgery. Some people might have suffered or felt bitter after this incident, but I choose to look at it differently. I am very grateful that I was blessed with the gift of sight in the first place—I could have been born blind. I am very lucky that my eye looks normal—I could have had a scar or a severe physical handicap. I am blessed that I received excellent quality health care that allowed the doctors to save my eye—I could have lost it completely and had to resort to wearing a glass eye. The list goes on and on. The point I am trying to make is that we are very much in control of how we choose to react to the events that occur in our lives. We can choose to suffer, or we can choose to be grateful. I choose the latter because in my heart, I am always saying *"il hamd lil La'ah"*—because there is so much to be thankful for: loving parents, close family, caring friends, talent, success, love, admiration, the abundance and beauty of this incredible world we live in … etc. This is how

I manage to stay optimistic and enthusiastic. By adopting this paradigm, I feel empowered and maintain a deep sense of gratitude for all the gifts that I have received—regardless of what happens to me.

Are you happy? Have you ever asked yourself that question and really looked deep within to determine the answer? Well, whether you think you are happy or not, almost every person who's ever lived wants to be happy.

Think about that for a moment. The desire for happiness is universal. It brings us all together and unites us—despite our differences. While happiness might mean different things to different people, the truth is that we all desire this feeling and state of contentment, this belief that all is right with the world.

The good news is that *being happy is possible for everyone, no matter what the person's situation or circumstances.*

> Happiness doesn't depend on any external conditions, it
> is governed by our mental attitude. (Dale Carnegie)

Background

There are two words in Arabic that, when translated and read by non-Arabic speakers, would both appear to mean "happiness." However, there is a distinction between the two. The first word—*farah*—is generally taken to mean worldly delights and pleasures, things enjoyed by the senses. This word is referring to external happiness—that which is seen and brought about by things outside of the spirit. The second word—*suroor*—has another meaning altogether. It is referring to a different kind of happiness; the kind that is felt inside and resides within the heart. This kind of happiness comes from other sources. It is deeper and far less tangible.

What does this distinction mean? What can we learn from it? A closer look at these two very similar words gives us a strong hint as to the nature of true happiness. True happiness is something that is felt deep within. It is associated with meaning, emotion, and a feeling that goes beyond superficial possessions or relationships. It comes from your sense of self-worth; from satisfaction with being who you are. It does not come from others; other people cannot make you happy. (They can only make you happier.)

Being happy is vital to a productive and successful life and no success in life is really worth anything in the long run unless it leads to happiness of some sort. In order to fully develop your heart—the essence of who you are—you must first be happy. And only you are in control of that.

> True happiness ... is not attained through self-gratification, but through fidelity to a worthy purpose. (Helen Keller)

Definitions

Happiness: a state of being happy, i.e. content with life and satisfied with one's situation and self, accompanied by an optimistic outlook.

Materialism: believing that happiness comes from owning possessions; associating value, worth, and satisfaction with material things.

Optimism: an outlook characterized by a belief that, in general, things will be good or will improve.

Pessimism: an outlook characterized by a belief that, in general, things will be bad or will get worse.

Moods: periods of time dominated by a particular emotion or thought process. Moods can change infrequently or often and can be good, bad, or neutral.

The Process

> Joy is what happens to us when we allow ourselves to recognize how good things really are. (Marianne Williamson)

Do you know what true happiness is and how to find it? If not, you're in good company. You see, most people have no idea. However, the potential for true happiness is always there—if only we know where to look for it.

So What Is True Happiness?

Let's first understand what true happiness is not. True happiness is not superficial or shallow. Rather, it involves

- genuine contentment with your current situation and although you might prefer to be in a better place, you are able to be content where you are for now,

- recognition of obstacles and weaknesses, not an avoidance of them,

- confidence and inner peace,

- an optimistic outlook,

- acceptance of yourself,

- ways to motivate, entertain, and satisfy yourself and others,

- and the fulfillment of a greater purpose.

It's hard to be truly happy when you're missing any of the above. In fact, some of the world's most successful people are missing those things in their lives. Yet, we think they are truly happy even though, sadly, they aren't.

Happiness Is Up to You

The truly marvelous thing about happiness is that it is completely within your control. That may sound far-fetched, but it's true. You can't always control what happens to you, but you can always control how you respond to it and feel about it, as well as your attitude toward life in general.

Happiness isn't genetic. If your parents or grandparents weren't happy, that doesn't mean you're destined to a life of unhappiness—even if you're not happy right now. You can be happy; all you need to do is make the right changes and understand the true sources of happiness.

> Training yourself to live in the present—without
> regretting the past or fearing the future - is a recipe
> for a happy life. (Jonathan Lockwood Huie)

Sources of Happiness

Finding happiness isn't hard. Let's look at some of the basic sources of happiness.

Self

By far, the most important source of true happiness is your self—and really, this is the only source that brings true, genuine, sincere happiness and satisfaction.

Others

Being around others, such as your friends and co-workers, can make you happier, but it won't make you truly happy. However, surrounding yourself with positive people and enjoying their company certainly makes it easier to be happy.

Family

Your family is another source of happiness. Since many of us spend a lot of time with our families, enjoying them is a great way to energize ourselves and put a smile on our faces.

Happiness and Possessions

On the surface, having lots of nice things and being materialistic is one way to find happiness. However, the reality is that material possessions, no matter how many or how extravagant, do not bring happiness.

Here's a story that illustrates this point: there once was a rich young ruler who had everything he wanted—gold, silver, jewels, fine clothing, a magnificent palace, and slaves at his beck and call. In the eyes of the world, he certainly seemed to have it all—yet he was not really, truly happy. Seeking a solution to his lack of happiness, he asked a wise man, "Master, what can I do to gain true happiness? I have everything I could ever want, anything money can buy, and the power and authority to use it. But I'm not happy."

The wise man nodded knowingly and replied, "Young man, in order to be truly happy, sell everything you have, give the money to the poor, and find your heart."

The rich young ruler recoiled at the thought and banished the old man from the palace in anger. "How dare he suggest I give up all of my riches!" he said to himself.

Many years later, the rich ruler was now a very old man on his deathbed. He did not have any friends, for he was too focused on gathering more and more power and wealth and possessions to make friends. The few so-called friends he did have liked him only for his wealth. None of his family was still around; he had alienated them with his selfishness.

All he had was himself and his possessions—all piled into his room, from the floor to the ceiling. Yet, none of his possession brought him comfort. They brought no inner peace or happiness. And thus he died—a rich, powerful, and unhappy ruler.

Is it really worth gaining the whole world and never experiencing genuine happiness or satisfaction?

How to Become Happier

Perspective

One of the ways you can become happier is to change your perspective. When you look at things from only your own perspective, you become not only narrow-minded and self-centered, but unhappy as well. But when you choose to shift your perspective to one that is fresh and new, you can become happy—even when others wouldn't. For example, whenever you are sick, don't focus on your illness. Instead, be grateful you are still alive. Whenever you don't accomplish something, don't focus on your failure—take the opportunity to try again. If you are beaten out for a position, rather than focus on your loss, consider the other person's gain and how happy it makes them feel.

> Success is getting what you want. Happiness is
> wanting what you get. (Dale Carnegie)

Positive Thinking

There once was a very old woman who looked in the mirror one morning. As she peered at her reflection, she noticed there were only three hairs left on her head. Being a positive person, the woman said, "I think I'll braid my hair today." So she braided her three hairs and had a wonderful day. A few days later, she once again looked in the mirror and saw that she only had two hairs remaining. She said to herself, "Well, I think today I would like to part my hair in the center." So she did, and she had a wonderful day. A few days passed, and lo and behold, she found herself with just one hair remaining. As positive as usual, the woman said, "I think I would love a pony-tail." And she went along and had another wonderful day.

At last, the day came when she looked in the mirror and saw that she was completely bald. No hairs were left. The woman smiled.

"Finally bald, huh," she said. "How wonderful! Now I won't have to waste time doing my hair anymore!"

The power of positive thinking should never be underestimated. Choosing to be happy means choosing to think positively whenever possible.

Change

Making real, lasting change is another way to create never-ending happiness. These changes can be physical or mental. Physically, you could become happier by improving your diet and exercising more, or by changing how you look or how you dress and act. Mentally, you can become happier by creating a vision, accomplishing goals, changing your perspective, learning a skill, and finding ways to motivate and please yourself.

Change, at the end of the day, is what it is all about.

Happiness is a choice. (Anonymous)

Since you're the one who gets to do the choosing, why not decide right now to choose a life full of fun, a life loaded with excitement, a life full of high flying adventure? And more than anything else, make sure you choose a life in which happiness is the name of your game. Then be sure to share your good fortune with everyone you are privileged to meet every day, for the rest of your life. When you begin to do that each day, you are sure to earn happy returns

Exercises

For this module, try these exercises:

1. Create Your Happy List

   On a piece of paper, identify ten things, people, and/or events that make you happy. Write down why they make you happy. Explore yourself. What makes you smile?

2. Mood Diary

   For one week, record your daily moods. Whenever you feel your outlook is changing, write it down, along with the emotions you are feeling and what you are thinking. This teaches you to be observant of your emotions and your moods.

Action Plan

Building on what we discussed in the discipline module, here is an action plan you can use on a regular basis to develop mental discipline and control your thoughts.

1. Create a Happy Book

   ✓ Take a notebook, scrapbook, folder, etc., and create a happy book. In this book, place anything that makes you happy—words, pictures, cartoons, images, song lyrics, etc.

2. Happy List Fulfillment

   ✓ Try to experience at least one thing, or interact with at least one person, on your happy list every day.

3. Create Unhappiness Counters

   ✓ Using what you have learned in previous modules and gates (particularly the self-esteem module and the control your thoughts modules), develop counters to any unhappy stimulus you encounter.

✓ Turn the negative into positive. Remember: you control your happiness.

4. Track Progress

✓ Keep a record or journal of your journey and your moods and happiness level. Review your journal periodically

You Can Do It!

Being happy is something that is within your control. It is something you can make happen in your life—as long as you recognize that the power to be happy lies within you, and not within anyone or anything else. Take a look at how you see the world and yourself. Examine your heart. Learn what makes you truly happy—what you have a genuine passion for, and not just what gives you temporary pleasure and satisfaction. Show love to yourself and to other people, every chance you get.

The secrets to happiness aren't really secrets, after all. They are right there in front of you. You merely have to open your eyes—and open your heart.

> Most people are about as happy as they make
> up their minds to be. (Abraham Lincoln)

Further Reading

Orloff, Judith. (2005). *Positive Energy: 10 Extraordinary Prescriptions for Transforming Fatigue, Stress, and Fear into Vibrance, Strength, and Love.* New York: Three Rivers Press.

Ricard, Matthieu. (2007). *Happiness: A Guide to Developing Life's Most Important Skill.* Boston: Little, Brown, and Company.

Understanding Men

*You cannot teach a man anything; you can
only help him discover it in himself.*

—Galileo Galilei

Personal Portraits

Understanding a man is quite easy actually—I'll just talk about things that are important to me. Since this is a book with references to psychology, let me cover the basics first before moving into the realm of self-actualization.

Italian food, red wine, a beautiful and sensual woman, a cool car, new gadgets, a house by the beach, acoustic guitars, great friends and family and a fulfilling job—that's the easy part (*il hamd lil Laa'h*).

I am personally motivated by purpose and a sense of mastery over the projects that I choose to challenge myself with as well as by my contribution to society as a whole—whether it is through music, media, or psychology. This vital sense of freedom and power to achieve my mission in life is very empowering and is what motivates me.

In my journey to find love, which is vital to my existence as a man and as an artist, I have been blessed and am grateful for my experiences. I consider myself very lucky. To love and be loved is worth fighting for, even if it means making mistakes.

I nurture my spirit through faith and believe that a man can transcend (if he chooses) certain innate human traits, such as lust, vanity, and pride, to achieve a more balanced and peaceful existence. Of course it takes a lot of effort and is a continuous struggle, but it also helps me to take responsibility for my life and the results that I get. I think that finding a sense of balance, stability, and harmony in my life will lead me to sustained happiness.

The bonds that I share with my family, friends, and band of brothers are extremely important and vital to my well-being. Every guy needs to experience the transition from boy to man in the company of male role models who can guide him, test him, and lead him through the initiation to manhood. Then, he can embrace his true nature as a man and let go of fear—and act with courage and integrity in the face of doubt.

I love children, and I know that I must give to the next generation. I really look forward to the day when I can nurture my own children, teach them, play with them, and become a child all over again. However, I will only take that decision when I am ready to maintain a family, emotionally and financially.

All of that sounds really serious, and it is. The strange thing is that I really don't take myself too seriously. I love to laugh, play, and be amused by the world, and I accept my nature with a sense of grace, faith and humility.

There are basically two types of humans: men and women. For thousands of years, this is the way it has been—men and women living together in (relative) harmony. Every now and then, however, situations arise in which men and women see things differently and these differences in perspective often result in negative behaviors and unpleasant actions. Wouldn't it be easier if men and women understood each other? There would certainly be much less conflict—if only it were possible.

Understanding men is an important part of building successful relationships with them—just as understanding women is important for men. In this module, you will discover the keys to really understanding what makes men tick. Once you understand them, you can build truly rewarding relationships with all the men in your life.

Background

Communicating successfully with someone of the opposite sex can be very challenging and confusing. If you are a woman relating to this, you probably feel you are clearly communicating—everything you say should be easy to understand. However, men often get lost in the message and feel completely overwhelmed by the emotions and words you use to express how you truly feel. If you are like most women, you long to hear elaborate explanations and apologies for the insensitive or harsh treatment you have endured by your loved one. However, your man can be completely unaware of the issue at hand, leaving you even more infuriated than before. This causes many women to throw their hands up and say, "He just doesn't care."

But, you see, it almost never has anything to do with whether or not he cares. Rather, it's because men and women are entirely different creatures. Their differences include everything from how they deal with emotions to the style in which they communicate. We'll help break down those barriers a little by taking a closer look at the male personality. We'll explore the things that create barriers to communication as well as barriers to understanding.

Remember: the differences between men and women can be overcome with understanding. This is the key to developing strong and successful relationships.

> Understanding is the first step to acceptance, and only with acceptance can there be recovery. (J. K. Rowling)

The Process

There are many times when men seem like an alien species—it's as if they're from an entirely different planet. What makes us tick? What goes on inside our heads? Why is it so difficult to communicate with us at times? Finding answers to these questions and others you may have can help dramatically improve your relationships with men—both personally and professionally.

A Man's Values

It's vitally important to understand that men generally have different values than women. They have some similarities, of course, but the differences tend to be much more pronounced. Men place a high value on the following:

- being providers and caring for our families,

- respect,

- purpose,

- solving problems,

- control,

- and assertiveness.

Respect is especially important to men. You see, if a man has to choose between being respected and being loved, he will almost always choose being respected. This is one area in which men and women are very different. Women are very relational beings, so they tend to place a much higher value on being loved. Conflicts often occur because women don't understand why being loved isn't as important to the men in their lives.

Unlike women, men typically place a high value on solving problems. A woman, on the other hand, may talk about a problem to her significant other just as a way of relating. She isn't necessarily seeking a solution—yet he will almost immediately go into problem-solving mode. She just wants to be heard—and he wants to fix it rather than just listen. This also leads to a lot of conflict.

Men and women both fall victim to subscribing to the roles created by society. However, many of those roles exist because of the inherent differences between a man's nature and a woman's nature. Men have come to see those values as important—not just because society says they are, but also because these values align with their nature.

> When women are depressed, they eat or go
> shopping. Men invade another country. It's a whole
> different way of thinking. (Elayne Boosler)

Importance of Work to Men

One concept that men generally regard as highly important is work. A man doesn't really feel like a man unless he is being productive. He takes great pride in his work and his profession, even if he may not particularly like the type of work he is doing.

If most men had to choose between caring for children at home and working around the clock to provide for their families, they would choose working. Both activities are difficult and noble, but unlike many women, men feel a strong need to contribute something substantial—to themselves, their families, and the world around them.

Men also identify strongly with their work. Ask a man who he is, and often the first thing he will tell you pertains to his work, such as "I'm an engineer" or "I'm a fireman."

Because working and being productive is so important to men, retirement can be a very difficult transition for them. Many men do well if they continue doing some type of work—even if it's only a few hours a week or volunteer work—once they retire.

A retired husband is often a wife's full-time job. (Ella Harris)

Men and Emotions

One of the most important things that women need to understand when it comes to men is emotion. Contrary to what women may think, men do have very strong emotions. Women often get frustrated because they feel that men do not show emotion nearly as openly and often as they do. Regardless of how it may appear at times, men feel emotion just as much as women. However, the primary difference is that most men keep their emotions inside. They appear guarded as a result, which women often interpret as them being insensitive, cold, or uncaring.

Part of the reason men tend to not show their emotions is because of what they were taught as young boys. They may have been told things like "Big boys don't cry" or ridiculed if they let their feelings show. They may have been given the message that they have to "be strong"—and that showing emotion is a sign of weakness. To a young boy, those are powerful messages.

Women, as part of their makeup, also tend to be more emotional than men. This is why many men take offense when their lack of emotion is regarded as something negative. It's part of their makeup.

Conflict usually occurs because men don't always show their emotions the way a woman would like. When they remain guarded and refuse to openly express their feelings—or if they do so only grudgingly—problems occur in the relationship. This is a common issue for most men, because they don't openly communicate their feelings without substantial poking and prodding.

One of the best ways to overcome this issue in a relationship is to find a happy medium—one in which the woman understands that men keep things a bit closer to the vest, and the man understands that he needs to make more effort at communicating his feelings.

> Men are taught to apologize for their weaknesses,
> women for their strengths. (Lois Wyse)

What Motivates Men

Understanding what motivates men is a great way to connect with them and get closer to them. Men, generally speaking, are motivated by the following things:

- ambition,

- power,

- control,

- security of loved ones,

- well-being of loved ones,

- praise for accomplishments,

- and status.

Of course, women can be motivated by all of these as well. After all, most women care deeply about the security and well-being of loved ones. But, in general, men are the ones who are the most strongly driven by these things.

If you have a hard time figuring out what drives a man—or need to know how you can connect with a man and find out what really makes him tick—chances are it will be something on that list.

> It takes a woman twenty years to make a man
> of her son, and another woman twenty minutes
> to make a fool of him. (Helen Rowland)

Communicating with Men

This is perhaps one of the most contentious concepts when it comes to talking about differences between the genders. More fights are caused by communication problems between a man and a woman than probably any other issue. You see, men have two main tendencies when it comes to communicating with women:

- they prefer a woman to be straightforward and direct,

- and they like to give advice or provide a solution when presented with a problem or situation.

Many women have a tendency to beat around the bush or go into elaborate detail when talking to a man. This drives most men crazy, and they often become impatient and frustrated. Men typically just want the facts—they would prefer the woman just to get right to the point.

Along these same lines, many women also expect men to be mind readers. This leads to many conflicts because rather than just state what's bothering them or on their mind, they assume that the man in their life should know them well enough to figure it out. These impossible expectations leave men feeling frustrated and inadequate.

Never assume that a man knows what you're thinking. Even the most amazing man doesn't have superhuman powers. The more clearly you communicate, the better your relationship with him will be.

Men are also wired to solve problems and fix things. If you talk to them about a problem or a difficult situation, their first reaction is almost always to tell you what you should do. This isn't because they view you as incapable—although you may interpret it that way. Rather, it's because men have a genuine desire to help—it's their nature. They also have a strong need to feel needed, although they'll rarely admit it. This issue frequently causes problems because quite often, a woman just wants to be heard and acknowledged rather than given advice.

Again, you need to find a happy medium. Your part is to be more direct and straightforward. If you just want him to listen—say so upfront. Tell him you would just like him to listen—that you just want to be heard and understood, not given advice. At the same time, be careful to avoid endless details, unless you want him to tune out halfway through. He, on the other hand, will need to work on refraining from giving advice unless you ask for it. And, he'll need to be patient with all the details and do his best to listen and understand.

Men's Need to Feel Needed and Appreciated

Ever since the caveman era, men have been the providers and protectors. As mentioned above, they have an inherent need to feel needed. They also need to feel appreciated. Unfortunately, over the past few decades, women have become increasingly self-sufficient. Most women have full-time jobs and earn almost as much or even more money than a lot of men. Many women today don't need a man to support them financially. In fact, highly independent women often have problems in their relationships with men because they have a hard time letting a man feel needed. Many women (and men) also tend to take their partner for granted. Men have a deep need to feel appreciated by the women they love. When they are taken for granted, it creates a rift in the relationship.

One of the primary reasons men have affairs is because they don't feel needed or appreciated by their wives. When this need starts being fulfilled by someone else, it can be very powerful—because this need is so strong.

If you tend to be very independent, one of the most important things you can do to improve your relationship is to find ways to show the man in your life that you need him. It may mean asking him to open a jar or fasten your necklace (even though you could easily do either), asking him to hold you when you're having a difficult day, or seeking his input on a project you're working on. When he does these things, thank him. Let him know—often—how much you appreciate him. You'll be amazed how these seemingly small gestures will draw him to you and improve your relationship.

Men like to be the hero—let him be that for you.

Sex and Men

Men are inherently sexual creatures. Not that sex isn't important to women—it is. But the differences between men and women when it comes to sex often create a lot of conflict in romantic relationships.

Many women get frustrated because they think that all men think about and want is sex. What they don't realize is that men express much of their love and affection for their partners through sex. If you're in a serious relationship with a man, it's important that you realize this. If you assume that he's just treating you as a sexual object and get frustrated and push him away, you're denying him the opportunity to feel emotionally close to you and connected with you.

> Part of the reason that men seem so much less loving
> than women is that men's behavior is measured
> with a feminine ruler. (Francesca M. Cancian)

A Further Look at Key Differences Between Men and Women

Robert Glover, PhD, provides powerful insights into primary masculine and feminine traits (and thus, men and women). [4] These insights may be helpful in trying to better understand the man in your life and your typical responses to him. For example, individuals with masculine traits tend to be powerful, disciplined, and focused. They are providers, protectors, and leaders. They strive for mastery and freedom, and they put supreme value on consistency. Those with primary feminine traits, on the other hand, tend to be receptive, open, and inviting. They seek connection and security. They are nurturers and tend to follow rather than lead. Trust is extremely important to them.

Exercises

For this module, try these exercises:

1. Write Down Five Men You Know Well

    Identify five main traits of each. For example, "Kind, impatient, helpful, arrogant, intelligent."

    Look for common traits. Learning more about a man is always a good way to understand him.

---

4   Please see www.nomoremrniceguy.com.

2. The Male Perspective

> Take events, activities, or situations that have caused
> you irritation or frustration because of how a man acted
> or reacted. Try to place yourself in his shoes and see the
> situation from his viewpoint. You still may not agree, but
> the changing perspective is very helpful.

Action Plan

To better understand the men in your life, try this action plan:

1. Interview

   ✓ Choose a close male friend, relative, or co-worker and ask
     him questions about his personality, drive, motivation,
     values, etc.

2. Observe Men Closely

   ✓ Try to get in the habit of watching men to see how they
     act, behave, etc.

3. Track Progress

   ✓ Keep a record or journal of your journey and what you
     learn about men. Review your journal periodically.

You Can Do It!

Understanding men, just like understanding women, can be complicated
and frustrating at times. Men pride themselves on being simple, clear, and
to the point, but often they do not realize how unclear the full range of
their emotions, thoughts, and behaviors can be.

The benefits of understanding the men in your life cannot be understated,
though, no matter how challenging the process may be. If you want
healthy, positive, and beneficial relationships with men, you should work
on trying to see things how they see them, and understand a few key
concepts about what makes them tick. Men want to be understood deep

down inside, just as women do. And once you understand a man and he knows that you do, you will earn a friend[5] and possibly more.

Remember this: men are different from women. Not better, not worse; just different. Celebrate the differences as you learn about them, and you will have success with men in your life.

> To effectively communicate, we must realize that
> we are all different in the way we perceive the
> world and use this understanding as a guide to our
> communication with others. (Anthony Robbins)

Further Reading

Gray, John. (2004). *Men Are From Mars, Women Are From Venus: The Classic Guide to Understanding the Opposite Sex*. New York: Harper Paperbacks.

Farrell, Warren. (1988). *Why Men Are the Way They Are*. New York: Berkley.

---

5   Please see www.nomoremrniceguy.com.

Understanding Women

All truths are easy to understand once they are
discovered; the point is to discover them.

—Galileo Galilei

Personal Portraits

I've been stuck on this module for weeks now because I wasn't sure how to tackle this subject. One idea was to leave it blank, but women are way too deep for that and warrant at least an attempt. Another idea was to write, "Women are made to be loved and not to be understood." This statement actually works for some, but others would say that a woman needs a lot more than just love.

I know a few things about women—but definitely not everything.

A woman wants to feel desired and respected at the same time. She will test you to make sure that you are strong and have conviction. She will beg you to tell her all your secrets and then leave you because there's no mystery left. Not all women are like that, however. Some women would die for you—because they love you.

A woman thrives on emotion, and if you can provide constant positive emotion for her, then she will make you very happy. If you neglect her or take her for granted, her need for emotional engagement will breed negative emotions, such as jealousy, doubt, and insecurity. Many men are aware of this and use it well to their advantage. For a woman it's all about how it feels, and even if there is a lot of "drama," that is much more fulfilling than being with someone who is just a plain "nice" person. That may be sad—but it's true.

Some of the books that I've read on this subject talk about the importance of connection, acceptance, and intimacy for women. When I watch two girls who are really good friends having a conversation, it is so obvious that they are much better communicators than men. They listen to each other, mirror each other's feelings, show compassion and empathy, and really "connect." A subtle body language cue can make a world of difference in the meaning of the message. It's quite funny, actually, compared to two guys having a beer and reciting their weekly to-do lists to each other.

I also think that a woman craves to be completely accepted for who she is and, in turn, loved unconditionally. It's a very deep romantic notion from childhood, and I believe it remains well into adulthood. Women tend to love being lost in the moment—dancing, singing, playing, and feeling "something." That's why when you read about seduction, it always echoes a similar theme—the enemy of any interaction with a woman is boredom.

A man's biggest challenge is to feel a deep sense of intimacy without it being linked to a sexual experience. For women intimacy is a very easy and natural emotion, and I think they sometimes wish that men could just listen and connect first—before they show their true male nature.

"A man doesn't know what a woman wants because a woman doesn't know what a woman wants," was another succinct option for tackling this subject—and in some cases this is very true. If you think about the statement, "He swept her off her feet," it tells of a man who just did everything right, without asking questions or seeking permission. Everything flowed smoothly until the girl realized she was totally in love, and extremely happy, too.

Of course a woman wants a strong, confident, passionate, and intelligent man who knows what he wants from life and is not afraid to reach out and grab it. However, there's a lot more to it than that.

It has been said that one of the greatest treasures ever created on Earth is a woman. Men have been intoxicated by women for thousands of years and will continue to be drawn toward them for thousands more. This is because, to men, women are incredibly alluring and intriguing—most of the time.

Sometimes, however, men are just annoyed by them. Men and women naturally clash with each other because they are so different, despite all they have in common. These differences are what make men and women unique and special, but they also can drive them apart if they are not understood.

If you want to build strong relationships with the women in your life, the first step is to strive to understand them as much as you can.

Background

> What a strange thing man is; and what a
> stranger thing woman. (Lord Byron)

For a man, communicating with a woman can be very frustrating (just as communicating with a man can be equally frustrating for a woman). The problem is that miscommunication is the most common roadblock to understanding. It could be said that men and women sometimes speak two entirely different languages.

For a humorous example, read this popular tongue-in-cheek guide to a female's language for men:

"We need …" = "I want …"

"It's your decision." = "The correct decision should be obvious by now."

"We need to talk." = "I need to complain."

"Do I look fat?" = "Tell me I'm beautiful."

While that may have made you laugh, the reality is that men and women are so different that understanding each other can be really challenging. Throughout this module, we'll talk about breaking down these communication barriers. We'll also help you understand the women in your life more completely.

The Process

> A woman's sense of self is defined through her feelings
> and the quality of her relationships. (John Gray)

Understanding a woman means trying to see things from her point of view. However, before you can do this, you need to understand what a woman's point of view entails in the first place.

A Woman's Values

Women and men have different core values. They also share some values, but for the most part, the differences are more noticeable. Besides, men and women rarely have conflict over what unites them.

A woman places value on the following:

- family,

- love,

- empathy,

- compassion,

- romance,

- and security.

A woman would generally rather have the things listed above than the things that men tend to value the most, such as respect, control, and status. Both men and women place high value on family and relationships, of course, but women tend to place more of an emphasis on the ties that bind people together.

Importance of Relationships to Women

> Man's love is of man's life a thing apart, 'tis
> woman's whole existence. (Lord Byron)

This isn't to say that relationships aren't important to men; it's just to say that, for the most part, they are more important to women. This is generally because women, as a whole, are more compassionate and empathetic than men, and they are probably more forgiving as well. They see value in establishing and nurturing relationships, even at the expense of their careers, their status, and many other things.

If you want to really know a woman—and truly get into her good graces— you need to know, understand, and value her friends and family. Those people, in the end, are the source of a woman's strength. They also have a significant impact on how she views life.

Whereas men tend to identify primarily with their work, women identify primarily with their relationships. This is why many single or divorced women struggle with their identity to some degree. This doesn't mean that women don't identify to a significant degree with their work or career; but, for most women, having a significant other is very important to them. Not having someone special in their lives can negatively impact their self-esteem and senses of worth—especially if they are alone for a long period of time. This is also why women often put their marriages ahead of their careers—and why they have a difficult time understanding when their spouses put their careers first.

> I see when men love women. They give them
> but a little of their lives. But women when
> they love give everything. (Oscar Wilde)

Women and Emotions

Women and men also differ drastically when it comes to emotions. For the most part, a woman and a man feel the same emotions. They just don't communicate or express these emotions the same way. Generally speaking, women wear their hearts on their sleeves. They are open with their feelings and seek to establish emotional connections when they interact with others. To observe this difference more clearly, just listen to two women talk, and then listen to two men talk. You will notice a big difference in what is being discussed.

One thing that frustrates men about women is that they often perceive women as too open with their emotions. Men often pride themselves on being strong, silent, and stoic. Women, on the other hand, tend to be the complete opposite and see themselves very differently.

A woman wants a man to understand her emotions. This is really important to her and is one of the biggest requirements—if not the biggest requirement—for a man to have a successful relationship with her.

What Motivates Women

What motivates women and drives them, for the most part, is different from what motivates and drives men.

Women are motivated by the following:

- the security of self,

- the security of loved ones,

- the well-being of loved ones,

- being valued for who they are,

- being heard,

- and being shown interest.

Every woman, deep down inside, yearns for a man to show interest and see value in her. Even if she doesn't hold a high-powered job or have a lot of status or have wealth or power, a woman can still feel worthy and successful if a man sees her as such.

Of course, not all women are as driven by these traits. However, if you want to truly understand a woman, you should start by looking at what motivates her and fulfills her life.

> A woman is the full circle. Within her is the power to
> create, nurture and transform. (Diane Mariechild)

Communicating with Women

This, perhaps, is the issue when it comes to men and women: men and women communicate differently. That is a simple fact. There are three main characteristics in how women communicate:

- they want to be heard, not necessarily given advice,

- they place an emphasis on emotions and feelings,

- and to them, words have deeper meaning.

Details—it's important to note that most women love to share all the juicy details when they talk. They don't like to just give you the essential facts—which might seem illogical to a man. Rather, they want to tell you the whole story—including everything that led up to what happened, how it felt to them, and so on.

This can be really frustrating to you—especially if you tend to be impatient. However, talking about the situation is a way for her to process her feelings and connect with you. This is, in large part, where the first two characteristics above come into play.

When a woman talks to you about a situation or a problem, it does not mean she wants you to provide a solution. In fact, it's probably safe to say that about 90 percent of the time, that isn't what she wants. She wants to be heard. When you listen to her, it makes her feel validated and loved. In fact, listening is one of the most loving things you can do for the women in your life. Try to refrain from offering advice—if she wants it, she'll ask you. She may say, "What do you think?" or "What should I do?" Those are your cues to offer the solution or advice you're dying to give.

If she doesn't say anything that suggests she's seeking advice, respond with empathy—in other words, try to put yourself in her shoes. For example, if something upset her you might say, "That must have felt awful." When you respond with empathy, it lets her know that you were listening and really heard what she said. Quite often, that is all she really wants from you—a listening ear, empathy, and understanding.

The last one—that words often have deeper meaning—is especially confusing for men. How often have you asked a woman, "What's wrong?" only to hear "Nothing" in response? I bet you soon found out that "Nothing" didn't really mean "nothing." In fact, many of the words and phrases that women use have other, deeper meanings. You may have to probe a little to find out what she really means. If her demeanor or her behavior suggests that something's bothering her, but her response is "nothing," you might try saying something like, "Are you sure nothing's bothering you? I sense that you're frustrated, and I really want to know what you're feeling. I'm here for you if you want to talk about it."

Sometimes a woman will hold back if she thinks you don't really want to be bothered. By letting her know you're willing to listen, she'll feel more comfortable opening up to you. Giving her "permission," so to speak, can be very powerful and she will appreciate it.

What you, as a man, need to understand is that women want you to be genuinely interested and concerned. They want you to communicate on a deeper level. And they want you to put effort into talking with them to show that you care. Once you understand this, you'll find it much easier to talk to a woman and connect with her.

Women and Sex

When it comes to sex, men and women are very different. For most women, sex is far more than just a physical activity—it is something that is very meaningful. Most women are not able to become sexually involved with a man without feeling an emotional attachment—even if they say otherwise. This is the reason why, once sex enters the picture, a woman will often assume that the man has feelings for her and will expect more. Don't assume that you can have sex with a woman and then just walk away as if nothing happened. Men who truly understand this will save themselves a lot of grief and trouble.

This is also why many women appreciate sufficient foreplay before sex and cuddling afterwards. Those two things help them feel more emotionally connected to you. They also show her that you care about her needs as well as your own.

The bottom line is, the more you show that you care about her feelings and sexual needs, the better your sexual relationship with her will be. If you're selfish or disrespectful in the bedroom, it will breed resentment, and she'll become increasingly less interested.

Women and Romance

It's a rare woman who doesn't enjoy and appreciate romance and romantic gestures. This doesn't mean you have to hire a pilot to fly overhead and pull a huge banner declaring your love and devotion (although that would most certainly be memorable). Sometimes it's the little romantic gestures that are the most special. A single rose "just because" or a sweet note tucked away where she'll be sure to see it when she least expects it will touch her deeply. Romantic gestures are important because they say "you're special to me—in a way that *no one* else is."

Of course, don't forget the important dates for romance—anniversaries, Valentine's Day, and birthdays. Make a point of doing something romantic on those days as well. Romance helps keep the spark alive in a relationship

> Be to her virtues very kind. Be to her faults
> a little blind. (Matthew Prior)

Exercises

To improve your understanding of women, try doing the following exercises:

1. Write Down Five Women You Know Well

   Identify five main traits of each. For example, "Kind, cold, exciting, charming, intelligent."

   Look for common traits among these women. Learning more about a woman is always a good way to understand her better.

2. The Female Perspective

   Take events, activities, or situations that have caused you irritation or frustration because of how a woman acted or reacted. Try to place yourself in her shoes and see the situation from her viewpoint. You still may not agree, but looking at things from a different perspective is often very helpful and enlightening.

   Man has will, but woman has her way.
   (Oliver Wendell Holmes)

Action Plan

Use this action plan to help better understand the women in your life and enhance your relationships with them:

1. Interview

   ✓ Choose a close female friend, relative, or co-worker and ask her questions about her personality, drive, motivation, values, etc.

2. Observe Women Closely

   ✓ Try to get in the habit of watching women to see how they act, behave, etc.

3. Track Progress

   ✓ Keep a record or journal of your journey and what you learn about women. Review your journal periodically.

You Can Do It!

Women are very different from men, and understanding them can be tough. Just because something is tough, though, doesn't mean it isn't worth it. In fact, nothing worth having in life is usually easy to obtain.

Understanding a woman is one of those things that may be challenging, but it is very worthwhile. You will find that your life is enriched by truly understanding and connecting with the women in your life. You'll have better, stronger, and closer relationships with them.

> Tell me and I'll forget; show me and I may remember; involve me and I'll understand. (Chinese proverb)

Further Reading

Gray, John. (2004). *Men Are From Mars, Women Are From Venus: The Classic Guide to Understanding the Opposite Sex*. New York: Harper Paperbacks.

Miller, Alisa. (2010). *Understanding Her*. New York: New Line Publishing.

SUCCESSFUL RELATIONSHIPS

*The more connections you and your lover make, not
just between your bodies, but between your minds,
your hearts, and your souls, the more you will
strengthen the fabric of your relationship, and the
more real moments you will experience together.*

—Barbara de Angelis

Personal Portraits

When I am asked what is important to me in my relationships, I always answer the same—peace, love, joy, and harmony.

Peace is a feeling of acceptance, trust, and respect. It flows from a sense of maturity and helps consciously to control any "negative" reactions in the relationship. It teaches us to show compassion and even transcend our own egos at times.

Love is inspiration and passion. It is the capacity to compromise happily—and not even call it compromise. It is acceptance and grace. It is the feeling that can only be lived and never described. It is a precious gift to be grateful for.

Joy is vital. It is the ability to laugh with each other and to share experiences that create sustained happiness and positive feelings. Great sex is also a very important part of joy. Love cannot thrive in sadness. Love cannot flourish within a relationship where there is no physical affection.

Harmony is the balance between yin and yang. It is the ability to understand and appreciate each other's differences and constantly celebrate them. It is accepting each other and being grateful for sharing such love. Harmony is the dialogue of the souls.

So I wish you peace, love, joy, and harmony.

A boy was born to a couple after eleven years of marriage. They were a loving couple, and the boy was the apple of their eye. One morning, when the boy was around two years old, his father noticed that a bottle of medicine had been left open. He was late for work, so he asked his wife to cap the bottle and keep it in the cupboard. His wife, preoccupied in the kitchen, totally forgot the matter.

The boy saw the bottle and playfully went after it. Fascinated by its pretty color, he drank the entire contents. Unfortunately, this was a potent medicine intended only for adults in small doses. Shortly after he drank it, the little boy collapsed. His mother rushed him to the hospital, but it was too late. The little boy died.

The mother was stunned and devastated. The thought of facing her husband terrified her. When the distraught father came to the hospital and saw his child, he looked at his wife and uttered just four words.

What were they?

"I love you, darling."

The husband's totally unexpected reaction is known as proactive behavior. The child was dead and could never be brought back to life. The husband understood that there was no point in finding fault with his wife. Besides, if he had only taken the time to cap the bottle and put it away himself, this tragedy would never have happened.

There was no point in blaming anyone.

The boy's mother had lost her only child. What she needed at that moment was consolation and sympathy—not judgment, criticism, or harsh reprimand—and that is what her loving husband gave her.

If everyone could look at life with this kind of perspective—with love, understanding, compassion, and empathy—there would be far fewer problems in the world, as well as in all our relationships. If you can find a way to let go of all your envy, jealousy, and fear, you will find that relationships are not nearly as difficult as you think.

So what is the lesson to be learned here? A successful relationship requires falling in love many times—with the same person. Learning how to have successful relationships means learning the lessons in the story above and applying them in your own life. That is what we'll be discussing throughout this module.

Forgiveness is the oil of relationships. (Josh McDowell)

Background

As humans, we're social creatures. We were designed to be with other humans—to interact with other people—to build relationships and develop bonds that bring us together.

Personal relationships can define your life and make it what you want it to be. As the English poet John Donne once wrote, "No man is an island." This is echoed by an old Arabian proverb that says, "Without human companions, paradise itself would be an undesirable place to live."

We have relationships with our friends, our families, and our co-workers—but arguably, the most important relationships we have is our relationships with our significant others. Few bonds in life are as strong as that between two partners linked by love. We'll talk about how you can strengthen not only your relationships with your friends and family but also your relationship with your boyfriend, girlfriend, husband, or wife.

> Shared joy is a double joy; shared sorrow
> is half a sorrow. (Swedish proverb)

The Process

What is a successful relationship? What, exactly, does it mean to have a successful relationship? Generally speaking, a successful relationship between partners is based on certain core attributes that should be present at least to some degree. These core attributes are good communication, respect, selflessness, common interests and values, intimacy, understanding, chemistry, trust, and compatibility.

Good Communication

As we've discussed in previous modules, the ability to communicate well is vital to any kind of success in life. Imagine living in a world without good communication—with misunderstanding, misperceptions, and distrust occurring on a daily basis.

Unfortunately, for some, that is the case. Good communication involves the following:

- giving and receiving from both partners,

- sharing feelings openly,

- talking freely without fear of judgment,

- and honesty.

The last one is a particularly important aspect of good communication. Yes, it is especially difficult for some people. Even though it may sound like a cliché, honesty really is the best policy—always.

> When men and women are able to respect and accept their differences then love has a chance to blossom. (John Gray)

Respect

A successful relationship is also based on mutual respect. Respect means that you see value in what your partner thinks, says, and believes. You also expect the same from your partner in return. Equality in relationship is extremely important, and it can exist only when there is mutual respect.

Selflessness

No one likes to be with a selfish partner—with someone who always thinks of himself. A selfless person doesn't go into a relationship thinking, "What can I gain?" Instead, he goes into a relationship thinking, "What can I give?" After all, if you take care of your partner, she will take care of you—and vice versa.

People who are selfless put the needs and interests of their partners above their own. They don't do things or make decisions without considering how it will affect the other person. When you are truly selfless, you'll always have your partner's best interests in mind. You're willing to make sacrifices and give generously within the relationship.

The best relationships are based on mutual selflessness.

Common Values and Interests

It's often been said that opposites attract. While that is often true to some degree, the best relationships are based on a foundation of common values and at least some common interests. That doesn't mean you and your partner have to have everything in common—in fact, it's healthy to have some different interests.

However, when it comes to values, major differences inevitably lead to conflict. Common values help to create a strong bond in a relationship.

Common interests and values help to bring two people together initially. They also help keep them together over the course of the relationship. If you've ever had a difficult time holding a conversation with someone so completely different from you, then you know the importance of common values and interests.

Intimacy

When does the word "intimacy" really mean? For many people, the first thing that comes to mind is physical closeness, including sex. Sex is a major part of intimacy between two people who love each other. Understanding the importance of sexual intimacy in a relationship is crucial to having a truly successful relationship with your significant other.

Most men seek validation through their sexual relationship with their partners. It is one of the primary ways they express their love and affection for their partners. It is a vital part of emotional intimacy for them. Most women, on the other hand, seek acceptance and emotional intimacy before becoming sexually intimate in a relationship. Understanding these differences between men and women, as well as what your partner personally feels about sex, can help you overcome differences in your relationship. Also, being truly open and selfless will go a very long way toward creating a truly healthy sexual relationship.

Understanding

Strong, successful relationships are built on understanding. Generally, the more two people know about each other—and use that knowledge to understand each other—the closer they become. They learn how to share their innermost secrets, darkest fears, and highest hopes. They also feel comfortable sharing their wants, desires, and needs—and also, their expectations.

It's impossible to understand your partner without open communication. No one can read your mind - so don't expect your partner to be one. You can help your partner understand what you are feeling or thinking by allowing yourself to be open and vulnerable. By letting your partner in, you break down the barriers that lead to misunderstanding and conflict.

The more you understand your partner—what makes him "tick" or why she does certain things, even those things that may annoy you at times—the more accepting you can be of your partner's quirks. Also, with understanding comes greater compassion and empathy. When you understand your partner, it is much easier to see things from his or her perspective.

Make it a priority to learn more about your partner—to get to know him or her on a much deeper level. And then use that knowledge to understand, to truly "get it."

Chemistry

Chemistry is that elusive quality that draws two people together. Whether it's an important friendship or a sexual relationship, you know you have chemistry when you feel that you "click" with the other person. You might also regard it as a special connection that you can't quite put your finger on—but you definitely know when it's there. When there's chemistry, being together is easy—it just feels natural. You don't have to force the relationship or try to make it work when there's good chemistry.

In your relationship with your partner, chemistry plays an important role in the passion and sexual intimacy that you share. Without it, relationships often fizzle or seem to take a lot of work—they usually feel very platonic and unexciting. Good chemistry doesn't necessarily mean there are fireworks when you first meet—it can definitely grow over time. However, if there's not at least some chemistry early on, you may not be a good fit.

Trust

No relationship can be truly successful without trust. Trust goes hand in hand with honesty. If you aren't honest with your partner, how can you expect your partner to trust you? Trust enables both partners in a relationship to feel emotionally safe—to know that you have each other's back. When there is trust, you can be yourself. You can be completely open and vulnerable without worry. With trust comes the freedom to be fully yourself—to be genuinely you without feeling the need to put on a façade or pretend to be someone you're not. That kind of freedom in a relationship is validating and empowering—and it allows the relationship to blossom to its fullest potential.

Compatibility

In order to have a successful relationship with someone, you need to be compatible. When someone's personality complements yours, and other aspects of your lives mesh, then you are compatible.

This doesn't mean you can't be opposites in many areas. In fact, often the person who is a good "fit" for you possesses strengths that you lack—and vice versa. For example, it's not uncommon for someone who is somewhat reserved to be a good fit for someone who's more outgoing. Together, they complement each other well.

Compatibility isn't just about personality. It also applies to interests, values, and background as well. The more compatible you are, the more likely you will have a successful relationship—especially when it comes to romantic relationships.

Handling Conflict

> Whenever you're in conflict with someone, there
> is one factor that can make the difference between
> damaging your relationship and deepening it.
> That factor is attitude. (William James)

When talking about successful relationships, it's important to talk about the importance of learning how to appropriately and effectively handle conflict. You see, no matter how compatible two people are—no matter how much they love each other—there will be conflict from time to time. No two people will always see things the same way or want the same thing. Life just doesn't work that way.

Conflict can (and often does) destroy even good relationships. But it doesn't have to be that way. Couples (and friends) who learn how to handle conflict have a significantly higher chance of success than those who don't.

> There are times when two people need to step apart
> from one another, but there is no rule that says
> they have to turn and fire. (Robert Brault)

Following are some guidelines for handling conflict effectively:

- No matter how frustrated or angry you are, avoid personal attacks at all costs.

- Focus on the things you agree on—look for the common ground and build from there.

- Let go of the need to be right (if that's hard for you, ask yourself what's more important—being right or keeping the relationship intact).

- Put yourself in the other person's shoes—genuinely try to see things from his or her perspective.

- Take responsibility for your part in whatever led to the conflict—remember that it always takes two people to have a conflict.

- Genuinely listen to the other person rather than just focusing on what you want to say next.

- Find ways to compromise—and be willing to do so.

- Choose your words carefully—words do hurt and can cause permanent damage.

- If you're really angry, take some time to cool off before trying to talk things out—this will help you avoid saying things you may later regret.

- Don't fight in front of others—always discuss conflicts in private.

- Never resort to name-calling or other types of verbal abuse.

- Keep your voice calm—shouting in anger is not effective.

- Let the other person speak without interrupting.

- Strive to respect the other person's feelings and perspective, even if you don't agree with him or her.

- Don't try to force a conversation if the other person isn't ready to talk.

- Don't dig up the past.

- Don't hold a grudge—it will only hurt you and the relationship.

Whenever you are feeling frustrated or angry with your partner, remind yourself of all the things you love about him or her. This will help you keep the issue in perspective and prevent the conflict from getting blown out of proportion.

> Oh, the comfort—the inexpressible comfort of
> feeling safe with a person—having neither to weigh
> thoughts nor measure words, but pouring them all
> right out, just as they are, chaff and grain together;
> certain that a faithful hand will take and sift them,
> keep what is worth keeping, and then with the breath
> of kindness blow the rest away. (Dinah Craik)

Exercise

To help you better understand the secrets to a strong relationship, try this exercise:

1. Close Relationship Analysis

   Identify a close relationship that you have had, currently have, or see in two other people. Ask yourself the following questions:

   ✓ What is the nature of this relationship (friendly/platonic, romantic, etc.)?

   ✓ What brings these two people together?

   ✓ What differences exist?

   ✓ How well do these two people communicate?

   ✓ How do they work out problems?

   ✓ Would you rate this as a successful relationship?

   Soul-mates are people who bring out the best in you. They are not perfect but are always perfect for you. (Anonymous)

Action Plan

Use this action plan to better understand and improve your own relationships:

1. Look at the Weaknesses in Your Relationships

   ✓ Create ways to correct the weak spots in your relationship. For example, if you don't feel like you two talk enough, try to talk regularly about deep, personal matters.

2. Interview Family/Friends/Loved Ones

   ✓ Ask others for their honest perception of you. Talk with them about your honest perceptions of them.

3. Practice Main Attributes

   ✓ Give compliments.

   ✓ Ask questions.

   ✓ Give/seek advice (when warranted).

   ✓ Do things for others.

   ✓ Open up.

4. Track Progress

   ✓ Keep a record or journal of your journey and interactions between you and others. Review your journal periodically.

   Man is a knot into which relationships are tied. (Antoine de Saint-Exupéry)

You Can Do It!

A strong, effective, successful, and mutually satisfying relationship is a wonderful, beautiful thing—arguably one of the most beautiful things you will ever experience in life. However, starting a relationship is the easy part; anyone can start a relationship. Keeping it going is something else entirely.

Remember the story at the beginning? That story, as touching and sad as it is, has elements of the main attributes we talked about. The true test of a relationship isn't the happy moments; it's the challenges—the sad, difficult, and trying situations that are part of life.

I guess you could say, then, that a successful relationship is one that endures throughout all the ups and downs.

Strive to develop the attributes discussed in this module. Work on developing good relationship habits. As with all things, good relationship skills take practice. Every relationship teaches us something, so seek to learn from every relationship. Make your relationships a priority in your life. You will not regret it.

> Some of the biggest challenges in relationships come from
> the fact that most people enter a relationship in order to get
> something. They're trying to find someone who's going to
> make them feel good. In reality, the only way a relationship
> will last is if you see your relationship as a place you go to
> give, and not a place that you go to take. (Anthony Robbins)

Further Reading

Covey, Stephen R. (2008). *The 7 Habits of Highly Effective Marriage*. New York: Covey.

Richo, David. (2002). *How to Be an Adult in Relationships: The Five Keys to Mindful Loving*. Boston: Shambhala.

SUCCESSFUL FAMILIES

No matter what you've done for yourself or for humanity,
if you can't look back on having given love and attention
to your own family, what have you really accomplished?

—Elbert Hubbard

Personal Portraits

Breathing in a surreal Sinai sunset, frozen by a natural Vancouver vista, immersed in the diverse culture of seductive Cordoba, lost in the ruins of ancient Athens, and testing technology in trendy Taiwan; I've experienced some amazing moments in this diverse world we live in. (*Il hamd lil La'ah.*)

Traveling makes me feel like a child all over again, lost in moments of astonishment or admiration. I have also met and befriended incredible people from all races and religions, and some of them are still my friends. But my home is Cairo. That is where my family lives, and that is where my heart resides.

We live in an old four-story building in an affluent part of Cairo called Mohandessine. My great-aunt and her son live on the ground floor. We greet them on the way out and sometimes rush in for an early dinner on the way in. My aunt used to buy interesting food from abroad—duck fois gras and smoked salmon were my favorites. On the first floor lived my grandmother. She was a beautiful, kind, and generous woman who gave us all that she could and more. Every Saturday, twenty hungry monsters would storm her apartment and sit around the table and in the living room—eating, playing, and shouting. She sat quietly and watched us all, and I always noticed a gracious smile of contentment on her face. Then there was my other aunt, who made the best Egyptian sweets in the world. Upstairs in my room I could smell the sweet aroma of the pastries baking. They lived right beneath us. Once, inspired by some horror film, my cousins and I re-created a dramatic experience complete with floating ghosts, creaking coffins, and strange sound effects. We sold tickets to our parents and they supported our madness.

The point is that as a large family unit, we did nearly everything together. When I was eight, the whole family traveled to Italy and hired a giant bus—it was insane. By sharing such amazing childhood experiences with my cousins and family, I have formed a very deep bond with them. Now, well into adulthood, we still laugh at our crazy memories, and we choose to bring up our children in exactly the same way. It's a great way to start life.

No matter where you live or where you were raised, family is important. Every culture in the world regards family as a high priority and a significant part of one's life. Even the most isolated societies in the far corners of the earth have family units and base their societies around this primary unit.

Western cultures tend to put a lot of emphasis on the individual. Individual accomplishments are encouraged and praised, and independence is considered an important trait to develop. However, the family has a special place and role in Western societies.

The cohesiveness of the family also has a significant impact on society. Studies have shown, time and again, that many problems in a community— such as high levels of crime—can be traced back to one common factor: broken homes. Communities in which family life is strong fare much better than those in which it is not.

Problems in the home spell trouble for just about anyone, and they are very difficult to rise above. This is one of the primary reasons why the family is so important. Your happiness and your success ultimately depend on the relationships you develop throughout your life. The quality of those relationships are strongly influenced by your family.

> A happy family is but an earlier heaven.
> (George Bernard Shaw)

Background

What makes a family so great? When I was growing up, I had a large family. Sometimes, we fought constantly—argued, kicked, punched, yelled, shoved, and disowned each other repeatedly. A large part of the reason we behaved that way was due to the fact that we were cousins who were growing up and being, well, cousins. But still, we were very noisy and difficult for our poor parents to control—and they would definitely tell you the same thing.

Now, years later, we regularly talk with each other, keep each other updated on what is going on, and even though we live in different places many miles away, we still view each other with love and care and concern. This is because the ties that bind a family together are also what make a family great.

In this module we will discuss something very important: how to build strong, successful relationships within the family—relationships that last a lifetime.

> The advantage of growing up with siblings is that you
> become very good at fractions. (Robert Brault)

The Process

Have you ever really thought about what makes a family strong and successful? Do you think your own family is that way? Did you grow up in a strong, successful family?

Just as there are commonalities in families all over the globe, there are common traits that bind each and every successful family together.

Communication

This word has popped up quite frequently already, and it will continue to do so during your journey. This is because communication plays such an important role in having healthy relationships and living a life that is successful and fulfilling.

The family that communicates openly, honestly, and with trust and respect is a family that stays together. Good communication among all family members is one of the key traits of healthy, happy families. Without it, families have many problems, and relationships within the family suffer.

Time Together

A healthy family thrives on spending quality time together. Sadly, the fast pace of many modern societies often pulls families apart. It can be subtle, but over time family members become increasingly disconnected if they do not spend time together regularly.

Spending time together as a family doesn't mean that you have to be with each other every waking moment. It's healthy to spend time apart and have individual activities and interests as well. In order to ensure that your family spends quality time together, plan a regular "family time." Do something that brings you all together—preferably something that everyone enjoys. For example, some families have a designated "game night" during which they play games (such as board games or card games) with each other. Another example may be a special dinner night each week, in which the family has Mexican food, or Italian food, or goes out to a restaurant together.

Day outings and vacations are a great way to bring the family together to share a fun experience. Be sure to bring along a camera and take plenty of photos for the family album. Speaking of the family album—all the shared memories and experiences help to keep a family united. The more that are created over time, the stronger the family becomes.

> Rejoice with your family in the beautiful
> land of life. (Albert Einstein)

Commitment

In a happy, healthy family, there is a true sense of commitment to one another—an allegiance to the family through tough times as well as the happy times. Every person within the family is considered important, and everyone supports each other. When one member is hurting or struggling, the rest of the family is there for him. When something good happens for one member, the rest of the family is happy for him.

Each family member places a high priority on the family. Often, a family activity is given priority over an individual activity because of this commitment. Committed families spend more time together than families that lack commitment. They play together, take trips together, work together on common goals, and, in religious families, worship together as well.

There is a strong sense of unity, with each person being proud to be part of the family.

Common Bonds

Successful families have strong common bonds that help keep them together. Often, these bonds are spiritual or religious in nature. In fact, families with strong common religious or spiritual bonds tend to stay together and be happier than families that don't have them.

Families that have a strong religious or spiritual belief system also have extra support, which comes from their religious community. Their mutual belief system also gives them a strong sense of purpose. Their shared beliefs can help provide guidance and strength during difficult times as well.

Another common bond that can be very powerful is a family-owned business. In fact, family-owned businesses tend to be more successful than those owned by partners or individuals. Why? Because of the common bond—a business to run—that not only involves and unites each member of the family, but that also impacts the family's well-being as a unit.

Clear Roles

Families are just like a sports team in many ways. Take football, for example. Every player on the team has a specific, clearly defined role:

- the goal keeper, who defends the goal,
- defenders, who help the goal keeper prevent the other team from scoring,
- midfielders, who mainly pass the ball and transition from defense to offense,
- and attackers, who primarily attempt to score.

What would happen if these roles didn't exist? There would be complete chaos—and the team would break down and cease to function.

A healthy family has clearly defined roles within it. Each member knows and understands what he contributes to the overall success of the family. There is only one head of the household, even though both parents are usually equal partners. Children understand obedience and responsibility, and parents see value in their children, which includes having regard for their feelings. When each member contributes according to their role, it makes the family stronger.

> If the family were a fruit, it would be an orange, a circle of sections, held together but separable—each segment distinct. (Letty Cottin Pogrebin)

Traditions

Traditions play a strong role in healthy societies, and they also play an important role in a healthy, successful family. This is because traditions provide a sense of meaning, stability, and direction in our lives. They enrich our lives and unite us—bringing us together during holidays and other particularly meaningful occasions.

Family traditions can be carried on for generations. They serve as a powerful reminder of the family unit—of that special bond that each family member shares. When they are honored and continued, they strengthen that deep sense of family identity.

Appreciation

Do you appreciate your family? What does it mean to appreciate someone? Appreciating a person means enjoying spending time with them, interacting with them, and being a part of their life. It also means valuing and respecting that person.

Every human has a deep longing to be valued and appreciated. Healthy, strong families openly express their love and appreciation for each other. When you appreciate the people in your family, it bolsters their self-esteem. This creates a sense of closeness, unity, and love within the family. This is so very important because, at the end of the day, your family may very well be the only place where appreciation can be found in this crazy world. As a wise Arabic proverb says, "The knife of the family does not cut."

Feelings of worth can flourish only in an atmosphere
where individual differences are appreciated,
mistakes are tolerated, communication is open, and
rules are flexible—the kind of atmosphere that is
found in a nurturing family. (Virginia Satir)

Ability to Adapt

Finally, strong families learn how to adapt and be flexible. They are able to
cope effectively with the challenges that life inevitably throws their way.
Of course, in order to endure, there must be a foundation of love, respect,
and commitment.

Every family has to deal with stress, conflict, and difficult times. The world
cannot be controlled, and life can be very unpredictable. Everything may
be great one day and suddenly a crisis changes everything. Successful
families are able to weather the storm. They do this by adapting to the
changes that occur, many of which are beyond their control. Many of
these changes, in fact, occur within the family. For example, children are
born, grow up, marry, and have children of their own. Family members
move away and pass away. The family must adapt to each of these changes
in order to survive, grow, and prosper. With each adaptation, the family
will only grow stronger.

Your family and your love must be cultivated like
a garden. Time, effort, and imagination must be
summoned constantly to keep any relationship
flourishing and growing. (Jim Rohn)

Exercises

To help you build powerful bonds and habits in your own family, try these
exercises:

1. Rate Your Family

    Take an honest look at your family, and then rate them on
    the above characteristics and traits of a strong family on
    a scale of one to ten, with ten being strong and one being

weak. A good minimum score should be thirty-five. This will help identify the weaknesses in your family.

Bonus: have your family members do the same, and compare and discuss scores.

2. Role Identification

Identify each member of your family, and then identify the roles and responsibilities that each member has. Are there any overlapping areas? You should be able to clearly see what each person brings to a family. If you cannot see what a family member contributes, chances are he probably feels alienated and not needed—and that is dangerous.

Action Plan

As with all things, to strengthen your family and make it more successful requires action and habit. Follow the action plan below to make your family stronger and more successful:

1. Scheduled Family Time

   ✓ Have a regular time every week to spend together.

   ✓ Alternate between inside/outside activities.

   ✓ Have the entire family help plan the events.

2. Family Council Time

   ✓ Schedule time for the family to talk about family issues.

   ✓ Identify roles, but also give each person a chance to talk.

   ✓ Focus on respect and openness.

3. Retest

   ✓ Take the "Rate Your Family" survey again, and do it once a month.

   ✓ See how you've progressed together as a family.

4. Show Appreciation Regularly

    ✓ Voice on a regular basis your approval and appreciation of your family members. Encourage this behavior in others.

5. Track Progress

    ✓ Keep a record or journal of your journey and how your family is performing. Review your journal periodically.

I don't care how poor a man is; if he has family, he's rich. (Dan Wilcox and Thad Mumford)

You Can Do It!

It is very difficult to be successful in life without a strong, stable family giving you support and love. At some point, no matter what, we are all weak. Having a family there to encourage you, love you, and support you during the difficult times is truly a blessing.

Make a commitment to building a strong, successful family—one that can withstand the challenges that will come from time to time. Strive to develop the traits of successful, healthy families that we discussed earlier in this module. Establishing and developing these traits will help create an unmovable foundation for your family. Your family is a part of you—and you are a part of them.

When you look at your life, the greatest happiness is family happiness. (Dr. Joyce Brothers)

Further Reading

Covey, Stephen R. (1997). *The 7 Habits of Highly Effective Families*. New York: St. Martin's Griffin.

Taulbert, Clifton L. (1999). *Eight Habits of the Heart: Embracing the Values that Build Strong Families and Communities*. London: Penguin.

PEOPLE

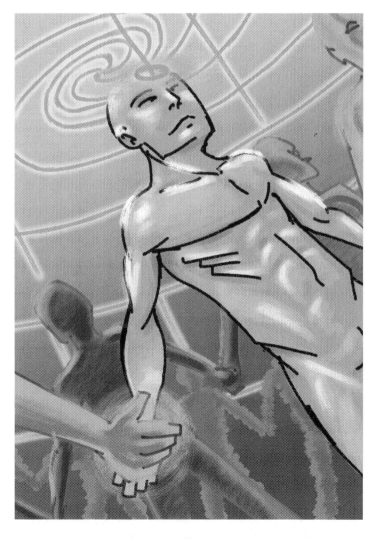

PERSONALITY TYPES

Personality to a person is what a sweet smell is to a flower.

—Charles Schwab

Personal Portraits

I've been called a lot of things: artist, genius, joker, and sage … but I don't know if any of those things are true. I know that I am an INTJ (mastermind) on the Myers-Briggs index. I'm also a "creative relator" on the Leonard Personality Index and nearly integrated on the KWML Jungian Archetype index.

What does all of this mean, and why does it matter?

Well, I've always been very interested in psychology and never really found all the answers in Freud or Maslow. I always sought to know myself better and understand my basic temperament. I think it is because I am driven to become the best that I can be; I'm always trying to figure out how I can utilize my strengths. I've always been very creative—I'm a musician, poet and songwriter. I don't waste time and energy on things I cannot influence. I can be very social and anti-social all at once. I can be very funny. I'm generous and selfish, disciplined and relaxed, vain and humble.

But I wasn't always like this—I used to be very different. It is possible for a person to change, to actively transform their personality. The secret is that change becomes a perpetual cycle between behavior and result, which cements the new habits into the self.

I truly believe we can teach our minds and thus change our lives.

Who Are You?

Are you the type of person that becomes energized by being in a large group of people? Or, do you draw your energy by spending some quiet time alone?

Many people have heard the terms "introversion" and "extroversion" but seem to miss the underlying aspects of "energy" and "preference" when discussing these two concepts. Typically, for example, the guy sitting apart from the crowed is identified as shy or introverted, while the girl who's the life of the party is classified as very outgoing or extroverted. We fail to understand that these key differences in preference not only reveal a lot about a person's personality but also indicate which types of situation energize him. Leave an introvert in a crowded room for too long and he'll be completely drained and in serious need of relaxation. On the other hand, an extrovert thrives off of social interaction and will be completely depleted if forced into solitude for too long.

Personality differences can be the underlying cause of many disagreements and misunderstandings. Remember our earlier discussion about different communication styles for women and men? The same goes for communication styles and preferences for individuals with different personality characteristics.

Imagine a newly married couple. The wife is extroverted, very clear, and organized. On the other hand, her husband is introverted and somewhat messy. Despite any similarities they may have, these differences can be a recipe for disaster as each of them struggles to understand the other. This, in essence, is why it is important to understand not only your own personality type, but also the personality types of those around you. Even though you may have many things in common with the people in your life, you also have your own unique ideas, viewpoints, interests, and tastes. That's how it should be, because that unique combination is what makes you who you are. But sometimes, those differences can cause you to clash with others. The more aware you are of this, the more prepared you will be to navigate those differences, and the better off your relationships will be.

> If you have anything really valuable to contribute
> to the world it will come through the expression of
> your own personality, that single spark of divinity
> that sets you off and makes you different from
> every other living creature. (Bruce Barton)

Background

The topic of personality has been studied extensively for hundreds of years. Ancient Egyptians and Greeks both pondered what makes people the way they are; that same train of thought has continued without interruption ever since. It's an interesting question—perhaps one you've even asked yourself many times: why do you think you are the way you are?

In this module, we'll discuss several theories in psychology—the science of the mind, of personality, of who we are, and of what those mean when it comes to personal development and the process of change. Keep in mind that personality does matter, and that understanding the personalities of other people—just as you understand your own—is one of the most important keys to success in life.

Definitions

Personality: the pattern of collective character, behavioral, temperamental, emotional, and mental traits of a person.

Character: the features and traits that make up the individual nature of a person.

Extraversion versus introversion: a dimension of personality that determines how a person seeks gratification. Extroverts seek it from outside themselves, while introverts seek it from within themselves.

Sensing versus intuition: a dimension of personality that determines how a person gathers information. Sensing people prefer information that is tangible and can be seen, touched, heard, etc. Intuitive people trust "hunches" or information that is abstract and theoretical.

Thinking versus feeling: a dimension of personality that determines how a person makes decisions. Thinkers decide things from a detached, logical, and rational perspective. Feelers make decisions based on empathy and emotions.

Judgment versus perception: a dimension of personality that determines how one judges the outside world. Judging types like to "have matters settled," while perceivers tend to be more open and abstract.

Attractiveness and magnetism of man's personality
is the result of his inner radiance. (Yajur Veda)

The Process

What, exactly, is personality? Simply put, personality is a term used to describe who you are and what you tend to do or think or feel in any given situation. Everyone has a personality. Personality develops during childhood and essentially crystallizes around the age of six for most people. In other words, who you are at the age of six is, for the most part, who you will be for the rest of your life.

You might be wondering, *what's the point of learning about it if we can't change it?* Well, while you may not be able to completely change your personality, you can learn to adapt. Besides, learning about your personality increases self-awareness, and without self-awareness, you will not be able to make any lasting change in your life at all.

Tips to Improve Your Personality

- Be genuinely interested in people.

- Assume that most people like you.

- Understand your strengths and your weaknesses.

- Associate with people who are successful and happy.

- Always be learning new things.

History of Personality Research

As you can imagine, personality has been studied by psychologists and psychiatrists for many years. Let's take a brief look at two of the most prominent theorists and their famous theories:

Sigmund Freud

Perhaps the "father" of modern-day psychological thought on the personality, Freud was an Austrian psychiatrist and thinker who philosophized about what makes people the way they are.

Freud believed that the personality is made up of three components:

- The id, the primitive, subconscious drive that seeks pleasure.

- The ego, which sees reality and understands that behavior has consequences. It is constantly striving to balance the id and the superego.

- The superego, the conscience or moral compass. It determines how one perceives right versus wrong.

One of Freud's most important discoveries is that we are not really aware of most of what goes on with our personalities. They're like icebergs; the vast majority is hidden beneath the surface, and we see only a very small part of it. In other words, most of what goes on in your mind is not within your conscious awareness. This is why it often takes a lot of introspection or "soul searching" to really understand what uniquely makes you "tick."

Carl Jung

One of Freud's colleagues, Jung sought to thoroughly understand this unconscious part of our personalities that Freud described. He is best known for his concept of personality typologies or "archetypes" and functions that describe who we are.

For example, Jung was the one who created the distinction between introverts and extroverts. He also suggested that we have four functions that explain how we deal with the world, both internally and externally. These functions are sensing, thinking, intuiting, and feeling.

The combined work of Jung and Freud was adapted by two psychologists, Katharine Cook Briggs and her daughter, Isabel Briggs Myers, to form the Myers-Briggs Type Indicator.

> We continue to shape our personality all our life. If we
> knew ourselves perfectly, we should die. (Albert Camus)

Myers-Brigg Type Indicator

This is a very popular tool used by psychologists to help people understand their personalities and have a better sense of who they are. Remember the definitions above? Those are the four main categories of the MBTI. The sum of who you are can be determined by taking a test and looking at the combination of attributes you share.

For example, when it comes to extraversion versus introversion, which are you? Are you more comfortable when you're around people, in crowds, going out, doing things with others, and being sociable? Or, do you feel more comfortable being by yourself, thinking, or doing solo activities?

The four typologies—extraversion/introversion, sensing/intuiting, thinking/feeling, and judging/perceiving—in the Myers-Briggs Type Indicator are used to determine your personality's natural preferences in dealing with yourself and others.

The MBTI is a good tool to use to learn more about yourself—to understand how you handle yourself, how you prefer to interact with others, and how you function in life.

Changing versus Adapting

With all of this talk about self-discovery and personality types, you may wonder if you can actually change anything about yourself.

The good news is that you can. You can improve your personality and make changes in your life. However, you need to understand that there is a difference between making changes and changing who you are. It is very difficult to change who you are, especially as an adult. If you constantly try to change the very essence of your personality, it will create significant stress in your life—because it's an exercise in futility.

Instead, it is much better to accept who you are and learn how to adapt yourself in ways that make your life better. It's not difficult to learn to adapt your behavior and personality to new situations and to those around you. You are still you, but you are managing yourself in the most effective way. It's like wearing clothing. Underneath your clothes, your body looks a certain way—in other words, it is what it is—a certain height, shape, skin color, etc. It's very hard to make permanent changes to your physical self—and even then, you'll at best be only partially successful. But you can change your clothes to fit different situations. For example, what you wear to work is very different from what you'd wear for playing sports or sleeping. You are still you underneath, but you've learned to adapt your appearance as needed.

Adaptation

Okay, so you're probably wondering how, exactly, do you adapt yourself? First, identify a trait that you would like to possess. For example, if you are an introvert, you may desire to be more sociable and outgoing. So focus on that.

Next, examine your current behaviors. Are they compatible with your desired trait? If you stay inside all the time, don't communicate much with others, and generally just keep to yourself, you'll notice that these are largely incompatible with being sociable.

Finally, identify ways to adapt your behaviors to fit the trait. Instead of going to the coffee shop alone, invite a friend. If you like to read a book in private, find others who also enjoy the book and discuss it with them.

You will still be the same person at the core—those attributes won't change. You've learned, instead, to adapt—rather than permanently and totally change—your behaviors to align with the type of person you want to be. With this example, you've adapted and become a more sociable introvert.

> A human being is a single being. Unique
> and unrepeatable. (Eileen Caddy)

Exercises

To help you with understanding personality, try these exercises:

1. Who Am I?

   Visit www.humanmetrics.com and take the Myers-Briggs Type Indicator. Then, discuss your type with others who have also taken the test.

2. Family/Friends Identification

   Think about the personalities of your friends and family members. Identify conflicts that you have with them.

Discuss why they happen and how they can be minimized or avoided.

Action Plan

Use this action plan to help you take your understanding of personality and apply it:

1. Resolve Personality Conflicts

   ✓ Not every conflict can be easily resolved, but you can use your understanding of personality to figure out the best ways to deal with conflict.

   ✓ Find ways to work with people by considering their personalities—how they tend to act and what they prefer.

2. Self-Evaluation

   ✓ Think about why you act the way you do on a regular basis.

   ✓ Pay attention to your initial impulses in various situations. This will help you know yourself better and predict how you will act in similar situations in the future

3. Adaptation Goals

   ✓ Set goals to adapt your personality.

   ✓ Identify difficult situations in your life.

   ✓ Think of ways to adapt your personality to these situations.

4. Track Progress

   ✓ Keep a record or journal of personalities in your life and how you handle them. Review your journal periodically.

You Can Do It!

Once you understand something, only then can you deal with it and make necessary changes. Understanding who you are and who other people are is a big step when it comes to having a successful life. This is because you will handle yourself and others more effectively throughout your whole life.

Remember: you still have control over who you are. It's all about adaptation. Play to your strengths. Seek to limit and improve your weaknesses. You can make a positive difference. It all starts with truly understanding who you are.

> If you have anything really valuable to contribute
> to the world, it will come through the expression of
> your own personality, that single spark of divinity
> that sets you off and makes you different from
> every other living creature. (Bruce Barton)

Further Reading

Baron, Renee (1998). *What Type Am I?: The Myers-Brigg Type Indication Made Easy*. New York: Penguin.

Hudson, Russ. (1996). *Personality Types: Using the Enneagram for Self-Discovery*. New York: Mariner Books.

Social Intelligence

If your emotional abilities aren't in hand, if you don't have self-awareness, if you are not able to manage your distressing emotions, if you can't have empathy and have effective relationships, then no matter how smart you are, you are not going to get very far.

—Dr. Daniel Goleman

Personal Portraits

I entered the slick corporate boardroom feeling apprehensive—this was a big meeting. I was involved in negotiating a content acquisition deal for television. There were about seven or eight people in the room from the legal, commercial, and marketing departments of both companies. When the meeting started, everyone was very courteous, smiling, and happy. You could sense rapport from the way people interacted, with open arms and gestures as well as sustained eye contact. It was all very pleasant.

After about fifteen minutes, we started discussing the commercial terms. I remember noticing the volume of their voices start to increase. At some points, I noticed people turning away on their chairs when they felt uneasy or were in disagreement. Their behavior reflected their internal emotional states. I felt the conflict begin to form from the subtle changes and escalation of their body language.

Then we got to the legal terms, and things really heated up. I recall somebody standing up and storming out of the room, upset and angry. Then someone broke a coffee mug accidentally and spilled coffee all over the contracts. The energy in the room was very different now—and a bit uncomfortable. There was an extreme change in everything that I saw and heard. Compared to their behavior at the beginning of the meeting, this was a totally different social dynamic.

Eventually, we managed to pull the meeting together, and things got underway again.

Then it was my turn, and I started asking everybody questions. I was trying to gather information about everyone's specific objectives and priorities. All the while, I had to concentrate on maintaining a diplomatic and courteous communication style. I had to appear very confident and also respectful of everyone's individual paradigm. The group began to listen to each other and understand each other. Eventually, we managed to reach a mutually beneficial agreement.

As the ancient Greek philosopher Epictetus taught, we have two ears and one mouth so we can listen twice as much as we speak. It is amazing to realize that most of the time human beings want exactly the same things. We are all the same. We need somebody to listen to us, to respect and appreciate our opinions and beliefs. We need to be admired and respected for our individual differences. We need to be treated with dignity. And we all love to laugh—but some of us just take life a bit too seriously, forgetting to be happy.

Inevitably, we also all need to share with and belong to a social group.

Imagine this situation: a woman learns she has just been diagnosed with breast cancer. Distraught, she runs home to her husband for comfort, love, and assurance. Her husband instead starts naming off the different types of procedures and treatments for surviving cancer. He tries to explain the various stages of cancer development and predict what stage she might be in. How will the woman feel? Most likely, she'll feel alienated, alone, and emotionally distant from her husband—all because he doesn't understand what she is going through, try to connect with her, or empathize with what she's feeling.

The man in question is demonstrating his intelligence—in the sense of his intellectual understanding of cancer—but his "social intelligence" is sorely lacking. You see, in life we often place a premium on knowledge—on knowing facts, figures, concepts, theories, solutions, and answers. But what is often far more important than intelligence (in the typical sense of the word) is social intelligence—the ability to understand and connect with other people.

> Neither a lofty degree of intelligence nor imagination nor
> both together go to the making of genius. Love, love, love,
> that is the soul of genius. (Wolfgang Amadeus Mozart)

Background

Everyone feels awkward at one time or another around other people. Sometimes we don't know what to say or how to act or what to do—or a million other things that run through our minds when we interact with people. However, over time, we learn how to act around others. We learn what to say and what to do. We develop a feel for them and what they need, want, like, and dislike. In other words, we develop our social intelligence when we interact with people and come to understand them.

Throughout this module, we'll discuss social intelligence and how you can improve yours. You will see improvements in how you deal with people and how you relate to them—and I'm sure the people in your life will notice and appreciate the change.

> If there is any one secret of success, it lies in the ability to get the other person's point of view and see things from his angle as well as your own. (Henry Ford)

Definition

Social IQ: the ability to fully understand your environment—including those within it—and react appropriately to ensure success in your social interactions.

The Process

Often being socially intelligent is a stronger guarantee for success in life than being conventionally intelligent. The higher your social IQ, the more likely you are to succeed in life—especially if your goals involve interacting with others on a regular basis. Researchers who study interactions between individuals and how the human brain works have discovered the correlation between social intelligence and personal success. Now you can learn to take advantage of this knowledge in your own life.

The S.P.A.C.E. Model

One tool used today to help us understand social intelligence is the S.P.A.C.E. model. Developed by Karl Albrecht, a successful German author and businessman, this model is used to describe the five key components of social IQ:

- situational awareness,

- presence,

- authenticity,

- clarity,

- and empathy.

Situational Awareness

Situational awareness refers to one's awareness of what's going on in various situations. In other words, it involves paying attention not only to what is being said but also to the gestures, facial expressions, and body language of those around you.

Presence

Presence involves the verbal and nonverbal behaviors that define you in the minds of others. For example, how you hold yourself, carry yourself, control yourself, etc.—these are the things that define your presence. Being open and receptive, for example, exude a positive presence. Crossing your arms, frowning, and being stand-offish convey a negative presence.

Authenticity

Similar to sincerity, authenticity includes the behaviors—nonverbal and verbal—that cause other people to believe whether or not you are being genuine and "real." Saying something positive in a negative tone, for example, comes across as inauthentic.

Clarity

Clarity is your ability to explain your ideas and voice your views to others so that they can understand you—and so you can understand them. Being clear is an important part of social intelligence. When you have clarity, there is no ambiguity in your message and others can interpret it without any misunderstanding.

Empathy

Perhaps the most important component of social IQ, empathy is your ability to put yourself in the other person's shoes. It enables you to "connect" with others because you can understand where they are coming from and what they are feeling. It also involves sharing their emotions—feeling what they feel.

> When you listen with empathy to another person, you give that person psychological air. (Stephen R. Covey)

You can evaluate your own social IQ by examining how well developed each of these traits are within you. Looking more closely at these traits within yourself provides an excellent framework for improving your own social IQ.

Did you know that your brain actually links up with other peoples' brains without you even being aware of it? This is made possible by parts of your brain called "mirror neurons." An interesting study found that when two people are in sync emotionally, their bodies and brains link up physically. Researchers, such as Dr. Daniel Goleman, have described two brains engaged in connections and conversation as two dancers dancing together in harmony. Empathy is when your emotions dance together with another person's emotions, which helps build those connections on which relationships thrive.

> Live authentically. Why would you continue to compromise something that is beautiful to create something that is fake! (Steve Maraboli)

Improving Social Intelligence

There are simple concepts you can understand and use to improve your social IQ. By doing so, you will become more successful in your interactions with others.

Observation

Observation is the key to improving your social intelligence. It is very important that you spend time observing how others act in various situations. This will help you learn how they treat others, as well as how they expect to be treated. For example, if you marry someone, you subconsciously pick up on their habits, routines, and behaviors over time. This is why you may have a lot of conflict in the early stages of your marriage, but you then gradually adjust to each other over time.

If your social IQ is low, unfortunately this will often lead to a lot of problems in your relationships. This is why observation plays a vital role in minimizing the potential friction in any relationship.

Etiquette

Simply having good manners is often a very good way to exhibit a strong social IQ. Having good manners shows people that you understand the importance of social harmony. Good manners also convey a genuine respect for others.

Do you think you have good manners? If you do, ask others this question to see what they would say about your sense of etiquette. People are often surprised at the response they get—but don't take it as an insult. Instead, appreciate their honesty and use their feedback to help you improve your manners. After all, etiquette is something that must be learned.

> Good manners will open doors that the best
> education cannot. (Clarence Thomas)

Solutions

Finally, having a mind that is open and willing to find solutions is an essential component of social intelligence. All through life you will encounter problems with others. Problems occur even between people who have high social IQs. Being receptive and diplomatic when it comes to resolving these problems—instead of insisting on getting your way or ignoring the other person's needs—is the proper mental mindset of someone with a strong social IQ.

> In the last decade or so, science has discovered a
> tremendous amount about the role emotions play in our
> lives. Researchers have found that even more than IQ,

your emotional awareness and abilities to handle feelings will determine your success and happiness in all walks of life, including family relationships. (John Gottman)

Exercises

If you want to build your social IQ, these exercises should help:

1. Perspective Exercise

   Practice seeing things and situations from others' perspectives. Start by choosing one person with whom you often have conflict. Try to see his perspective on an issue that comes between you two. Ask this person how he feels about it if you're not sure.

2. Elicit Feedback

   Talk to people who know you. Find out how they perceive your social IQ with regard to the components described above.

Action Plan

Want to work on your social IQ? Here are some steps you can put into practice:

1. Turn Negatives into Positives

   ✓ Learn from your failures and mistakes in your interactions with other people.

   ✓ Think of ways to improve for next time, and commit to them.

   ✓ For example, if you said something that offended someone and didn't really understand what happened, ask the person about it and resolve to do better in future conversations.

2. Ask Questions

✓ Get in the habit of asking questions of other people. What behaviors would they prefer from you?

✓ The goal isn't to become passive or a "people-pleaser." It is to develop empathy and correct wrong behaviors.

3. Track Progress

✓ Keep a record or journal of social interactions you have in your life and problems that arise. Review your journal periodically.

You Can Do It!

Working with people—truly understanding them, comprehending them, and "getting" them—is such a major part of life. Having an underdeveloped social IQ can hurt you and keep you from achieving and realizing the success you want.

The good news is that humans are hardwired to be social and interact well with others. It's in our blood. This means that you can improve your social IQ and get better at dealing with people and emotions by observing others, practicing good habits, and seeking to improve by soliciting feedback and making adaptations. Seek out others, and seek to understand them. Then you will have yet another tool for success.

> It is very important to understand that emotional intelligence is not the opposite of intelligence, it is not the triumph of heart over head—it is the unique intersection of both. (David Caruso)

Further Reading

Albrecht, Karl. (2009). *Social Intelligence: The New Science of Success*. San Francisco: Pfeiffer.

Goleman, Daniel. (2007). *Social Intelligence: The New Science of Human Relationships*. New York: Bantam.

COMMUNICATION SKILLS

*Communicate unto the other person that which you would want
him to communicate unto you if your positions were reversed.*

—Aaron Goldman

Personal Portraits

My very first corporate training program was about basic communication
and presentation skills. I was still twenty years old, had just completed my
media and psychology studies, and was curious to learn more about the
subject of presenting information.

The training took place in a large hotel meeting room with bad coffee,
savory biscuits, and bland doughnuts during the break. The trainees were
all cramped around a U-shaped table that faced the white roll-up projector
screen.

The first order of the day after introductions was to prepare a five-minute
presentation on a random subject. We were told to do this prior to learning
about basic concepts, such as good posture, eye contact, and tone of voice.
I decided to do a presentation on graphic design. I was already confident
by nature and a good communicator, so I did not see this as a major issue.
When I was younger, I used to breakdance in the school hallways—doing
backspins during the break—and according to my mother, I was always
a very active, friendly, and curious child. So, I was fine with delivering
a presentation on graphic design. It was amazing to see the reactions
of other trainees when the assignment sunk in and they realized what
it was they were expected to do. Social phobia, which includes the fear
of public speaking, is the second most common fear among us, after
the fear of spiders. One of the girls had an anxiety attack and started
hyperventilating—it was quite amusing actually, but I felt bad for her and
decided to go first.

I strolled to the podium and greeted everyone in a friendly manner. I sensed
my heart contract and quicken, and sweat broke out on my brow. I wiped it
with my sleeve swiftly and began to introduce myself. My voice came out
weak and tentative. I cleared my throat. My body language and posture
were slumped, and I had no idea what to do with my hands. I waved

them around, folded them, put them behind my back, and eventually just dropped them to my side. I presented the information in a very dull manner—reading off my PowerPoint slides like a robot for the blind. I did not take the time to try to understand the audience. I did not involve anyone. There was no eye contact, and when I managed to focus and remembered eye contact, I directed my presentation to the trainer himself. It was a massacre.

That was twenty years ago, and I don't do that anymore. I'm very grateful that I have completed more than thirty courses in subjects ranging from emotional intelligence to guerrilla marketing. However, I have chosen to focus on knowledge transfer methods and have made a conscious decision to learn about the skill of teaching.

After completing a program called "Train the Trainer," I found that delivering information effectively is a very powerful and important ability. I know that my purpose is to transfer knowledge as a teacher and express art as a musician and that they are both vocations that can positively affect others. So at the end of the day, I am a communicator.

Have you ever played the telephone game? I played this game in school when I was a kid. The teacher would whisper a simple sentence, such as "The boy ran through the park," into the ear of one child. This child, in turn, would then whisper what she heard in the ear of the next child. This would continue until the message got to the last child in the room, who would then say out loud what he heard.

The ridiculous phrase that emerged—always drastically different from the original sentence—would always cause the class to burst into laughter. "The boy ran through the park" could easily turn into something like "A toy can't do a bark"! It's a fun game to play that also provides a powerful lesson. Observing how distorted the original sentence becomes as it is passed from one person to the next is a perfect example of how important communication is to everyone—and how easy it is for communication to become really messed up.

> Take advantage of every opportunity to practice
> your communication skills so that when important
> occasions arise, you will have the gift, the style,

the sharpness, the clarity, and the emotions to
affect other people. (Anthony Robbins)

Background

Communication has existed in nature for a very, very long time. Animals communicate to each other just as humans do. Dolphins, for example, use various clicks and beeps to communicate in the ocean. Wolves in a pack howl to each other. Birds chirp and whistle to relay messages.

Humans are perhaps the best communicators on the planet because we have developed and learned to use language—a higher-order means of communicating. With language, we are able to communicate vastly more complex messages than other animals can. However, with words we can also significantly mess things up and easily misinterpret or misunderstand each other in the process.

Developing good communication skills can help you bridge gaps, avoid misunderstandings, and clearly convey your message across to others. Good communication skills also enable you to more accurately interpret the messages of others.

> Communication—the human connection—is the
> key to personal and career success. (Paul J. Meyer)

Definitions

Communication: the activity of conveying and relaying information to another person through a common system of symbols, signs, sounds, and/or behaviors.

Medium: the method by which information is exchanged.

> Communication leads to community, that is, to
> understanding, intimacy and mutual valuing. (Rollo May)

The Process

> Great speakers are not born, they're trained. (Dale Carnegie)

As you'll see, communication is a two-way street. Improving your communication is almost always beneficial to everyone. Before we talk about how to improve communication, we need to first understand what communication is and how it works.

Types of Communication

There are two types of communication, verbal and non-verbal.

Verbal communication involves the spoken and written word. It includes what you say. People receive what you say either by listening to your words or reading what you write. The key point here is that verbal communication occurs through words that have specific meanings.

Non-verbal communication is further broken down into four subtypes:

- Physical: facial expressions, tone of voice, touch, smell, body movements, and gestures.

- Aesthetic: creative expressions, such as music, dancing, art.

- Signs: mechanical communication, such as signals, flags, sirens, etc.

- Symbolic: symbology or the use of symbols that represent different things.

Did you know that only about 7 percent of your communication is verbal—that is, expressed with the actual words you say? In comparison, approximately 38 percent is conveyed through vocal communication, which includes the tone, volume, and pitch of your voice, as well as the rhythm, etc. The other 55 percent of your message is communicated through your body movements—primarily via your facial expressions. That should help you realize just how crucial non-verbal communication is between two people.

Tips for Good Non-verbal Communication

- Posture—standing tall with shoulders back.

- Eye contact—solid with a "smiling" face.

- Gestures with hands and arms—purposeful and deliberate.

- Speech—slow and clear.

- Tone of voice—moderate to low.

Components of Communication

All communication between two people features the same essential components:

- Message: the message is what is being said or conveyed—in other words, whatever it is you are trying to get the other person to understand. Most miscommunication is due to an ambiguous or flawed message.

- Sender: the person initiating the message.

- Receiver: the person who receives the message—regardless of whether or not the message was intended for that person.

- Interference: anything that gets in the way of a successful, clear transmission of the message. In the telephone game, for example, the original message was passed through several filters and came out garbled in the end.

- Medium: the means by which the message is transmitted.

- Feedback: communication from the receiver to the sender in response to the message. This lets the sender know if the message has been successfully received and interpreted, or if there was a breakdown in communication along the way.

  Effective communications starts with listening. (Robert Gately)

Importance of the Medium

Have you ever heard the phrase, "The medium is the message"? It really is true—the medium you choose for your communication goes a long way in conveying your message, especially if you are communicating through media like art or music. Art, music, dancing, performing—all of these are forms of communication, just like speech and writing. Making sure you select the proper medium is a crucial step in communicating effectively.

Keys to Successful Communication

> You can have brilliant ideas, but if you can't get them
> across, your ideas won't get you anywhere. (Lee Iacocca)

There are four essential keys to successfully and effectively sending a message to ensure that it is received and interpreted properly: paying attention, empathy, framing, and clarity.

Paying Attention

You have to pay attention, not only to the person you are communicating with, but to the situation and environment as well. Keep your eyes and ears open, and give the person you are talking to your undivided attention for effective communication.

Empathy

Remember, communication isn't just about technical details involving transmission, sending, receiving, and so on. It is also about sending a message that is received and interpreted accurately. If you want your messages to be received and interpreted properly, you need to be empathetic—you need to put yourself in the shoes of those receiving your message. Otherwise, telling someone you are sorry will come across as insincere. Respect and authenticity are major components of good communication.

Framing

Pay close attention to how you "frame" your message. Frame it appropriately by following these steps:

- Think about what you want to say.

- Think about how you're going to say it.

- Think about how it will be received.

With practice, you will frame your messages effectively without really needing to think about it first. However, it is always a good idea to take the time to thoughtfully consider your message before sending it out.

Clarity

Being clear is vital to good communication. Without clarity, the message will quickly become distorted. A lack of clarity is a common form of interference, just like static on a radio station. In order to improve the clarity of your message, first ask yourself if you would be able to understand the message if someone relayed it to you.

> You are not only responsible for what you say, but also for what you do not say. (Martin Luther)

Exercises

Try these fun and challenging exercises to improve your communication:

1. Give a Speech

   Remember our module on overcoming your fears? Well, this may be the perfect opportunity for you to put that into practice. Think about one of your favorite memories of all time. In an informal three-to-five-minute speech, share this memory with others and explain why it is important to you. This will help you learn how to communicate a message effectively.

2. The Mime Game

   Take a picture, preferably from a coloring book that features simple lines but several designs, shapes, etc. Don't let your partner see it. Give your partner step-by-step instructions so that he or she can replicate the picture as closely as possible. This will teach you the importance of delivering clear messages.

   > When all other means of communication fail, try words. (Anonymous)

Action Plan

Improving communication skills can be accomplished by using this effective action plan:

1. Framing

   ✓ Develop a habit of framing your messages on a regular basis.

   ✓ Framing also works in reverse, when you hear a message. Think about what the person is trying to say before replying.

2. Solicit Feedback

   ✓ Develop a habit of asking people if they understand what you are saying. This reinforces clarity.

3. Interpersonal Feedback

   ✓ Ask others who know you what your weaknesses are in communication.

   ✓ Commit to correcting these weaknesses.

4. Track Progress

   ✓ Keep a record or journal regularly of how you communicate with others and any challenges you face and have to overcome. Review your journal periodically.

   Communication works for those who
   work at it. (John Powell)

You Can Do It!

If you can communicate effectively on a regular basis, you can be well on your way to becoming a confident, assured, motivated, and successful individual. So much of what we do in life is based on communication, so being good at it is not an option—it's a necessity.

Remember: most of what you "say" to another person is non-verbal in nature. Be mindful of how you look, the expressions you make, the gestures you use, and how you are portraying yourself.

You can also drastically improve your communication skills by simply taking the time to listen, thinking about what you are saying before you say it, and seeking feedback from others.

Just like the telephone game, if your communication is flawed, your message will be as well. And that is something you should now understand loudly and clearly.

> The difference between the right word and the
> almost right word is the difference between
> lightning and the lightning bug. (Mark Twain)

Further Reading

Bolton, Robert. (1986). *People Skills: How to Assert Yourself, Listen to Others, and Resolve Conflicts*. New York: Touchstone.

McKay, Matthew. (2009). *Messages: The Communication Skills Book*. Oakland: New Harbinger Publishing.

LISTENING SKILLS

Deep listening is miraculous for both listener and speaker.
When someone receives us with open-hearted, non-judging,
intensely interested listening, our spirits expand.

—Sue Patton

Personal Portraits

When I was still fresh out of college, I could be a real smart-ass sometimes. If I now met that old me, I would probably give him a piece of my mind. I was arrogant and very hungry to prove myself. I was lucky to be mentored at a young age by much more experienced professionals who taught me a lot about corporate protocol within a large organization. I listened to them for hours raving on about strategy, marketing, operations, finance, and the perils of life. I never contributed much to these conversations, and it seems that I served as a mirror to reinforce their own knowledge base. I listened a lot, learned a lot, and am very grateful to them all.

However, in other aspects of my life, I didn't listen at all. I think this was because I was seeking some sort of validation from others; so much of what they said to me about their own personal experiences didn't register at all. I was too involved in my own thoughts to care about their feelings and interests. It may sound a bit harsh looking back now, but I am aware of many incidents that would testify to my narcissism.

It is ironic that it was in music that I was taught about the importance of listening. I had just bought my brand new sunburst Fender Stratocaster guitar and was rushing down to a local bar in Vancouver to jam along with other blues musicians. After a few drinks and a couple of conversations about Stevie Ray Vaughn, it was my turn to play. I remember being lost in a dark distorted daze of screeching blues notes when suddenly the abrupt buzz of my guitar cable being jerked out of the amp ended my fifteen minutes of fame. I was far too loud and was playing too much. My eyes were closed shut and I could not see the others signaling to me. The sweet music continued without me—but my guitar had been killed. I was very upset and I marched to the large well-built keyboardist who had done the deed. He just waved me off the stage and told me we would talk later.

"Later" turned out to be important lessons in the courtesy of listening and understanding others. I was ashamed of myself for being so self-centered. The guys all took it lightly and told me that it was probably going to make me a much better musician. As the keyboardist put it—"Music, my young grasshopper, is the evolution of conversation." Lesson learned.

"Honey, I need you to do me a favor," the wife said as her husband continued to prepare for work.

"What's that?" he replied, not really paying attention but not wanting to upset his wife.

The wife replied, "Our daughter needs to be picked up at school today at 3:30, but I can't do it because I have an important meeting at work. Could you pick her up?"

The husband, trying to tie his tie and focused more on the task at hand than what his wife was saying, half-nodded and said, "Yeah, yeah, I'll do it."

The wife then left the house and went to work.

Later that afternoon, she called her husband after her daughter—hysterical and in tears—called her from a school phone. "You said you would pick up our daughter at 3:30! It's 4:30—she's still at school, and she's terrified!"

The husband had forgotten to pick up his daughter like he had said—or is *forgotten* really the right word? Can you forget something you never really put into your memory in the first place?

This is a perfect example of how bad things happen when people don't take the time to really listen.

> You cannot truly listen to anyone and do anything
> else at the same time. (M. Scott Peck)

Background

> The greatest motivational act one person can do
> for another is to listen. (Roy E. Moody)

What does it really mean to have good listening skills?

We've already discussed why good communication is so important. If you'll recall, a big part of communication is receiving the message. In order to do that, you have to listen. Of course, you don't only listen with your ears. You can "listen" to the messages from others with your eyes as well—by paying attention and being observant.

In this module, we'll discuss how you can develop good listening skills so that you'll be able to communicate effectively with others. Just as in the story above, not listening can lead to bad outcomes. Sometimes the outcome is minor, but in some cases, it can be serious. Failing to really listen can cause a relationship to fall apart—in fact, it's often the underlying cause of many divorces because it breeds contempt and resentment. We all long to be truly heard—especially by those closest to us. This is why learning how to listen—and not just hear—is vital to your success in all areas of life.

> When we talk about understanding, surely it takes
> place only when the mind listens completely—the mind
> being your heart, your nerves, your ears—when you
> give your whole attention to it. (Jiddu Krishnamurti)

Definitions

Active listening: the process of listening to a person and giving active feedback to the sender of the message to ensure accuracy and comprehension.

Feedback loop: a loop that begins with a message being sent and ends with the interpretation of the initial message being received by the original sender.

The Process

> To meet at all, one must open one's eyes to another;
> and there is no true conversation no matter how
> many words are spoken, unless the eye, unveiled and
> listening, opens itself to the other. (Jessamyn West)

Let's look for a moment back at the previous module on developing good communication skills.

When you send a message, you start a loop. The message goes to the receiver, and the receiver interprets the message and sends feedback. The feedback is then received by the sender of the original message. Listening allows you to fill in any gaps in the loop. When you do not listen well, there will be holes in the loop. As a result, the message can easily be misunderstood, and you don't get the feedback you intended.

The husband in the story did not listen to his wife, so he never properly received the message or stored it in his memory. Since he didn't listen, his feedback wasn't accurate. His wife thought he had listened, however, because of the response he gave her—even though he would later fail to pick up his daughter as he had promised.

What Happens When You Don't Really Listen

What happens when you don't listen? Well, usually there are three primary consequences:

- Alienation: the person you're not listening to will resent you for not paying attention, just as you would if the situation were reversed.

- Distance: listening brings people closer, but ineffective communication pushes them away.

- Inefficiency: simply put, not listening is inefficient. Nothing can get done if instructions or messages aren't heard.

   To listen is an effort, and just to hear is no
   merit. A duck hears also. (Igor Stravinsky)

Active Listening

There's a crucial difference between hearing what someone says and actually listening to him. Hearing is really nothing more than picking up a sound. Listening, on the other hand, involves interpreting a message, understanding it, and storing it in your short-term memory.

Active listening takes this a step further. With active listening, you strive to eliminate any misunderstanding and misinterpretation of the message. When you actively listen, you are engaging with the other person in a two-way feedback loop to make sure everything is being transmitted and received properly.

In order to actively listen:

- When someone says something to you, listen to the message.

- Then, rephrase what you just heard and ask her for confirmation.
  - Example: "Okay, if I heard you correctly, you want me to pick our daughter up at 3:30 this afternoon because you won't be able to. Is that right?"

- This gives the other person a chance to confirm that you understand.
  - Example: "Yes, dear, 3:30 this afternoon."

This works especially well when you are discussing intangible concepts, such as emotions. If your partner says, "What you told me the other day made me feel unloved and unappreciated," active listening would sound something like, "Honey, it sounds like you're saying my comments made you feel like I wasn't showing love or respect to you. Is that right?"

What if you said something like, "Okay, so, you felt angry at me, right?" Your partner would correct you by saying, "No, I said I was feeling unloved. Your comments made me sad and hurt, not angry."

By going through this process, you will significantly increase your understanding of your partner's feelings. Rather than assuming the meaning of your partner's words, you clarify it with active listening and then can prevent any misunderstanding.

Tips for Effective Listening

- Concentrate on what others are saying. Convey the nonverbal message that you are really listening.

- Avoid assumptions or early evaluations.

- Avoid getting defensive.

- Practice paraphrasing.

Normal Listening versus Active Listening

Following are some differences between hearing (or "normal listening") and active listening:

- Normal listening is passive; active listening is interactive and engaging.

- Normal listening is susceptible to distraction; active listening requires focusing on the message.

- Normal listening can lead to misunderstanding; active listening fosters mutual understanding.

- Normal listening can create disharmony; active listening increases respect and fosters harmony.

Non-Verbal "Listening"

As mentioned above, you can also "listen" to non-verbal signals. This simply involves paying attention to the other person's

- posture,

- tone,

- volume,

- gestures,

- and facial expressions.

When you pay attention to what your partner is doing non-verbally, you will significantly enhance your understanding.

Remember: non-verbal signals and tonality make up *93 percent* of communication. Listening to the words alone will give you only 7 percent of the message being conveyed.

I'm glad I understand that while language is a gift,
listening is a responsibility. (Nikki Giovanni)

Exercises

The exercises below can help you practice active listening skills and improve
on them:

1. Practice Active Listening

   Have a partner tell you a personal story or relate his feelings
   about an important topic to you. Rephrase what he says to
   you to show how you interpreted the message. See if you are
   listening correctly.

2. Charades

   With a partner, play charades. Think of an emotion, feeling,
   or important event in your life and act it out without using
   words. Try to see if your partner can guess what you are
   trying to represent. Switch roles and repeat.

   Give me the gift of a listening heart. (King Solomon)

Action Plan

Improving listening skills can be accomplished by this effective action
plan:

1. Make a Habit

   ✓ Engage in active listening regularly.

   ✓ Use active listening whenever you need to make sure you
     interpret something correctly.

2. Solicit Feedback

   ✓ Get into the habit of asking people if they understand what
     you are saying. This reinforces clarity on both sides.

3. Interpersonal Feedback

    ✓ Ask others who know you what your weaknesses are in listening.

    ✓ Commit to correcting these weaknesses.

4. Track Progress

    ✓ Keep a record or journal of how you are listening with others. Review your journal periodically.

You Can Do It!

Being a good listener is such an important part of being a good communicator—and an effective person—that picking up solid listening skills is a must.

Learning how to actively listen can be challenging at first, because for the most part, it is not an innate skill. Most people have to learn how to do it. That's okay, though, because it can definitely be learned.

I used to be bad at active listening. I would frequently misinterpret what was being said to me because I did not commit myself to really listening to the message. Now, though, I focus and actively listen when I interact with people. It has drastically increased the success of my interpersonal relationships with others because it shows them that I genuinely value what they have to say—and respect them for saying it.

Try active listening, and you will quickly find that people want to talk to you and share their thoughts and feelings with you. After all, why wouldn't they? Wouldn't you want to share your thoughts with someone who was ready and willing to listen to you?

By developing your listening skills, you will improve not only your listening but also the listening skills of those around you—and everyone will be better off.

> So when you are listening to somebody, completely,
> attentively, then you are listening not only to the words,
> but also to the feeling of what is being conveyed—to
> the whole of it, not part of it. (Jiddu Krishnamurti)

Further Reading

Donoghue, Paul J. (2005). *Are You Really Listening?: Keys to Successful Communication*. New York: Sorin Books.

Goulston, Mark. (2009). *Just Listen: Discover the Secret of Getting Through to Absolutely Anyone*. AMACOM.

TIME

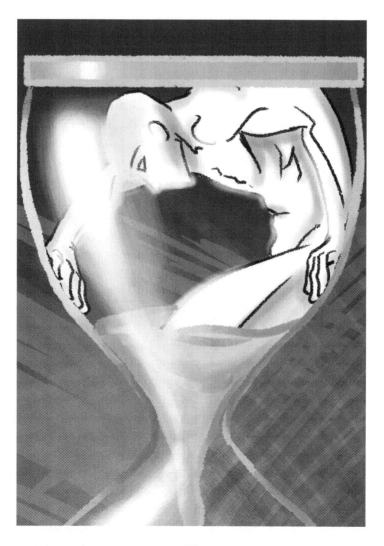

TIME MANAGEMENT

The key is not in spending time, but in investing it.

—Stephen R. Covey

Personal Portraits

Covey was right about the importance of investing time rather than simply spending it, and he taught me an extremely valuable lesson about the effectiveness of time management.

Many people may consider my approach a little too scientific, and that is their right—not everyone wants to live life in such a meticulous manner. I generally make a conscious decision not to get caught up in the exactness of it all. I use time management to manage the random chaos of life and make sure that I don't wake up one day wondering where my life went. I also believe that I am strongly motivated by my fear of not accomplishing my purpose. So it works for me because I am also spontaneous in the way I react to things in my life and do not feel that having structure negates the ability to improvise. But that's just me.

When I first read about the concept of "goals via roles," a light bulb exploded in my head! It wasn't that I was wasting time—I am considered someone who views watching TV, smoking shisha in cafes, playing cards, and clubbing as petty and time-wasting activities and would much rather invest my time doing something much more productive. Mind you, I still go clubbing and watch TV—but it is conscious recreation and not mindless habit.

When I started the task of managing my time using Covey's method, I quickly reviewed the different "roles" that I portrayed in my daily routine. There were social roles, such as spending quality time with loved ones and maintaining my social network. There was the athlete, the musician, and the entrepreneur. There were spiritual and professional roles as well. All in all, I created seven distinct personas, which I used to build my usual week.

I started with exercise, filling up the week's evening slots with a variety of activities from swimming to intense circuit training. Next, I focused on my personal projects, such as music and knowledge transfer. I set aside at least four hours of the week for practice with my band and learning new musical concepts. I also set aside time to read and study. I ensured that I spent at least three nights a week with my girlfriend, switching between dancing, dinner with friends, and weekend getaways. Saturday mornings were always for errands and grocery shopping. I made it a point to attend social functions, networking events, and new product launches. I also made sure that I set aside time for some volunteer and charity work at least once a month.

The great thing about starting with "roles" is that it's a great a way to balance all the things that are important. By the end of the week I really felt fulfilled by what I had accomplished. It is an amazing feeling to know that I have given every important aspect of my life enough attention and time.

To some, this method may seem too methodical and verging on insanity, but to others it may seem like the answer to the question, "Where did all the time go?"

When my father passed away, I was struck by the fragility of life and the fleeting nature of time. I am sure that he wanted to give, say, and do so much more. I am also sure that his time had come—and there was no use denying or resenting that truth. However, his passing left a bitter aftertaste in my mouth. It was then that I truly "realized." We really are completely ignorant of our own inevitable demise. It was the first time death had come so close.

I then chose to experience every moment as though it might be the first and the last time. I chose to reach my best potential and never be complacent. And I chose to refuse to waste time—except by choice. ☺

It's okay to go on vacation, sit around the house doing nothing, watch ten movies in a row, play video games, and sleep for twenty hours. I just make sure that this kind behavior is the exception and not the rule.

A professor came into class one day and, without a word, took a large, empty glass jar and filled it to the brim with large rocks.

"Class, is this jar full?" he asked. The class unanimously agreed that it was.

He then picked up a box of pebbles and emptied the box into the jar. The pebbles filled the empty spaces.

"Is the jar full now?" he asked. The class again indicated that the jar was indeed full.

So the professor took some sand and poured it into the jar. The class watched as the sand naturally filled in the rest of the space in the jar.

"Class," he said, "I want you to look at this jar and pretend it is your life. The big rocks represent the important things in your life—your family, your partner, and your children. These are the most valuable people and things in your life, without which you probably wouldn't have a very happy life.

"The pebbles represent other things in your life that are still important, but not nearly as much as the rocks. For example, your job, your car, and your home—these are the pebbles.

"Last of all, the sand represents everything else in your life—the small, trivial things that fill your days.

"Class, if you put the sand or pebbles in first, there won't be any room left for the rocks. The same goes for life. If you spend all your time and energy on the small stuff, or on the things that don't really matter that much, you won't have any time for the truly important things in life."

As the class remained silent, the professor smiled. "Learn how to use your time wisely. Take care of the important things first. The rest is just pebbles and sand."

Background

> Once you have mastered time, you will understand
> how true it is that most people overestimate what they
> can accomplish in a year—and underestimate what
> they can achieve in a decade! (Anthony Robbins)

Why talk about time? Why is time management such an important topic? Everything revolves around time. You only have so many minutes and hours in a day, and only so many days in a year, and only so many years in a lifetime. You simply can't afford to waste them—especially because you don't know how much time you actually have. Your life could end abruptly in the next five minutes—or go on for another fifty years.

Managing your time—your most valuable resource—is absolutely crucial. We're not talking about wasting time here. You see, poor time management can lead to disastrous consequences and a lifetime of missed opportunities, failure, and regrets.

In July, 1187, a Crusader force led by the reigning king of Jerusalem, Guy of Lusignan, marched from Acre to meet Salah ad-Din in battle. Impatient, Guy of Lusignan sent his outnumbered forces to attack Salah ad-Din in open battle, instead of waiting until he could attack from a position of strength. This premature, ill-fated attack resulted in the Battle of Hattin, a devastating defeat for the Crusaders that would lead directly to the capture of Jerusalem by Salah ad-Din just three months later.

Proper time management is important. Knowing when and where to act—and keeping track of time—is vital to your personal success.

> Time is what we want most, but what
> we use worst. (William Penn)

The Process

Time, of course, is viewed differently depending on your culture and society. Westerners—especially Americans—are known for being very punctual and time-oriented. Everything is done according to the clock and planned right down to the minute.

In many other parts of the world, time is viewed more casually. People may or may not be on time. Whether or not something happens when it is supposed to is not viewed as a major concern. With that said, time management is still important in these societies. If a person does not manage their time wisely in life, it will be much more difficult for them to attain success and a sense of fulfillment.

> If you want to make good use of your time,
> you've got to know what's most important and
> then give it all you've got. (Lee Iacocca)

Keys to Effective Time Management

What are some ways you can manage your time effectively? How do you focus on the rocks—the truly important things in life—and not on the pebbles and sand?

Let's look closely at the keys to using your time wisely: keeping a schedule, knowing your pace, setting realistic expectations, and scheduling breaks.

Keeping a Schedule

You should create a schedule for each day, week, and month. This way you'll know when you have meetings, important events, and other things you need to attend to or accomplish. It will also enable you to prioritize those events and goals.

A schedule will help you assign a specific time and place to a specific task. For example, if you want to take your partner out on a date, choose a time in advance—say, next Wednesday at 7:00 p.m. at a specific restaurant. Each important event should have a specific time set aside for it.

Knowing Your Pace

You should realize what you can actually accomplish and how fast you can work. Know your pace. Don't schedule events that will overwhelm you or overload you with more work than you can handle. By pacing yourself appropriately, you'll be more effective and enjoy your life more as well.

Setting Realistic Expectations

It's very important that you're realistic with regard to your goals and obligations. Don't take on more than you can reasonably accomplish. When you are considering how long a given task will take, be realistic and objective. It helps many people to err on the side of being conservative—assuming a task will take longer than it really will in order to be on the safe side.

You don't necessarily need to plan everything right down to the minute, but it does help to be realistic about what you have on your plate.

Scheduling Breaks

Life should never be centered on one activity. Instead, make sure you give yourself time to rest and relax. Scheduling breaks is very important because it allows you the time to rejuvenate—which will also make you much more effective at everything you do. Give yourself the gift of free time in your schedule, and always allow some room for flexibility as well.

> One cannot manage too many affairs: like
> pumpkins in the water, one pops up while you try
> to hold down the other. (Chinese proverb)

Tips for Good Time Management

- Keep paper or a calendar with you to jot down the things you have to do or notes to yourself.

- Put up reminders in your home or office about your goals.

- Plan your day each morning or the night before and set priorities for yourself.

- Do first things first.

Developing Good Time Management Habits

What are some good habits to develop when it comes to managing your time well?

Foresight

Make a habit of looking ahead so you know what's coming up before it happens. This will help ensure that you're not caught off guard.

Planning

Take this phrase to heart: "If you fail to plan, then you plan to fail." Those words are very true—if you begin a major endeavor or project without a good plan, your chances of failure increase dramatically.

Prioritization

Prioritizing plays a huge role in effective time management. Just as with the story at the beginning, it's very important that you decide which things are truly important in your life. Make them a priority by moving them to the top of your "to do" list.

> Learn from the past, set vivid, detailed goals for the
> future, and live in the only moment of time over
> which you have any control: now. (Denis Waitley)

Setting Goals and Roles

Personal development guru Dr. Stephen R. Covey teaches the concept of "roles and goals" in his books. Covey states that you fulfill a variety of roles in life, such as parent, daughter or son, teacher, employee, student, friend, etc. These roles determine what you do and who you are—and you need to learn how to create specific goals for each role you that have. Start with the more general goals, followed by the more specific ones. This will allow you to schedule the appropriate time to meet these goals. If you do this, you'll be a well-rounded person who can develop in each area as needed.

For example, if your role is "teacher," one of your goals may be, "Spend three hours grading papers today, from 5:00 p.m. to 8:00 p.m." Understand your roles and use that understanding to create appropriate goals.

Creating a Balance

As with everything in life, you need to create a balance. Time management is important, but don't overdo it. Becoming obsessive with tracking your time and planning every single detail is just as bad as not planning at all. You'll make yourself miserable. Strive to strike a good balance. Allow yourself to be spontaneous from time to time. Allow yourself to stay flexible, using your schedule as a guide rather than a burdensome ball and chain. Time management should be like floating down a river in a boat: go with the current, but use your oar—time management—to help you steer where you want to go and how fast you want to travel.

> Time = life; therefore, waste your time and waste of your
> life, or master your time and master your life. (Alan Lakein)

Exercise

Try this exercise to become more realistic with your time management and the tasks you can effectively handle:

1. Time Yourself

    Choose a day filled with routine activities and time yourself. See how long it takes you to do each task. This makes you aware of what you do during a day and how much time you really spend on tasks.

    It's not enough to be busy, so are the ants. The question is, what are we busy about? (Henry David Thoreau)

Action Plan

Time management is all about planning, so here is an action plan to help you do it more effectively:

1. Keep a Daily Schedule

2. Identify Time-Killing Obstacles

    ✓ What causes you to be late?

    ✓ Why do you waste time?

    ✓ Identify ways to overcome or avoid these obstacles.

3. Track Progress

    ✓ Keep a record or journal of how you are listening with others. Review your journal periodically.

You Can Do It!

Every time you need to remember the importance of time management, just think of the jar in the story at the beginning of this module. The lesson it teaches is powerful. The rocks—spending time with your children, your family, your partner; taking time to care for your health; learning about your passions; relaxing and enjoying the world—are what matter, and they should be your highest priority. Give the majority of your attention to them. Attend to your pebbles next—your job, house, car, hobbies, and other important things. Let the sand—the trivial things in life—take care of themselves.

As Stephen Covey says, time is not spent. It is invested. Invest your time wisely.

> Lost time is never found again. (Benjamin Franklin)

Further Reading

Allen, David. (2002). *Getting Things Done: The Art of Stress-Free Productivity.* New York: Penguin.

Morgensten, Julie. (2004). *Time Management from the Inside Out: The Foolproof System for Taking Control of Your Schedule—and Your Life.* New York: Holt Paperbacks.

PLANNING

Planning is bringing the future into the present
so that you can do something about it now.

—Alan Lakein

Personal Portraits

It was like a well-oiled machine, churning out content efficiently every day. Teams of producers would run around, managing the madness that was *Fear Factor*. Every week, five new contestants from three different countries would arrive to take part in this strange audio-visual ritual. They had all traveled sixteen hours around the world on cheap economy tickets, and they were all very angry when they arrived in Buenos Aires.

I went there three times in three months. I was managing the production process for one of the countries, and my team was responsible for making sure that the seventy-eight Arab contestants traveled from the Middle East to Argentina and back safely. The scariest part was that they were there to jump out of helicopters, eat cans of worms, and run through sheets of glass to win a cash prize. It was very intense.

The last time, I told my boss that I wouldn't go again if he didn't send me on business class—it had been a nightmare flight. Sitting eight hours in a transit lounge after a seven-hour flight and fearing the next eleven-hour trip to Argentina is enough to kill anyone's sense of hope. And I had already done the twenty-six hour trip twice.

The project involved specific sets of challenges, and producing any audio-visual content requires high-level planning. Finding the contestants, interviewing them, screening them, getting their visas on time, and securing their plane tickets and hotel bookings in the right time-frame—all of these were issues that we had to plan for.

The legal aspect of the business also required intricate attention to details. Besides the main contract with the mother company, we also had a stream of crew and cast contracts that we had to draft and sign. And counter-sign. And then send back to the other party. I remember that the intern who was responsible for chasing this constant volume of administrative work kept a contract-tracking excel workbook which enabled her to know the status and place of every document at any point in time. That was essential planning.

The actual production process from script to screen also required a blueprint that everyone had to follow. What cameras are we going to use? What lenses? Soft lights or reflectors? What will the cast wear? Who has the permits? Where's the gaffer tape? What about ambience recording? Did you back it up? Most importantly—who has the answers to all of these questions? It was an incredible adrenalin-inducing experience, and I loved every moment of it.

By nature, film production is crippled with problems. Things go wrong all the time. Things don't work at exactly the worst moment. People get sick. Generators fail. Clients change their minds. It's all very normal. Everyone knows that planning is not enough—you also have to counterplan. And then you need a contingency plan. It's a very dynamic challenge.

Suffice it to say that it is impossible to accomplish anything without a plan.

Artists may improvise and create, lost in a "stream of consciousness," and that's something that I relish. But I would never rely on such a fleeting and unpredictable force to achieve my professional and personal objectives. Once I have set the structure and built a good base, then I can afford a bit more freedom to create.

Background

In this module, we'll be discussing time—the value of time in your life, what it means for you, and how you can manage it correctly.

Planning is another big step in the process of managing your time wisely. As we've said earlier, if you fail to plan, you plan to fail—in your personal life as well as your professional one. Fortunately, planning is easier than you think. If you can nail down good planning habits, you can manage your time, set goals, and be more productive and successful.

> Unless commitment is made, there are only promises and hopes; but no plans. (Peter F. Drucker)

Definition

Methodology: the process needed to complete an objective, with defined steps, deadlines, and guidelines.

The Process

Do you have good planning habits? If you're not sure, ask yourself these three questions:

- Do you tend to start tasks right away?

- Do you usually have a good idea of what you want to do ahead of time?

- Can you describe the tasks you have to do, in detail, for the next week?

If you answered yes to the questions above, you probably have a good grasp of planning already and just need a few tips to help you improve your skills.

If you answered no to those questions, though, that's okay. Planning involves first understanding what can happen when you fail to plan.

> Organizing is what you do before you do something, so
> that when you do it, it is not all mixed up. (A. A. Milne)

Historical Examples of Failure

If you think planning is something you can ignore, think again—the following people wish they had planned better;

- In 1986, a nuclear reactor in Chernobyl, Ukraine, experienced a catastrophic meltdown, destroying the plant and sending massive amounts of poisonous radiation into the environment. The cause? The reactor was poorly designed from the beginning—due to faulty construction plans.

- In 1258, a Mongol army under the command of Hulagu Khan approached the city of Baghdad. The ruler of Baghdad, Caliph Al-

Musta'sim, not only refused Khan's offer of surrender but failed to prepare at all for the siege—and didn't plan to reinforce the city, rebuild and strengthen the city walls, order an evacuation, or seek assistance. The result? Due to poor planning, the Mongol army ransacked and destroyed Baghdad, which, at the time, was the cultural capital of the world.

In each of these examples, poor planning led to disaster. Of course, this isn't to say that all your planning failures will result in the same. But still, you can see how a good plan can come in handy and maybe prevent consequences you'll regret.

> Planning is bringing the future into the present so that
> you can do something about it now. (Alan Lakein)

Hallmarks of a Good Plan

What makes a good plan? Have an objective, a step-by-step process, a deadline, and alternatives.

Objective

Every good plan needs an objective—a goal, a purpose, a reason for the plan. You need something that needs to be accomplished in order to make a plan.

Step-by-Step Process

A good plan also contains a process that shows you what you need to do each step of the way. This is so you know in advance everything that needs to be done—how much time it will take, what resources you will need, where you need to go, and what you need to do.

Deadline

No plan is complete without a deadline. You need specific deadlines that tell you exactly how much time you are giving yourself to complete a task. Otherwise, your plan will fall victim to poor time management and fail as a result.

Alternatives

Things happen in life, and even the best plans can fall victim to unforeseen circumstances. Since you never know what will happen, putting alternatives—a "plan B" that you'll resort to just in case—into your plan is a wise idea.

Good planning

- conserves resources,

- prevents wasted effort,

- saves time and money,

- and prevents small problems from becoming big problems.

    If you don't design your own life plan, chances are you'll fall into someone else's plan. And guess what they have planned for you? Not much. (Jim Rohn)

How to Develop a Good Plan

So just exactly how do you create a good plan for your personal and professional life? No matter how big or small, simple or complex a plan may be, you can create one by following the same process:

- Know how much time you have.

- Know the exact requirements you need to fulfill or meet.

- Cover each requirement in the plan.

- Create a methodology.

Creating a Methodology

This step is particularly important because it shows you exactly how to fulfill your goal.

Let's say that one day you want to plan something relatively simple like cleaning the house. You want to clean it in the most efficient and effective manner possible, because you have a busy week and can't afford to waste any time. You can create a methodology in advance that will help you prioritize your tasks, figure out what needs to be accomplished first, and so on. For cleaning your house from top to bottom, you could create a methodology by ordering the rooms that you will clean, from the first one to the last. Then, within each room, you'll start by picking up any trash first, then putting things in their proper place, followed by dusting, and finally vacuuming or sweeping the floor. This way, as you move from room to room, you are doing the same steps, organized in the most efficient manner. This also helps ensure that you don't miss a spot or skip over a step.

> He, who every morning plans the transactions of the day, and follows that plan, carries a thread that will guide him through a labyrinth of the most busy life. (Victor Hugo)

Exercises

For this module, try these planning exercises:

1. Plan Your Day

    Pick a day and create a plan for that day, from start to finish. Schedule your events. Create alternatives in case of delays, traffic, bad weather, etc. This will teach you to create a plan and see what your day will look like before you begin it.

2. Plan an Activity

    Choose an activity that you do. It can be a part of your routine if you want, and it doesn't have to be complex. Create a detailed plan for the activity. A plan is especially useful when multiple people are involved in your activity, such as your family members.

Always plan ahead. It wasn't raining when
Noah built the ark. (Richard C. Cushing)

Action Plan

You can also improve your planning skills by carrying out this action plan:

1. Diagram a Problem

   ✓ Take a major problem, task, or event in your life.

   ✓ Follow the steps outlined above to create a good plan.

   ✓ Create one to two alternative plans in case something goes wrong.

   ✓ Write everything down, and keep it handy. This allows you to identify potential problems before they arise.

2. Identify Mistakes

   ✓ Has something gone wrong with an activity? If so, see if the failure was due to poor planning.

   ✓ Identify ways you can correct this step.

   ✓ Track Progress

   ✓ Keep a record or journal of your journey and how plans are working in your life. Review your journal periodically.

   When planning for a year, plant corn. When planning for a decade, plant trees. When planning for life, train and educate people. (Chinese proverb)

You Can Do It!

Planning is essential to both personal development and professional achievement. It is another part of the overall time management process. Remember, though, that plans can and do fail. Stay flexible and open-minded. Prepare for the possibility of your well-laid plan going south and being interrupted by unforeseen events.

Learning how to successfully plan will help you overcome these hidden pitfalls and obstacles in your life as well as fulfill your goals and objectives.

Get into the habit of planning for major events so that you can ensure they go smoothly. Failing to plan almost definitely means you are planning to fail. Keep your eye toward the future, use the time management skills we've discussed, and focus on your goals. That is a plan for success.

> Let the sword decide only after the plan
> has failed. (Arabian proverb)

Further Reading

Bradford, Robert W. (2004). *Simplified Strategic Planning: The No-Nonsense Guide for Busy People Who Want Results Fast.* Worcester, Massachusetts: Chandler House Press.

Blankson, Samuel. (2005). *Planning and Goal Setting for Personal Success.* Lulu.com.

GOAL SETTING

All successful people have a goal. No one can get anywhere unless he knows where he wants to go and what he wants to do or be.

—Norman Vincent Peale

Personal Portraits

We can learn a lot about the science of goal setting and truly begin to manifest change in our lives by focusing on and pursuing our dreams. We can also learn about the art of affirmations and how to visualize our future desired states. However, I also believe that goal setting is an innate human ability that comes naturally to all of us.

I was exposed to BMX bicycle tricks and stunts at an early age. I loved watching the freestylers soar off their ramps into the skies, twirling and twisting their bikes. I imagined that the sense of freedom must have been incredible. I guess that at the age of seven, I "set a goal" to learn to fly and do tricks on a BMX. I was motivated by the desire to experience that wonder and awe. I hadn't read any self-development books back then and didn't know what a SMART objective was either—I just wanted to be a freestyler.

And that's exactly what I did. We didn't have the Internet back then, so I could only learn by watching others. Our old silver AKAI player got jammed many times from re-winding, playing, and pausing the VHS tapes—trying to freeze the moment where the freestyler makes his move. I remember being caught up in a jumble of magnetic tape reels, trying to glue the ends back again so I could watch the stunt one more time. I immersed myself in BMX culture.

A year later, I was a freestyler myself. I had mastered "fish-tails," "curb-endos," "bunny hops," and "twisters." I used to spend hours flying off the squeaky ramp we had built, as my older brother took instant Polaroid pictures. Yes, I had set a goal for myself and applied my energy and focus to achieve it—and now, at eight years old, I could fly.

Il hamd lil La'ah, this has been an ongoing pattern in my life. I have the ability to go after what I want and to achieve my desires. However, this is not always the case. I am only human and suffer from setbacks, incorrect decisions, procrastination, and other negative traits. But my goals act as a compass for me, and I refer to them to ensure that I am aligned and on track. Every time I read the list, I get a positive boost that leaves me with a sense of clarity and focus.

Here are two of my goals that I wrote at the beginning of 2010:

Musician/Artist

I will continue my musical journey with my band Dahab, and we will successfully record our second album *Qabeela'h* by September 2010. We will have access to some of the most creative and talented musicians in the Arab World.

(The album was recorded in the summer of 2010, was very well received by fans and critics alike, and featured some of the best musicians in Egypt.)

Trainer

By February 2010, I will have identified a certified program that is either offered online or in Dubai that will prepare me for the path of becoming a certified trainer.

(This took a bit longer, but in June 2011, I completed the "Train The Trainer" course, which started me on the path of becoming a trainer.)

My "goals via roles" plan contains about fifty individual goals under seven different headers. It is a dynamic document that I constantly refer to, update, and try to live by. I highly recommend you get one. ☺

Imagine a football pitch—a large green field with twenty-two players, one ball, and two goals. The object of football is for each team to maneuver the ball and get it into the designated goal. The goal represents a target—which is why a well-aimed shot is said to be "on target."

Life, believe it or not, is just like football. You are on the pitch, dribbling the ball, weaving past the opposing team players—the obstacles—in your path, with your objective waiting for you at the end. Your aim is to place your life on target and score a goal—and win. Goals in life are the same in football. They're what you're aiming for—what you want to achieve. However, in life, they are much more important.

Learning how to set and reach goals is the same as trying to plan a winning strategy that will take a football team to victory on the pitch. In this module, we'll talk about how you can be on target by setting good goals and pursuing them.

> The major reason for setting a goal is for what it makes of you to accomplish it. What it makes of you will always be the far greater value than what you get. (Jim Rohn)

The Process

What's the big deal behind a goal? Is it really necessary?

Consider this story. A few decades ago, in a class at a famous world-class business school, researchers looked at a group of students' grades and other metrics to determine who would be successful. They were then re-evaluated ten years later to see how the students progressed—who became successful, who didn't, etc. What the researchers found surprised them. The most successful students weren't the ones who had the highest grades ten years earlier. Instead, the most successful students were the ones who had created specific goals for themselves.

Successful people have their goals in mind, whereas unsuccessful people often don't. And even though not all goals can be achieved, the point that successful people realize is that they should still be pursued.

A goal, simply put, gives us something to pursue.

> Far away there in the sunshine are my highest aspirations. I may not reach them, but I can look up and see their beauty, believe in them, and try to follow where they lead. (Louisa May Alcott)

Traits of a Good Goal

What makes a good goal? A good goal

- is realistic, but not too easy,
- has a timeline and a deadline,

- and is tied to a greater vision, mission, or purpose.

It's important that your goal shows you where you want to be, when you will get there, and why you are going there in the first place. It should challenge you, but it should not be so difficult that you cannot possibly achieve it. It shouldn't be too easy, either.

After all, as Robert Browning, a famous poet, once wrote, "Ah, but a man's reach should exceed his grasp, or what's a heaven for?"

The Process of Creating a Good Goal

Goal setting really is quite simple, once you know the process. Every goal, no matter what it is, essentially follows the same process from start to finish. The process is this:

- Identify your purpose.

- Identify key objectives.

- Determine how long will it take.

- Gather necessary information and resources.

- Break the goal into smaller goals or intervals.

Identify Your Purpose

What do you want to achieve? Why is it important? Why should you spend the time and effort to accomplish this goal?

Identify Key Objectives

What, specifically, must get done in order to achieve this goal? For example, if you want to earn a promotion at work, what must you do in order to earn it?

How Long Will It Take?

Always be mindful of deadlines and timelines. How much time do you have? Is there a limit? This may be external, such as a deadline imposed by your boss, or internal, a deadline you create to keep yourself on track.

Gather Information and Resources

What do you need in order to accomplish this goal? What do you need to know? What resources are required? Identify any gaps in your current knowledge and seek to fill them.

Break the Goal into Intervals

Every goal has a process behind it, and every process requires steps. Break your goal into smaller goals or steps so that you can manage them more efficiently. Doing this will also make the goal seem more doable and less challenging. Getting a promotion, for example, is a big task. Getting a top-notch rating on your next semi-annual employee evaluation might be one of the smaller goals to achieve as part of accomplishing the bigger goal.

Goals: Making and Achieving Them

- Pick *one* goal.

- Start small and easy.

- Simplify.

- Write it down.

- Keep track every day.

- Prioritize.

- Be firm yet flexible.

- Make the time.

> Setting goals is the first step in turning the invisible into the visible. (Anthony Robbins)

SMART Goals

In 1981, a man named George T. Doran coined the term "SMART" method for setting goals. The method is used to remind you of the key characteristics of your goals that are necessary for success:

- **S**pecific: your goal needs to be specific so you know exactly what you are aiming for.

- **M**easurable: vague goals are bad goals. You need to be able to measure it in some way so you will know when it is achieved.

- **A**ttainable: a good goal is one that can be achieved and isn't unrealistic.

- **R**elevant: does it matter? Is your goal tied to a greater purpose?

- **T**ime-based: all goals must have some kind of time limit imposed on them. Otherwise, you won't be able to plan for them.

Use the SMART method for setting goals in your life as a way to create proper objectives for yourself and keep yourself on the right path.

> Many people fail in life, not for lack of ability or brains or even courage but simply because they have never organized their energies around a goal. (Elbert Hubbard)

Exercise

Try this exercise to help you set solid goals that align with your purpose in life:

1. Create Three Goals

    Select three goals for yourself. One will be short-term (within five to seven days); one will be medium-term (within three to five weeks); one will be long-term (within three to six months or greater). Create plans for each of these goals.

    > All who have accomplished great things have had a great aim, have fixed their gaze on a goal which was high, one which sometimes seemed impossible. (Orison Sweet Marden)

Action Plan

Here is an action plan you can follow to get the most out of the goals you set for yourself:

1. Create Plans for Your Goals

    ✓ Whenever you have a goal, you need a plan for it.

    ✓ Follow the guidelines given in this module.

    ✓ Make sure your goals meet the criteria above.

2. Set Varied Goals

    ✓ Each area of your life needs goals:

    • personal life, such as relationships

    • career

    • family

    ✓ Follow the guidelines previously discussed.

3. Review Goals Regularly

    ✓ Take time to revisit and analyze your goals on a routine basis.

    ✓ Do they need to change?

4. Track Progress

    ✓ Keep a record or journal of how you are setting goals and working toward them. Review your journal periodically.

Goals provide the energy source that powers our lives. One of the best ways we can get the most from the energy we have is to focus it. That is what goals can do for us; concentrate our energy. (Denis Waitley)

You Can Do It!

Undoubtedly, you already have goals in your life. You more than likely have goals created right now, in your head—you just might not be aware of them yet.

A good goal doesn't necessarily have to be written down, but it definitely helps. That being said, some experts say that if you write down your goals, you'll be much more likely to achieve them. More importantly, though, you should be aware of your goals and keep them in your mind.

Remember: without a goal to shoot for, you will never be on target. It's like dribbling a football aimlessly up and down the field. To put it another way, if you aim for nothing, that's what you'll hit. Can you score points that way? Can your team possibly win if they never take a shot at the goal? Don't let goalkeepers and defenders get in the way of setting goals and striving to reach them. You will experience obstacles frequently in your life, and you may never achieve some goals. But the purpose of life is to try our best always.

Try your best to set goals and reach for them whenever possible. Reaching for a dream is the only way to make it a reality. Create a goal, set yourself on target, and take a shot.

> You have to set goals that are almost out of reach. If
> you set a goal that is attainable without much work
> or thought, you are stuck with something below
> your true talent and potential. (Steve Garvey)

Further Reading

Ellis, Keith. (1998). *The Magic Lamp: Goal Setting for People Who Hate Setting Goals.* New York: Three Rivers Press.

Le Blanc, Raymond (2008). *Achieving Objectives Made Easy! Practical Goal Setting Tools & Proven Time Management Techniques.* Cranendonck Coaching.

Achieving Balance

Happiness is not a matter of intensity, but of
balance, order, rhythm and harmony.

—Thomas Merton

Personal Portraits

You want to know what balance is? It's very simple—eight hours of work, eight hours of play, and eight hours of rest.

Of course there will always be exceptions, like when I had to work for twenty-two hours straight to finish a presentation for the chairman of the company. I was still a fresh graduate, and I was worried about my job security, worried about getting replaced, and generally very passive when it came to corporate demands. It didn't matter that I had to stay in the office until ten every night for months on end. It didn't matter that I had no social life and no energy to work out. It didn't matter that I had no time to nurture the relationship with my girlfriend. All that mattered was to earn the blessing and grace of top management. I was so naïve back then. I thought that "work" was more important than everything else. I was wrong.

There are other exceptions as well, such as when I took three months off and decided to travel and explore the Sinai Peninsula on my own. There was no "work" in that equation—just finding "peace" and "harmony."

A friend of mine owns and operates an eco-lodge that he built on a beautiful bay in Nuweiba, where the brilliant azure waters of the Red Sea contrast with the stark majesty of the Sinai Mountains. I am always amazed at the sense of simplicity, tranquility, and peace that I experience when I visit him. He chose to design his life to co-exist within the beauty of this naturally serene environment—and his family adapted accordingly. He even hired a certified teacher to educate his children, and she decided to settle there and start a small nursery where Bedouin children were welcome as well. A constant stream of strangers visited them every day, and familiar faces regularly passed by to indulge in a traditional desert feast. We would gather around the dinner tables, surrounded by bright pillows and candles, and listen in on a shy musical jam as the fire crackled and heaved. I would break away from the crowd and stare at the explosion of galaxies in the Sinai sky—anticipating the next meteor. Was this a sort of balance that I had found? Even though I was very happy, I felt that my drive to accomplish my goals was not being nurtured. I couldn't just do "nothing" all the time. The owner had built a beautiful home and a successful business—but this was his "balance," not mine.

After being in the rat race for twenty years now, I have come to appreciate the importance of balance in my life. When I plan well, manage my resources effectively, do my best, and over-deliver on my tasks—while maintaining a professional and courteous work ethic—I find no reason to work for more than eight hours every day. Some jobs demand long hours, and this is part of the "deal," but it is not the norm to be expected to put in twelve-hour days all the time. That's just not right.

I have a fierce mentality when it comes to this sort of thing. I do not appreciate that companies sometimes use scare-tactics to pit employees against each other, taunting them and threatening them until they "break." Of course if you have three kids, a mortgage, and mounting credit card debt, you cannot afford to lose your job. Unfortunately, some people take advantage of this and expect their subordinates to give, give, and give. I say it's important to be assertive at times like those.

My view is that to achieve balance you have to have a very strong sense of purpose. You have to be confident of your abilities. You have to know what your priorities are. You have to be assertive and fair to yourself and others. You have to be 100 percent true to yourself. You have to invest time in exploring your varied interests. If you know your true worth and value, you will be able to stand up for yourself when someone makes unrealistic demands.

Achieving balance requires awareness of that which is most important to you.

Is it success that you want? Money? Love perhaps? Is it the power to influence people? Is it the admiration of a million fans screaming your name? Do you want a loving and secure family? Is it a life of spirituality and prayer that you seek? Do you long for vitality and health? Do you wish you had amazing and supportive friends? Do you imagine a beautiful home on a secluded Mediterranean beach, where you can be surrounded by family and friends as the sounds of music and laughter echo through the night?

Whatever it is you truly desire—you will need to find a balance between your needs and the needs of others.

It's good to plan for your life—to prepare, to set goals, to focus on time management, and to control your life as best as you can. It's also good, however, to venture outside of your comfort zone every now and then and take risks. This is how to achieve balance in your life. When there's balance, you're not hitting one extreme or the other in any area. Instead, you have a healthy mix of work and play, routine and spontaneity, excitement and rest. Balance means playing by the rules when you must—but also following your heart.

Is your life in balance?

> I've learned that you can't have everything and do everything at the same time. (Oprah Winfrey)

Background

Achieving balance is one of the most difficult paths of the personal development journey. The main reason for this is that it's a difficult concept to grasp. Also, many people don't fully understand the need for it.

What, exactly, does it mean to be in balance? Is it one of those concepts that can be defined in any way by anyone? Being balanced means having equilibrium in your life. In other words, you don't have too much or too little of any one thing.

If you work all day long and never have time for yourself or your family, your life is out of balance. If you spend time with your family and on your hobbies, yet never work or contribute or be productive, you are out of balance. If you are always hurried, with no time to relax, you are out of balance. If you have all the time in the world but never really get anything accomplished, you are out of balance.

Is your life in balance? Does one particular area of your life dominate everything else, or do you have a healthy mixture of all the important things in life? Is your life in harmony?

> Be aware of wonder. Live a balanced life—learn some
> and think some and draw and paint and sing and dance
> and play and work every day some. (Robert Fulgham)

Definition

Harmony: being in balance, with every aspect of your life in agreement; unity; avoiding extremes.

The Process

To understand how we can better achieve balance in our lives, we will discuss the areas of life that can and should be balanced with each other.

Our lives are complicated. We are always going from one thing to the next, doing this and that, talking to this person and that person, trying to juggle responsibility and pleasure, and worrying about one thing while trying to do something else altogether. This is why life can often be absolutely exhausting.

There are three areas in life that most people need to balance so that they're not stressed out, frustrated, or drained of all their motivation and energy. You need to find balance

- socially,

- professionally,

- and romantically.

Social Balance

Having a healthy social life is important. After all, we're social creatures. We're wired for social interaction. Not having enough social interaction leads to isolation and often depression as well. Too much social interaction, on the other hand, often results in resentment, pressure, and exhaustion.

Everyone should have friends, and you should make time for your friends—they'll make time for you in turn. But make sure your time with your friends doesn't overshadow the other two areas of your life. (For the sake of this discussion, I am including family as a part of social balance.)

Professional Balance

For some people, their work is their whole life. Many people live to work rather than work to live. That's not necessarily a bad thing. However, it is a bad thing when you work too much and lose sight of more important things. Remember that you need to balance work with the other aspects of your life.

Romantic Balance

The relationships in your life matter, but no relationship matters more than a committed, long-term romantic relationship with your significant other.

Achieving balance when it comes to love and commitment is difficult for some because they fail to realize one crucial thing: when you are in a committed, romantic relationship—particularly marriage—that relationship should never be pushed aside in favor of something else.

There are two common scenarios that occur:

- A person doesn't spend enough time or energy on his partner; as a result, the partner feels neglected, and the two grow apart.

- A person spends too much time and energy on their partner; as a result, he or she loses friends, alienates family, and suffers at work.

The first scenario is more common, especially if someone becomes too absorbed in work. In the second scenario, a person can suffocate their partner and lose touch with their social network.

> Next to love, balance is the most
> important thing. (John Wooden)

Key Components of Achieving Balance

If you want balance in your life, there are a few components and habits you need to adopt.

Managing Expectations with Abilities

Don't create expectations for yourself that aren't realistic. Be mindful of your abilities. Don't expect yourself to do something you simply aren't able to do. Likewise, don't create expectations that are too low. The best approach is to have high standards, not impossible ones.

Realism and Ambition

Ambition can be a powerful motivating force in your life. Everyone desires bigger and better things. However, when you take ambition too far, you can damage your relationships with others very easily. At the same time, you need to have some ambition.

With too much drive and desire for more, you will become greedy and crave power, influence, and status. Without enough drive and desire, you'll never achieve anything worthwhile.

Managing Commitment

We all want to achieve as much as possible, but it is very easy to overcommit and overload ourselves. Be careful that you don't bite off more than you can chew. Be realistic with regard to the workload you can handle.

Eye for Details and the Big Picture

Many people are either detail-oriented people or big picture people. Some notice the small things, have an eye for detail, and see the individual trees rather than the entire forest. Others are good at taking a step back and seeing how everything fits together. They notice the big deal or overriding purpose, and they see the forest instead of the individual trees within it.

A well-balanced person is able to do both. Even if you are a big picture person, you still need to be able to notice details when appropriate. And if you are a detail-oriented person, you need to know how to step back every now and then and look at the entire task, problem, or environment.

Assertiveness and Passivity

A well-balanced person is also an assertive person. Note that assertiveness is not the same as aggression. You can be passive (i.e. you fold easily, submit to others, and don't speak up), assertive, or aggressive (i.e. you speak up too much, never back down, and refuse to compromise).

Assertiveness is the more appropriate trait. When you're assertive, you have a healthy respect for yourself as well as others. You know when to sit back and keep quiet and when to take action. You are not afraid to defend yourself and act in your best interests, and you're able to do so without alienating others.

Let's say that you enjoy spending time with your family after work, but lately your boss has been unfairly pulling you in for more and more work after hours. As a result, your family barely gets to see you. A passive person would just agree and not say anything. An aggressive person would antagonize the boss and potentially lose the job. An assertive person, on the other hand, would calmly voice their concerns to the boss in a professional manner and stick to their values. She'd say something like, "Sir, I enjoy working here, and I'm dedicated to my job and to our mission. But I am also dedicated to my family. Lately I have been away from home far too often, and I would like my schedule to be adjusted. Work is a priority, but so is my family, and I will not sacrifice them for my job."

Whether or not the boss agrees is almost irrelevant. Assertive people stick up for their values and themselves while also respecting others.

> We can be sure that the greatest hope for maintaining
> equilibrium in the face of any situation rests
> within ourselves. (Francis J. Braceland)

Maintaining a Good Balance

What are some ways to keep a good, healthy balance in your life? To answer that question, let's consider the importance of spirituality, patience, and vision.

Spirituality helps many stay focused and balanced. It gives people a greater calling—a sense of guidance and purpose—one that can help them determine what is truly important and what isn't.

Patience is also a very valuable trait. Being patient with situations and events in your life helps ensure that you do not overreact to change. Overreacting can destroy harmony.

Finally, having a solid vision, one that is supported by goals and plans, goes a long way toward maintaining balance and harmony. When you create your vision, you know what you want to do. When you create goals and plans, you can make sure that your life is well balanced. These things give you control, and that can be a powerful tool for attaining harmony.

> Fortunate, indeed, is the man who takes exactly the right measure of himself and holds a just balance between what he can acquire and what he can use. (Peter Latham)

Exercise

A big part of balance lies in knowing where you stand at all times. This exercise can help you do just that:

1. Task Time Estimation

   Take a future day's schedule, preferably the next day. Predict how much time it will take you to complete each task. After the next day is over, see how close you are. This helps you properly estimate events in your life, so you can better manage time and plan properly.

   > Problems arise in that one has to find a balance between what people need from you and what you need for yourself. (Jessye Norman)

Action Plan

Here is an action plan you can follow to achieve balance in your life:

1. Keep Track of Your Daily Plan/Schedule

2. Pay Attention to Yourself

   ✓ Stay mindful of your physical and mental state.

- If you are getting stressed, slow down.

- If you are getting bored, speed up.

- Maintain harmony by listening to your mind and body.

3. Track Progress

   ✓ Keep a record or journal of the balance and imbalance in your life and what you are doing to correct it. Review your journal periodically.

You Can Do It!

Balance is possible. It is within your reach. Having a balanced life in which your family, friends, work responsibilities, and partner are all in harmony with each other—with no conflict—is a terrific goal in and of itself. And it's definitely attainable. Remember: staying in harmony means being aware of who you are, what you want, what is important to you, where you stand, and what is expected of you.

Perfect balance is not always possible, but you can achieve balance. The knowledge and skills contained in the previous gates all lead to balance. Master them, and the key to balance in your life is yours.

> The best and safest thing is to keep a balance in your life, acknowledge the great powers around us and in us. If you can do that, and live that way, you are really a wise person. (Euripides)

Further Reading

Brooks, Robert. (2004). *The Power of Resilience: Achieving Balance, Confidence, and Personal Strength in Your Life.* New York: McGraw-Hill.

Swenson, Richard. (2010). *In Search of Balance: Keys to a Stable Life.* Colorado Springs: NavPress.

CHANGE

CHANGE YOUR HABITS

Watch your thoughts, for they become words.
Watch your words, for they become actions.
Watch your actions, for they become habits.
Watch your habits, for they become character.
Watch your character, for it becomes your destiny.

—Anonymous

Personal Portraits

Throughout my life, I've had some success in changing my habits, but I still cling on to certain habits that I wish I could change. As you probably know by now, I hate smoking, but I still continue to smoke. I have also tried several times to become a "morning" person, where I would wake up at 6 a.m., work out, and have a good hearty breakfast before starting my day. I have been unable to accomplish that, too, since my energy levels peak around 7 p.m., which is the optimum time for me to exercise. I will keep trying, however.

One of the small habits that I did manage to change successfully about ten years ago that had a profound impact on my health is the amount of white sugar I consumed. Apparently, when sugar is refined, it becomes "lethal" to humans because it provides what nutritionists describe as "empty" calories. The refining process strips the sugar of all the natural minerals that were present in the sugar cane plant. In addition, the digestion, detoxification, and elimination of sugar drain the body of essential vitamins and minerals. Of course, I had no idea that this was the case. When I was younger, I would happily pour three spoons of sugar into my coffee, and it was normal for me to drink about five cups a day.

The first thing I did was switch to brown sugar and cut back from three spoons to two. I also made a point to drink no more than three cups a day. Then I discovered the benefits of green tea and spearmint. So I decided I'd have coffee in the morning, green tea after lunch, and another cup of coffee prior to working out to give my system a strong caffeine jolt. I then replaced the sugar in my tea with a spoonful of honey and managed to drop down to only one spoon of brown sugar with my coffee. In the beginning, I recall the experience was slightly unpleasant because the sweet taste of the sugar had previously completely overpowered any other scent or taste. Now I can actually sense the different nuances of the coffee flavors and can differentiate between them from their aromas. Although the drink became much more bitter, I began to enjoy savoring the variety of coffee. I also drink green tea with mint without any sugar, and I really enjoy the taste.

The interesting thing is that once I managed to change that annoying and useless habit, I found that it was easy to apply the same process to other things. The process starts with a sense of awareness about a need for change. It also requires a strong commitment and a sense of clarity about how you will feel once you have achieved the change. It is important to work in small increments and not expect quick results.

Every habit can be broken, and new habits are easy to form—it all stems from a steadfast desire to change.

An old woman walks up to an old man—rocking in a chair on his porch.

"You look so happy," she says. "What's your secret for a long, happy life?"

The old man smiles and says, "I smoke three packs of cigarettes a day, drink a case of whiskey a week, eat fatty foods, and never exercise."

"That's amazing, how old are you?" she asks.

"Twenty-six……"

As humorous as that may be, the "old" man is a victim of bad habits. You can see just how much of an effect bad habits can have on your life.

Fortunately, habits can be changed. You can get rid of your bad habits and replace them with new ones. As the quote at the start of this module says, if you change your habits, you basically change who you are—and your destiny.

> Winning is a habit. Unfortunately, so
> is losing. (Vince Lombardi)

Background

What is a habit? What does it mean to do things out of habit? And how, exactly, do you change your habits? We've talked about how difficult it is to completely change your personality. But you can adapt it—and that begins with adapting your habits.

Think about your routine—what you do on a regular basis. Most of the time, you probably aren't even aware of your habits, because most of them occur on a subconscious level. Becoming aware of your habits, then, is the first step toward creating real, lasting change in your life. In this module, we'll talk about how habits are created, how they can be changed, and how you can make sure that your new habits stick—permanently.

> The chains of habit are generally too small to be felt until they are too strong to be broken. (Samuel Johnson)

Definition

Habit: a recurrent, often unconscious pattern of behavior that is acquired through frequent repetition.

The Process

> "All human actions have one or more of these seven causes: chance, nature, compulsions, habit, reason, passion and desire." (Aristotle)

Every person, no matter who he is, has both good and bad habits. A good habit is basically one that helps a person be successful in her life—in relationships, work, personal development, and other important areas.

We all know what basic bad habits are when it comes to etiquette, such as talking with your mouth full, speaking out of turn, etc. We also all know what basic bad habits are when it comes to health, such as smoking and excessive alcohol consumption. All of these are habits, but for the purpose of this module, we're looking at the major habits—the entrenched routines and behaviors in your daily life that interfere with your interaction with others as well as with yourself.

We will talk about how to change bad habits and create new, positive ones.

You Are What You Do

> Your net worth to the world is usually determined
> by what remains after your bad habits are subtracted
> from your good ones. (Benjamin Franklin)

If you have ever wondered why habits are important, just think about this: you are what you do. In other words, the person you've become stems largely from your habits—the things you do regularly.

There is a reason why athletes train so much and so often. There's something called "muscle memory" that basically allows you to do certain movements without really thinking about them—you do them automatically. A basketball player, for example, does not have to consciously think about every single step he must take when he shoots the ball. If he constantly had to stop and think about it first, he'd fail miserably. Instead, he practices his shooting technique over and over again. When game time rolls around, he doesn't have to think—he just does.

The habits you've developed over time work the same way. You are what you do. That is why practicing and establishing good habits is so crucial.

> A habit is something you can do without thinking—which
> is why most of us have so many of them. (Frank A. Clark)

What It Takes to Change a Habit

So what does it really require to change a habit and alter your behavior consistently? Experts who have studied how people form and establish habits have reported that it typically takes about 40 days of continuous, sustained effort and behavior to create or change a habit. However, you can break a habit with only seven days of inaction.

Think about that for a moment. That's why you have to concentrate and focus on creating your routines and altering them. One to two months may seem like a lifetime, but if you can keep it up, it will get easier and easier with every day that passes.

Four Essential Qualities

There are four basic, essential qualities that you absolutely must have if you want to change a bad habit or create a new one: persistence, discipline, self-esteem, and the ability to plan.

Persistence

Being persistent means you don't give up—you stick with something once you start. It means you're dedicated and determined to change a behavior—and no matter how hard the going gets, you keep on going. It also means you keep working at it—even after failing or slipping.

Discipline

To be persistent and keep yourself on the right track, you also need to have discipline. Discipline means you hold yourself accountable. You're as tough on yourself as you need to be in order to succeed—in a positive, proactive, forward-moving way.

Self-Esteem

It takes a certain amount of self-esteem to successfully change a habit. This is because you have to actually believe you are worthy of positive changes—of having a better life. You do not have to have a high degree of confidence. Rather, you just need to believe that you are a worthwhile person, and thus worth the effort required to change.

Planning

None of your efforts to change a habit will succeed if you're not able to develop a plan. Planning gives you a path toward your objective so you can stay the course.

> Excellence is not a singular act, but a habit. You are what you repeatedly do. (Shaquille O'Neal)

Creating Good Habits

Following are the five necessary steps to create a good habit or change a bad habit to a beneficial one:

1. Identify Desired Behavior

Decide what new behavior—what new habit—you would like in your life. If you are lazy, you might want to be proactive and responsible. If you are a smoker, you may want to kick the habit once and for all. Picture yourself doing that behavior in your mind.

2. Identify Potential Benefits

    It's not enough to just mentally picture the behavior itself, though. You have to keep in mind the benefits you'll experience once you adapt this new behavior. By focusing on the benefits—the light at the end of the tunnel—you'll be much more motivated and focused as you work on making it a habit.

    For example, if you desire to start working out regularly, focus on having more energy, sleeping better, and having a stronger, more toned, and leaner body.

3. Create a Plan and a Schedule

    After you've considered the potential benefits, take some time to think about the process you're going to follow. Imagine, for a moment, that you already possess this desirable habit. How would you behave differently?

    If you're always running late, for example, imagining that you are always on time means you would probably set your alarm clock, keep a schedule, and so on. Create your plan and your schedule around the ways you imagine you'd do things differently. Plot out your path to establish your new behavior.

4. Set up Reinforcement

    Everyone needs reinforcement from time to time. You can get reinforcement from yourself as well as from others. Typically, people use a system of rewards and punishment when they're striving to change a habit.

    If you want to create an exercise routine, for example, you can reward yourself when you fulfill your obligations and stick to your schedule. Having someone else exercise with you and motivate you—or chastise you gently when you don't do what you'd planned to do—is a good example of getting reinforcement from others.

5. Track Your Progress

Finally, after you create a routine, be sure to stick with it. Habits develop out of continuous action, not sporadic action. Remind yourself often that you need a minimum of just forty days of continuous effort to make the new habit stick, along with a commitment to go beyond that.

Track your progress along the way. Track where you are going and how you are doing. Remind yourself of your original goal and all the progress you've made on a regular basis.

First we form habits, then they form us. Conquer your bad habits or they will conquer you. (Rob Gilbert)

Using Anchors

Previously, we discussed how you can use anchors to help control your thoughts. You can also use anchors to control your behavior and habits.

Anchors have been shown to be useful in helping people cope as they work on changing negative habits. Smoking is a popular example. If you use an anchor to associate an unpleasant feeling—such as being ill—with a cigarette, you will gradually begin to associate just picking up a cigarette with being sick.

Anchors can be powerful tools. Not only will they help you keep your mind on track, but they'll help keep you positive and relaxed as well.

Habits? The only reason they persist is that they are offering some satisfaction. You allow them to persist by not seeking any other, better form of satisfying the same needs. Every habit, good or bad, is acquired and learned in the same way—by finding that it is a means of satisfaction. (Juliene Berk)

Exercise

This exercise will help you further complete your habit and establish your routine by making you aware of your habits. Remember, most of the time, habits are subconscious. Being aware, then, is the first major step toward correction.

1. Good Habit, Bad Habit

    Take a look at good habits and bad habits you have. Think of all you can come up with, and then ask your friends and family for help. Evaluate why you have these habits. Is there a common thread? What could you accomplish if your bad habits were not there?

Action Plan

You can also improve your habit-changing skills by carrying out this action plan:

1. Create a Comprehensive Habit-Changing Plan

    ✓ For each bad habit, create a plan according to the schedule we discussed above.

    ✓ Use the steps outlined to create your plan, complete with a schedule.

    • Develop Sources of Motivation

    ✓ Gather resources you can use for motivating yourself and finding inspiration.

    • Refer to previous modules, especially the one on motivation.

    • Identify Potential Obstacles

    ✓ What could possibly trip you up? What are some possible roadblocks?

    ✓ Prepare plans to overcome them as they occur.

- Track Progress

✓ Keep a record or journal of your journey and how changing your behavior is progressing. Review your journal periodically.

A nail is driven out by another nail. Habit is overcome by habit. (Desiderius Erasmus)

You Can Do It!

You can do anything when you put your mind to making real, lasting change in your life. Making your habits into what you want them to be is how you accomplish this. Commit on a daily basis to change your habits and your actions. Look at your life from an objective standpoint and see what you are doing—or aren't doing—to be productive, responsible, assertive, positive, and effective.

You are what you do. Your habits will determine your success in life. Let your habits speak loudly for you by changing them for the better—today.

The second half of a person's life is made up of nothing but the habits acquired during the first half. (Fyodor Dostoyevsky)

Further Reading

Prochaska, James. (1995). *Changing for Good: A Revolutionary Six-Stage Program for Overcoming Bad Habits and Moving Your Life Positively Forward.*

New York: Harper Paperbacks.

Spackman, Kerry. (2009). *The Winner's Bible: Rewire Your Brain for Permanent Change.* Austin: Greenleaf Book Group Press.

CHANGE YOURSELF

Failure is not fatal, but failure to change might be.

—John Wooden

Personal Portraits

I have been lucky to be blessed with the ability to listen to and assist others in reaching their innermost potential. Although I manage to implement much of this advice in my own life, it is an incredible feeling to see someone else transform into the person he truly desires to be.

My friend Hassan is an excellent example. Hassan wanted a girlfriend more than anything in the world. Unfortunately, he had absolutely no idea how to attract girls. Throughout our lives as close friends, he suffered from the same issue: girls think he is too nice and automatically put him in the "friend" zone. Hassan was very frustrated and angry, and he used to complain to me about his lack of success with women.

As for me, I'm no player. Some guys are just born with the skills required to seduce women, while others need a little "polishing" up to become more effective. You know—get groomed, get active, be confident, have fun, make friends, and just go for what you desire. Others have absolutely no clue what to do.

I started to coach Hassan on his dating skills. I also got more involved in his life plan concerning his purpose, his goals, and his overall lifestyle. I gave him advice in all areas of his routine and actually told him to get his own stuff in order first and focus on that for three months before even considering going out on a date. We talked about changing his paradigm regarding the responses that he gets from girls. If a girl chose to reject him, it didn't mean that there was anything wrong with him. On the contrary—it was her loss. Hassan still didn't grasp this new "re-framing" paradigm in which one changes the meaning of the responses one gets in life.

There are courses on the Internet that teach men how to become more successful with women and, as with any body of knowledge, it is interesting to glance through it and read some of the concepts discussed. Some of the material is utterly insane, and some is quite interesting, but overall it all comes down to the same thing—a man needs to have total conviction in everything that he says and does. It doesn't matter if he is short or fat, tall or bald—what matters is what those things mean to him. If he is confident and takes action, most of the time, the woman will follow.

Hassan lost weight. He looked good. We bought him a new Armani suit and a cool Omega watch—to remind him of James Bond. We would go out every night, making new friends, having fun, and just interacting with girls in clubs and bars. Most of the time, we would end up meeting some cute girls, but Hassan was still afraid. He was living out some strange and dramatic outcome in his mind. He wasn't living in the moment and was unable to enjoy and learn from these interactions. I was doing most of the talking, while he stood there with a beer in his hand, nodding his head.

It was difficult to break his old mental routines. I would ask him to try to visualize the outcome in a positive way and change his paradigm about the "fear" associated with approaching strangers. Unfortunately, Hassan was by nature a shy introvert who still viewed himself as the total geek he had been five years before—but now things had changed. He was very fit and well groomed, and he looked very good in his new suit. The strange thing was that his mind was still stuck in the past. I remember telling him to walk with me toward a large mirror outside the club. As we stood there staring at our reflections, I asked him to slap himself really hard and scream as loud as he could. Hassan smiled and understood the meaning in my message. He stared into his "new" reflection for several minutes as he let go of the nerdy geek that still plagued his mind.

That evening, Hassan met his girlfriend. Things flowed naturally between them as they laughed and smiled. He played it cool and teased her about her big orange bag. They exchanged numbers, and he called her the next day, excited about the connection they had made. Strangely enough, she responded positively, and they had dinner that same night.

It made me proud; he had changed himself internally and externally to get the results that he wanted in his life. And he is much happier now.

A wise sultan gathered three of his sons together one day.

"My sons," he said, "the world is out there—dragons to slay, warriors to fight, maidens to rescue, and lands to discover. Go forth and conquer!" The three sons then left the palace to go out into the world.

Three years later, the first son returned. The sultan embraced him and said, "Son, what have you conquered?" The first son replied, "My father, I have slain dragons, conquered new lands far and wide, and expanded our territory!"

The sultan was pleased and said, "Well done, son, you will rule over these new lands forever."

Three more years passed, and the second son returned. The sultan asked, "My son, what have you conquered?"

The second son replied, "My father, I have rescued many damsels in distress and have done many amazing deeds. I have also conquered foreign lands for you, the sultan!"

The sultan was again pleased and said, "Well done, my son. I appoint you as ruler over these new lands."

Three more years passed, but the third son did not return. Another three years came and went, and still, no return.

Finally, after another three years had passed, a single, ragged stranger came up the steps of the palace alone and went into the court of the sultan. The old sultan recognized the stranger and said, "My son! You have finally returned! Tell me, what have you conquered?"

The son smiled slowly. "My father, I have danced and laughed and loved with maidens. I have traveled to distant lands of mystery beyond the imagination. I have feared, and lost courage, only to find it again. I have dared, and risked, and succeeded. I looked deep within my soul and lost myself over and over again, only to find myself time after time."

"I come here content, my father. I have no need of lands, or adventures, or riches. Today is enough, and I have all I need for a lifetime."

The wise old sultan thought, and then nodded slowly as he smiled knowingly. Speaking quietly but beaming with pride, he said, "My son, you have conquered yourself. And now, the world and the worlds beyond are yours, and everything in them."

> To conquer oneself is the best and noblest
> victory; to be vanquished by one's own nature is
> the worst and most ignoble defeat. (Plato)

Background

How do you change yourself? Why is it so important? The third son in the story above proved to be wise beyond his years because he did something truly amazing—he conquered himself. It's a feat that few people accomplish.

When you control yourself and make yourself into the person you truly want to be, you'll have everything you'll ever need for the rest of your life—and the world will be your playground. Changing yourself can be difficult, frustrating, and challenging, to say the least, but it is well worth it. Just imagine what you could do if you were exactly the person you wanted to be. That's why we'll talk about changing yourself and making yourself into your ideal—a conqueror of your own life.

> Everyone thinks of changing the world, but no
> one thinks of changing himself. (Leo Tolstoy)

Definitions

Paradigm: a model or pattern that you use to view yourself and the world.

Paradigm shift: a dramatic transformation in your perspective and way of thinking about yourself and the world at large.

What Brand Are You?

If you keep doing what you have been doing, you will end up getting what you have been getting. However, if you want better results, you have to re-brand yourself. You have to transform yourself into the best version of yourself.

The Process

> The greatest revolution of our generation is the discovery that human beings, by changing the inner attitudes of their minds, can change the outer aspects of their lives. (William James)

We have spoken previously about how difficult it is to change your personality. But that doesn't mean you can't change you—once you figure out who "you" are, at any rate.

Why Are You, You?

Why are you who you are? What is it that makes you uniquely you? Each person is essentially a sum of many different things— environment; all the events, influences, and stimuli in life; and all the different developments that have occurred along the way. Genetics also play a big role.

This does not mean, however, that who you are is something over which you have absolutely no control. Life is not just about what happens to us. We are not merely the result of thousands of random events. We are not just bystanders or observers of our own lives. We were created to be a rational and proactive species that will be held responsible for the results that we get in our lives. As Alfred Adler, a prominent theorist and pioneer in the field of psychology, once said, "The important thing is not what one is born with, but what one makes with the equipment." In other words, you are, first and foremost, who you decide you are and everyone has the capacity to change.

Why Change Yourself?

No one is born perfect, and no one is exactly who they want to be. It is only through growth that you can achieve a successful and fulfilled life.

We change our behaviors, thoughts, and attitudes because every human, deep down, wants something better in life. The only way to ensure that this happens to us is to take our lives in our hands and make them what we want them to be.

> One key to successful leadership is continuous personal
> change. Personal change is a reflection of our inner
> growth and empowerment. (Robert E. Quinn)

What It Takes to Change

Commitment

If you want to change, you have to first make a commitment. A commitment is a pledge to yourself to do something. It must come first.

Dedication

Dedication supports the commitment by resolving to stick with it, no matter what. Obstacles will come, but dedication will enable you to overcome them. Prayer can also provide strength at times of trouble and knowing that you are doing your best allows you to accept the outcome—no matter what the consequences are.

Motivation

Motivation is an essential quality when it comes to achieving anything in life. Motivation is the energy that supports your dedication, which, of course, allows you to fulfill your commitment.

Clear Purpose

Going into anything—especially something as challenging as really changing yourself—without a clear purpose to guide you is simply asking for trouble. Know in advance exactly what you want—set clear goals.

Internal/External Pressure

It's difficult to keep yourself going without some kind of pressure. Internal pressure comes from within—it's how you push yourself. External pressure is the reinforcement that comes from others, such as friends and family. External pressure helps keep you accountable. Both types of pressure are important, and they should be positive, optimistic, and supportive to help you keep going when the going gets tough.

> You must take personal responsibility. You cannot
> change the circumstances, the seasons, or the wind,
> but you can change yourself. (Jim Rohn)

Making an Internal Commitment

The reason why you make a commitment is just as important as making the commitment in the first place. If you don't have a compelling reason, you probably won't keep the commitment.

Ask yourself why you want to change. You should change because you want to be a better person, not because someone else is pushing you to change. Never try to change just for someone else's sake. Not only does that rarely work, but it often leads to resentment. The desire and drive must come from within, and the commitment must stem from a genuine, personal desire to change. A sincere, serious commitment made from personal desires and self-realization is always stronger than a decision made on a whim or made to please someone else.

How to Change Yourself

The steps to changing yourself are similar to the steps we discussed in the last module about changing habits. After all, your habits make up a big part of what you do, and ultimately, who you are.

To change yourself, do the following:

- Identify a desired trait or characteristic that you want to possess in your life, or that you want to modify.

- Brainstorm tangible, actionable steps you can take to adapt your behavior in order to develop this trait.

- Change your mindset to align with your new behavior.

You Are What You Do—And What You Think

You already know that you are what you do. But you are what you think as well. You see, everyone has a paradigm—the way in which one sees the world and one's self. Changing your paradigm is called a paradigm shift. A paradigm shift is a crucial step toward bringing about real and lasting change.

If you want to adapt your behavior and attitudes, start with how you see yourself. Make sure your perspective—your paradigm—is both positive and forward-looking. See yourself as the person you want to be, and you will move one step closer to making that vision a reality.

> Change and growth take place when a person has risked himself and dares to become involved with experimenting with his own life. (Herbert Otto)

Exercises

These exercises will help you with knowing yourself and envisioning what you want to have happen in your life with your personality, attitudes, behaviors, and thoughts:

1. Imagine the Changed You

    Envision how you will act, behave, think, and be when you have become the person you want to be. This will give you a clear picture of your goals; something to place in your mind to guide you toward your destination. If you can imagine it, you can do it.

2. Map Your Personality

    Write down who you are in as much detail as possible. Identify the major traits you possess—the key aspects of your personality. Who are you? Thoroughly explore yourself and who you are, and figure out what your most dominant traits are. Take enough time to be very introspective and explore your consciousness.

    Change has a bad reputation in our society. But it isn't all bad—not by any means. In fact, change is necessary in life—to keep us moving ... to keep us growing ... to keep us interested ... Imagine life without change. It would be static ... boring ... dull. (Dr. Dennis O'Grady)

Action Plan

Changing yourself is a difficult process at times. This is why it's important to have a well-conceived plan. The action plan outlined below will help you with the fundamentals of making lasting, permanent change:

1. Take It One Step at a Time

   ✓ Identify and work on one key trait at a time.

   ✓ Brainstorm ideas to correct this trait:

   • different behaviors,

   • different thoughts,

   • and different attitudes.

2. Consider Your Environment

   ✓ Your environment influences you significantly. Identify the things in your environment that impact you positively. What things have a negative effect on you?

   ✓ If there are a lot of negative things, you may need to move or find another way to change your environment to lessen the negative impact.

3. Track Progress

   ✓ Keep a record or journal of your journey and how you are making changes in yourself. Review your journal periodically.

   If we all did the things we are capable of, we would astound ourselves. (Thomas Edison)

You Can Do It!

The legendary philosopher Sun Tzu wrote, "If you know your enemy and know yourself, you need not fear the results of a hundred battles." Knowing yourself and knowing that you are in control of your life is a major component of change and of a successful life. Know yourself and know what you want for yourself, and you need not fear what happens.

Remember: you are in control. You can bring about change in your life. Just like the wise third son in the story, you can conquer yourself and gain all the wonderful and truly valuable things the world has to offer.

> If you don't like something, change it; if you can't change it, change the way you think about it. (Mary Engelbreit)

Further Reading

Hundreds of Heads. (2006). *Be the Change! Change Yourself. Change the World*. New York: Hundreds of Heads Books.

Chandler, Steve. (2004). *100 Ways to Motivate Yourself: Change Your Life Forever*. Pompton Plains, New Jersey: Career Press.

Success Principles

Success means having the courage, the determination, and the will to become the person you believe you were meant to be.

—George Sheehan

Personal Portraits

There is a concept in Jungian psychology that classifies our personalities based on four archetypes: the King or Queen, the Lover, the Magician, and the Warrior. For someone to achieve integration, he must be able to balance and display the characteristics of these four. In my study of this concept, I have created twelve actions that convey my approach to attempt to attain integration.

The King archetype reflects a combination of nurturing "feminine" energy, which includes empathy and compassion, along with a more left-brain oriented approach based on knowledge and logic. For this persona, I developed three key principles; learn knowledge, know truth, and serve justice. This manifests in my life in various ways. I am constantly seeking and transferring knowledge. I am very clear about my beliefs, values, and morality. I try to treat everyone with fairness and courtesy and stand up against oppression or injustice. It's like being a king in my own kingdom.

The Warrior archetype shares the logical and methodical mental approach of the King but replaces the nurturing energy with a more aggressive and active male force. Within this persona I developed the following three key principles: harness strength, get balance, and achieve discipline. I imagine a strong and focused warrior who has the clarity and discipline to be his best at everything he does. He knows how to protect himself and his loved ones and can balance his emotions as well as his life. He has a strong mind and a powerful desire to progress and evolve into his best possible form.

The Magician archetype shares the same assertive male energy with the Warrior but replaces the logical mind with the more emotional and unpredictable heart. In some cases, this is also viewed as the right brain; controlling emotion, language, and creative thinking. Within this persona, I developed the following three key principles: show honor, create art, and inspire change. I feel that for as long as I live, I will continue to create music, poetry, and other forms of art. I also feel that being true to my nature as an artist is an honorable way to live my life. If I can set a positive and proactive example for others—whether it is through writing, music, teaching, or just by the way that I lead my life—then I hope to inspire a constructive change in others.

The Lover archetype combines the nurturing energy of the King with the emotional framework of the Magician. Within this persona, I developed the following three success principles: care for yourself, love others, and feel passion. Yes, the first thing we have to do is to love ourselves, take care of ourselves, and treat ourselves with dignity and respect. I also think that one of the challenges of life is that happiness is about giving and not about taking. The capacity to be generous with everything that I have been blessed with allows me to be happier. I also believe that the most important success principle of all is to feel passion. If I am not passionate about my life, or my job, or my wife, or anything that is of vital importance to my well-being—then what's the point of it all? I cannot live trapped inside a mundane role that I am not inspired by. At the end of the day, we only get one chance at this life, so we had better do our best to get it right.

So there it is—my personal manifesto for building a better me:

Learn knowledge, know truth, serve justice, harness strength, get balance, achieve discipline, show honor, create art, inspire change, care for yourself, love others, and feel passion.

Now go create your own!

Self-development guru Jack Canfield has made a career out of showing everyday people the principles of success and how to apply them to significantly improve their lives. One of my favorite ways he accomplishes this comes from his book, *The Success Principles: How to Get from Where You Are to Where You Want to Be.* To demonstrate the power of taking action in his seminars, he holds up a $100 bill and asks the audience, "Who wants this $100 bill?" Most of the people in the audience raise their hands, others wave their hands vigorously back and forth and some even shout out "I want it" or "I'll take it" or "Give it to me." Jack Canfield just stands there calmly holding out the bill until someone jumps out of their seat, rushes to the front of the room, gets up on stage, and takes the bill from his hand.

The will to act is one of the success principles that Jack Canfield says is essential to achieving success in your life. There are many more—and applying them is the key to unlocking the future you want and deserve.

> Strive always to excel in virtue and truth. (Prophet Muhammad (Peace Be Upon Him))

Background

What does it really mean to succeed? As we've already discussed, the definition of success depends on the person. But what most people forget or fail to realize is that success is every bit as much about the process as the destination.

Life is filled with many journeys. We all have places and destinations we want to reach. But success is never really about just getting to the destination any way we can. Instead, it's about enjoying the journey as well. The journey—the process we use to reach our destination—should be fulfilling in and of itself.

Success, then, is something you should be pursuing every day of your life, not just something to admire from afar while you suffer and slog your way through a miserable life. Principles of success are guideposts on the road that leads to success on a daily basis. Adopting these principles will help you achieve a successful and fulfilled life, day in and day out, for the rest of your life.

> The difference between a successful person and others
> is not a lack of strength, not a lack of knowledge,
> but rather a lack in will. (Vince Lombardi)

The Process

Many of the principles that we'll be discussing in this module will probably sound very familiar. Reaching this point in the self-development journey means that you are ready to practice and apply solid, proven principles for success.

Commitment and Dedication

By now, you know that a commitment is a requirement for any meaningful action. Dedication is what keeps the commitment in your mind and in your heart, so you keep going and keep moving along the path before you.

Motivation

Motivation keeps your commitment and dedication going—it is the fuel that you need to maintain positive change for any meaningful period of time. Just as a car needs gas, you need motivation. We place so much attention on the price of fuel, yet we give little thought to motivation.

Enthusiasm and Passion

Another essential principle that flows from motivation is enthusiasm and passion. If you're not enthusiastic, it's almost impossible to really make yourself do anything. And when you are enthusiastic and passionate about something, you don't have to make yourself do anything.

The comedian George Burns once said, "I honestly think it is better to be a failure at something you love than to be a success at something you hate."

Discipline

Remember the module on discipline? You know why discipline is important. It's because it keeps you on the right track. Just like the rails on a railroad keep a train on the right track, discipline keeps you on the right track and helps you stay focused on your objectives, no matter what difficulties you may encounter.

> Success is the sum of small efforts, repeated
> day in and day out. (Robert Collier)

Courage

Courage is also essential for success. Life is full of uncertainty, which is something people naturally fear. Changing yourself is no different. Acknowledge the fear, but have the courage to act in spite of the uncertainty and the unforeseen obstacles ahead.

Confidence

All successful people have confidence in themselves. This doesn't mean you have to be the most confident person in the world. You just need to believe you can do it. Without that belief in yourself, nothing will happen.

Vision

You should have a clear vision. Keep it at the forefront of your mind along with the goals you have set for yourself that are specific to that vision.

Bruce Jenner is a former Olympic gold medalist in the decathlon. When he won that prestigious medal, he also earned the title of "World's Greatest Athlete." He was giving a speech one day to a crowd of people who wanted to become Olympic athletes themselves. He asked them a very important question: "How many of you have written down a list of your goals?"

Most people in the room raised their hands. Jenner then asked, "How many of you have that list with you right now?" Only one person did—and that person, Dan O'Brien, went on to win the gold medal in the decathlon at the 1996 Olympic games.

Always keep your vision and your goals in front of you.

> You must see your goals clearly and specifically before
> you can set out for them. Hold them in your mind
> until they become second nature. (Les Brown)

Support

No journey in life is ever possible without some kind of support. Remember, no person is an island. Support comes through cultivating dynamic and fulfilling relationships with other people, which you can do by applying communication and interpersonal skills.

Flexibility

Flexibility is another key to success because, again, life is often unpredictable. You never know what will happen. Keep an open mind. Reconcile yourself to the idea that your plans, no matter how good they may be, will backfire and fail from time to time. Be ready to act and to adapt no matter what.

Adaptation

Never be afraid to adapt yourself. In fact, you will have to adapt your behavior and attitudes and thoughts all the time—even multiple times a day every now and then.

The most successful people among us are masters of adaptation because they stick by their principles while also changing what they need to change to make the best of any situation.

Patience

Nothing truly amazing and worthwhile was ever achieved in one day. Even a championship won by a sports team isn't won by one game. Think about the long hours of practice, the many games that had to be fought and won (and lost), and the endless hours and days spent thinking, dreaming, planning, recovering, and hoping. Remember—you are in this for life.

Practical Skills

You also need practical skills that we've talked about in order to succeed:

Time Management

Knowing how to make the most of the time you've been given is critical. I don't know any successful people who are bad at time management.

Planning

The commitment to plan for your life is as much a principle of success as any of the others. You need to get into the habit of at least looking ahead to the future, even if you don't create a formal, written plan.

> The secret of your future is hidden in your daily routine. (Mike Murdock)

Interpersonal Skills

People are such an integral part of success. This is because no one succeeds by themselves—ever.

Communication

To communicate with others is to learn how to involve yourself in the world. Without proper communication skills, you will essentially be alone—and you won't succeed.

Listening

Remember, not all communication involves you talking. Most of the time, you will need to listen, and not just with your ears. Keep your ears, eyes, mind, and heart open at all times.

Initiative

Finally, all successful people have initiative—the urge to take action and do something. Remember Jack Canfield's story at the beginning of this module? Without proper initiative—the willingness to act—all the principles of success in the world and all the help, advice, and guidance are meaningless.

You have to act in order to make a difference. If you want that $100 dollar bill, don't just ask for it. Jump up and take it.

Success seems to be connected with action.
Successful people keep moving. They make
mistakes, but they don't quit. (Conrad Hilton)

Exercises

Integrating principles of success into your life can be helped by the following exercises, designed to create awareness of what needs to happen in your life:

1. Principles of Success Self-Survey

    Consult the principles above. Are you already applying them in your life? If not, think about how you can better incorporate them. Write it down and track it in a journal if you must—anything to make them a regular part of your life.

2. Identify Your Weaknesses

    In what ways are you falling short when it comes to following these principles? Identify them and make sure you know where your weaknesses lie.

    Don't wait until everything is just right. It will never be perfect. There will always be challenges, obstacles and less than perfect conditions. So what? Get started now. With each step you take, you will grow stronger and stronger, more and more skilled, more and more self-confident and more and more successful. (Mark Victor Hansen)

Action Plan

This action plan can help you internalize the success principles and make them part of your everyday life:

1. Create a Grand Vision

    ✓ Create a vision for your life that is the one statement you will use to explain where you want to go and who you want to be.

- You don't have to predict the future.

- It is a roadmap to where you would like to go.

- Incorporate success principles into your vision.

2. Review Vision Statement

   ✓ Remember the vision statement you created earlier in our journey? Revise what you wrote then in light of the principles you have just reviewed. See what has changed and what you need to focus more on.

3. Reaffirm Your Commitments

   ✓ You have made several commitments during this journey.

   ✓ Review them. Do you still feel the same?

   ✓ Recommit yourself every step of the way.

4. Track Progress

   ✓ Keep a record or journal of your journey and how you are incorporating success principles into your life. Review your journal periodically.

You Can Do It!

> Some people dream of success ... while others
> wake up and work hard at it. (Anonymous)

These success principles are guidelines and rules, not suggestions. Think of them in a positive way—as supports that you use to better your life.

Reflect on them and understand that this is a constant and evolving journey. Try to incorporate these principles into your life. If you can slowly master these skills—you will never be without the tools you need to succeed. Go slow and remember that the journey of self-development is an on-going and progressive path that requires constant re-evaluation.

Success is to be measured not so much by the position
that one has reached in life as by the obstacles which
he has overcome. (Booker T. Washington)

Further Reading

Canfield, Jack. (2006). *The Success Principles: How to Get from Where You Are to Where You Want to Be*. New York: Harper Paperbacks.

Hill, Napoleon. (1997). *Napoleon Hill's Keys to Success: The 17 Principles of Personal Achievement*. New York: Plume.

LEADERSHIP

> *A leader is one who knows the way, goes*
> *the way, and shows the way.*

—John C. Maxwell

Personal Portraits

Being a leader is an extremely difficult and challenging role, and many people actively shy away from this burden. It is not easy being the boss.

Throughout my career in media and also as a musician, I have been given the opportunity to lead some very exciting projects and initiatives. I have succeeded in some and failed in others. One of the hardest challenges in leadership is balancing between empathy and understanding while enforcing your own vision with conviction. Too many times, I have seen clashing egos and wounded pride sabotage the success of a project. Too many times, I lacked the assertiveness to make a firm decision at the right time. Sometimes I suffered from listening too much and being too nice. Other times, I was viewed as a tyrant and chose to do everything myself. Other times still, I fired the entire team and quickly hired replacements that were more professional and competent. Other times, I gave up.

Another key challenge of leadership is the paradox of accountability without authority. I have seen many adept leaders suffer from a lack of trust and autonomy from their superiors. Sometimes bureaucracy and the "one-man show" attitude also hinder the success of proactive visionaries who are not given the chance to manifest the totality of their vision. Even within my band Dahab, there are certain challenges in finding unity between the band members' different opinions. Yes, we are all brothers and share a common vision for the band—however, we sometimes disagree on the direction of the music or the name of an album. We challenge each other about songs, rhythms, and harmonies. I find that it is crucial to have a common vision in mind and also find harmony among all the stakeholders.

Think win-win, as Mr. Covey so eloquently stated.

I try to breed trust and a sense of harmony within my team. I also try as much as possible to give feedback to my team and my management. I choose not to anger easily or abuse people with callous and cold gestures. I am passionate about my ideas and am an excellent communicator. I share my vision with others and take their input into consideration. I share what I have learned and hope that others do the same. I do not care much for ego or pride. Because I always do my best and act with integrity, I have nothing to fear. I do not tolerate tantrums and gossip and respond assertively to any threats. I believe in the success of my team. I believe in the success of anything that I am part of—whether I am the leader or not. I make decisions quickly but always do the research first. I try to remain enthusiastic and treat everyone fairly.

But I am still very young at this complex role, and I still have a lot to learn. Perhaps leading from the heart is a good way to inspire change and bring about positive results. I still do not know.

Alexander the Great, the famous Greek conqueror, once led his troops across a hot, arid desert. After nearly two weeks of marching, he and his soldiers were near death from thirst, yet Alexander pushed ahead. In the noonday sun, two of his scouts brought what little water they were able to find. It barely filled a cup. Alexander's troops were shocked when he poured the water into the burning sand.

The king said, "It is of no use for one to drink when many thirst."

Alexander knew how to be a great leader because he understood what leadership is all about—setting an example, living the example, and showing others how to follow his lead.

Other great leaders throughout history—such as Salah ad-Din, Mahatma Gandhi, George Washington, and T. E. Lawrence—used motivation, courage, enthusiasm, foresight, and wisdom to influence large groups of people to achieve truly amazing things. You can do the same in your own life with leadership.

> Leadership and learning are indispensable
> to each other. (John F. Kennedy)

Background

A society can't exist without good leaders. Without leaders, a society doesn't have anyone to supply guidance and direction. Whenever you have groups of people living together, some form of leadership is needed to ensure survival and to keep things running smoothly. A great leader provides a vision and brings people together to work toward a common goal. When there is no leadership, chaos and dissonance quickly emerge—and the society inevitably crumbles.

The same is true for your life. Your family needs leadership. Your peers and colleagues and subordinates at work all need leadership. You need leadership as well—and it starts with you.

Before you can learn to lead others, you must learn to lead yourself. Throughout this module, we will discuss the tools and skills that are necessary for leadership. When you apply them to your life, you will be able to guide yourself and others as well.

> The very essence of leadership is that you have
> to have vision. You can't blow an uncertain
> trumpet. (Theodore M. Hesburgh)

The Process

Why Leadership Matters

Why do you think leadership matters? Why is it necessary? We'll answer those questions with another question: do you know any leaders in your life who have made a difference? Chances are, the answer is yes. Consider the various ways these individuals influenced your life for the better. Did they inspire you to be a better person, to do great things? Did they provide guidance when the path was unclear? Or were they bad leaders who had a negative impact on your life or the lives of others?

By taking a few moments to consider those who have influenced you, you see that leaders do matter—because people who are leaders can influence others to think, feel, and behave in certain ways. Leaders can inspire, motivate, and encourage. They can engage, persuade, and convince. They can provide direction and guidance, give orders, and issue commands. They can exert significant power over others.

Good leaders help people achieve common goals through personal and professional influence. They know how to make people want to do the work that is necessary in order to succeed.

> Leadership is the capacity to translate vision
> into reality. (Warren G. Bennis)

What Great Leaders Do

To say that leaders merely lead is overly simplistic and doesn't begin to do justice to all that is involved in being a leader. Let's look at a more comprehensive explanation of what a leader really does:

- motivates followers,

- sets the example,

- issues guidance and directions,

- encourages morale,

- unites a group toward a common purpose,

- handles conflict,

- instills discipline,

- provides inspiration,

- looks after the best interests of his followers,

- creates the vision,

- and gives clear guidance and direction.

As you can see, a leader has a tremendous amount of responsibility. In fact, it is probably easier to consider what a leader doesn't do.

> Absolute identity with one's cause is the first and great
> condition of successful leadership. (Woodrow Wilson)

Examples of Leadership

There have been many outstanding leaders throughout history. However, you don't have to be famous or legendary in order to be a good leader. In fact, you can find opportunities to lead in every aspect of your life.

Leading at Work

Your work place is a prime example of an environment that is ripe for leadership. You might be called upon to work on a team for a specific project. A project needs direction, vision, guidance, and motivation when things get tough—and that is what a leader provides.

Leadership is especially important when you are working with subordinates who look to you for guidance and direction. As a leader, you are responsible for upholding the values and standards of the organization and making sure that the greater vision is being pursued. You can also act as a mentor to them—transferring knowledge and helping them to progress in their careers.

Leading in Society

There are plenty of opportunities to lead in society as well, especially if you are involved in a variety of activities within your community. You can lead at your place of worship, at volunteer agencies and organizations, and even in recreational activities. In each of these places you can help guide others to fulfill an objective or live up to a purpose. When you do so, you are being a leader.

Your friends may occasionally need leadership as well, especially when they're going through a tough time. Leadership can be something as simple as organizing a get-together for your friends or checking up on a friend who is ill or struggling in some way.

Leading at Home

Your family—including yourself—perhaps offers the best opportunity for effective leadership. Families need leadership in order to be successful. A strong leader is a steady presence that can guide and steer others toward positive experiences and help them navigate smoothly through negative ones.

If you are in a relationship with someone, you can also lead your relationship by helping make sound decisions and providing inspiration and encouragement to your partner.

Relationship between Leaders and Followers

Leaders and followers enjoy a special relationship. It is one marked by trust, respect, communication, a strong bond, and mutual interests.

A leader is expected to be there for his followers and have their best interests at heart. A follower is expected to follow the leader and obey, while also giving constructive feedback to the leader so he is always aware of what is going on within the group.

A strong leader can inspire strong bonds between his followers. Strong bonds among the members can help a group survive anything. Books have been written about how much followers and leaders can come to rely on each other. Nothing can get done, and nothing great can be achieved, without this special relationship.

> A good objective of leadership is to help those who
> are doing poorly to do well and to help those who
> are doing well to do even better. (Jim Rohn)

Principles of Successful Leadership

Common Vision

A leader creates and shares a common vision with his followers. This common vision is the most important key in creating a successful relationship between leaders and followers. Followers have to buy into the vision and believe in it in order to be as effective as possible.

Direction

One of a leader's main responsibilities is directing others—telling them what to do and what not to do. Direction is needed in virtually every area, especially if the task is highly technical and complex.

Guidance

Leaders do not just give orders—they also guide. Leaders offer guidance and help to their followers so they can more effectively realize their goals and objectives. A leader's guidance can be specific to the job at hand, or it can be personal in nature to help with the emotions, uncertainty, and concerns of his followers.

Motivation

A major responsibility for leaders is to motivate a group of followers. Leaders encourage and inspire, and by doing so they increase motivation. They provide the fuel that keeps a group going. When times are tough, leaders are tough, too—but good leaders know how to be tough in a way that uplifts their followers. Being overly critical, condescending, or punitive is rarely effective—it typically deflates motivation.

> The challenge of leadership is to be strong, but not rude; be kind, but not weak; be bold, but not bully; be thoughtful, but not lazy; be humble, but not timid; be proud, but not arrogant; have humor, but without folly. (Jim Rohn)

Discipline

As we've discussed previously, discipline is a trait that everyone needs to develop in order to be successful. A good leader makes sure that discipline is present. He firmly enforces the rules and standards when needed.

Empowerment

In order to be effective, a person has to believe that he is capable of achieving something. Without that core belief and confidence, people simply will not be able to perform up to their potential. Empowering followers—making them feel capable of contributing something of value and succeeding—is a key responsibility of a leader.

Balance

Finally, a leader has to have balance. There are times when a leader needs to be firm, enforce the rules, exert discipline, and give orders. But there are also times when a leader needs to be compassionate, kind, and understanding—he often needs to be more of a mentor and guide than an authority figure.

Additionally, all leaders need to know how to follow and when to do so. A wise leader looks to his followers for feedback. No single person can do everything alone. Sometimes, succeeding requires incorporating a team's talents and skills into the equation.

> Do not go where the path may lead; go instead where there is no path and leave a trail. (Ralph Waldo Emerson)

Exercises

Being a leader means knowing yourself inside and out. This exercise will help you take an honest look at your leadership ability:

1. Self-Evaluation

   Are you a good leader? Do you exhibit the characteristics of a good leader? What do you need to change or improve in your life in order to be a better leader at home, at work, and in the world in general?

2. Let Go of Excuses

   In order to develop your true potential as a leader, you must be willing to let go of any excuses. A true leader takes full responsibility for himself and for those he leads. Take some time to consider any excuses you may be making for missed opportunities or failures, such as the following:

   ✓ If only I were younger…

   ✓ If only I'd started sooner …

   ✓ I'm not smart enough …

   ✓ I'm not educated enough …

   Write all of them down, and then go through them, one by one, and consider the payoff of each excuse. How is it serving you to keep making that excuse? Excuses let us "off the hook" in some way. Consider how you can turn each excuse around—from something negative that holds you back, to something positive that will propel you forward.

For example, "If only I were younger" could be turned around to "Because I'm older, I have a lot of valuable knowledge, experience, and wisdom."

If your actions inspire others to dream more, learn more, do more and become more, you are a leader. (John Quincy Adams)

Action Plan

This action plan can help you internalize the principles of successful leadership into your everyday life:

1. Identify Opportunities to Lead

    ✓ You won't always be a leader. Identify when you should lead and when it would be better to follow.

    ✓ What situations would benefit from your talents and skills?

2. Examine Your Potential Followers

    ✓ Who would you lead? Base your leadership style in part on what they need.

3. Set the Example

    ✓ Be an example of the standards you uphold and want to impart to your followers.

4. Track Progress

    ✓ Keep a record or journal of your journey and how you are leading yourself and others. Review your journal periodically.

An army of sheep led by a lion would defeat an army of lions led by a sheep. (Arabian proverb)

You Can Do It!

Everyone has the innate ability to become a leader. You can be a leader—not only for other people but also for yourself. You need to learn how to lead yourself and develop yourself before you can truly lead others—and the journey you have been on will help you develop effective leadership skills.

Leadership is all about setting the example, living the example, and guiding others to live the example as well. Look within yourself for the strength, courage, and wisdom needed to be a successful person and an effective leader. You possess all of those traits already—you just have to nurture them and allow them to blossom. When you do that, you will triumph.

> The most dangerous leadership myth is that leaders are born—that there is a genetic factor to leadership. This myth asserts that people simply either have certain charismatic qualities or not. That's nonsense; in fact, the opposite is true. Leaders are made rather than born. (Warren G. Bennis)

Further Reading

Maxwell, John C. (2007). *The 21 Irrefutable Laws of Leadership: Follow Them and People Will Follow You*. Nashville: Thomas Nelson.

Kouzes, James and Barry Posner. (2008). *The Leadership Challenge*. Hoboken: Jossey-Bass.

BEYOND THE 7TH GATE
(CONCLUSION)

This is where the journey begins. This is the point where you consciously enter a world of possibility and positive personal change. This is where you can begin to achieve progressive human integration.

You have gained basic awareness of the 'Self' and identified your true purpose. You now know why and how to live your life. You can motivate yourself. You possess confidence and high self-esteem. You know how to manage your fear and emotions.

You have a focused 'Mind' with a clear vision that is linked to your purpose. You have the power of discipline at your disposal and continuously strive to learn more and experience more. You have learned to control your random thoughts and have trained your mind to be your friend, not your foe.

You have conditioned your 'Body' and put your health and wellbeing as a number one priority in your life. You take responsibility for the results that you get in your life and don't make excuses. You strongly enforce the guidelines of healthy nutrition in your life and exercise your body to become stronger, leaner and healthier. You are fit, healthy and energized.

You know the importance of nurturing positive relationships in your life. You see with your 'Heart' and respect the differences between the genders. You apply the principles of building and sustaining rich loving relationships and strive to create joy and harmony in your life and others. You give more than you take.

You have a high degree of self-awareness and through observation and experience—you have begun to understand the personalities of other 'People' as well. You use empathy, compassion and assertiveness to communicate more effectively. You are socially intelligent. You practice active listening and as a result are forming deeper and more meaningful relationships with others.

You value the scarcity of 'Time'. You can set big lofty goals and can achieve them. You have a plan and nothing can stop you. You celebrate your successes and are not undermined by slight mishaps. You act with courage in the face of fear. You have achieved balance and are happy in all aspects of your life.

You also have the power to 'Change'. You have understood that the path of self-mastery is a constantly evolving state of being. You have mastered your thoughts and habits and know how to change yourself—if you choose. The principles of success are an integral part of your life. You are dedicated, committed, motivated and act with integrity towards yourself and others.

You are now ready to lead yourself beyond the 7th Gate—to the point of progressive human integration—the place where Phi resides.